本书为2021年度教育部人文社会科学研究青年基金项目
"基于机器学习的对标《量表》写作自动评估模型建构研究"（21YJC740038）
阶段性成果

本书出版承蒙浙江大学董氏文史哲研究奖励基金资助

外国语言学及应用语言学研究丛书

A Study on the Rule-Based Approach
to the Automatic Extraction of Grammar Patterns

基于规则方法的
语法模式自动提取研究

马　鸿　著

ZHEJIANG UNIVERSITY PRESS
浙江大学出版社
·杭州·

图书在版编目（CIP）数据

基于规则方法的语法模式自动提取研究= A Study on
the Rule-Based Approach to the Automatic Extraction
of Grammar Patterns: 英文 / 马鸿著. —杭州：浙江大学
出版社，2022.8
　　（外国语言学及应用语言学研究丛书）
　　ISBN 978-7-308-22847-3

　　Ⅰ．①基… Ⅱ．①马… Ⅲ．①英语－语法－研究
Ⅳ．①H314

中国版本图书馆CIP数据核字(2022)第129238号

基于规则方法的语法模式自动提取研究

A Study on the Rule-Based Approach to the Automatic Extraction of
Grammar Patterns

马　鸿　著

策划编辑　包灵灵
责任编辑　仝　林
责任校对　田　慧
封面设计　项梦怡
出版发行　浙江大学出版社
　　　　　（杭州市天目山路148号　　邮政编码　310007）
　　　　　（网址：http://www.zjupress.com）
排　　版　杭州林智广告有限公司
印　　刷　广东虎彩云印刷有限公司绍兴分公司
开　　本　710 mm×1000 mm　1/16
印　　张　13.75
字　　数　280千
版 印 次　2022年8月第1版　2022年8月第1次印刷
书　　号　ISBN 978-7-308-22847-3
定　　价　49.00元

CONTENTS

CHAPTER 1

Introduction

This book is designed according to the conceptualization that vocabulary knowledge is multidimensional (Jaen, 2007; Qian & Schedl, 2004) and the learning of grammatical and collocational patterns should be considered as important as, if not more important than, the acquisition of semantic knowledge of single words. The purposes of this book are to (1) propose a method of extracting grammar patterns for the most frequent content words (verbs, nouns, adjectives, and adverbs) in a given corpus, and (2) derive a tentative grammar pattern list for the 115 most frequent academic verbs. The extraction of grammar patterns was realized through a rule-based programming approach, where the researchers coded all possible patterns of the most frequent academic verbs and used the script to extract grammar patterns from a given corpus. The extracted grammar patterns were compiled in sequence according to the corpus-based frequency information and developed into a grammar pattern list for the most frequent academic verbs. The grammar pattern list is expected to complement the widely used Academic Vocabulary List (AVL) developed by Gardner and Davies in 2013, by specifying the frequency of each verb pattern (e.g. "provide N with N", "select N from N", "base N on N").

In Chapter 2, previous literature on frequency list development is reviewed with a focus on methodological concerns and specific procedures, given that this book revolves around the development of a frequency list of grammar patterns for the most frequent academic verbs per se. In this chapter, grammar patterns are viewed as an indispensable aspect of vocabulary knowledge. As argued in Chapter 2, vocabulary knowledge is significantly related to students' proficiency of a foreign / second language. Important considerations of list development have also been reviewed to establish the foundation for the frequency list developed in the current project. In particular, the argument concerning the existence of a core academic list (consisting of words that frequently occur in a range of different academic disciplines) has been reviewed in that it is related to this book. Researchers supporting the existence of such an academic core see frequency lists extracted from one single academic corpus as meaningful and useful. Nevertheless, researchers questioning the existence of such an academic core only support the existence of discipline-specific word lists that are extracted from specific academic disciplines. Besides, statistical measures adopted in previous research on word frequency lists are also summarized to shed light on the current list development and specific empirical studies are reviewed afterwards. Meaningful discussions in previous research on word list development are particularly conducive to this book.

Chapter 3 and Chapter 4 focus on theories and empirical studies on Construction Grammar (rooted in Psycholinguistics) and Pattern Grammar (accepted in Corpus Linguistics) respectively, since grammar patterns can generally be considered as constructions. The connection between grammar patterns and constructions was clearly articulated by Hunston and Su (2019), before which there had been little dialogue between the two fields (Cognitive Linguistics and Corpus Linguistics). By analyzing a list of 44 adjective complements extracted by Francis et al. (1998) through a local grammar approach, i.e. a grammar of discourse function, Hunston and Su (2019) proposed that a large number of meaning-pattern combinations (e.g. In the sentence *Some teachers may be **adept at** introducing their pupils to grammatical concepts*, the

"Adj at N" pattern indicating "(un)skilled" is a construction.) could be identified as constructions, form-meaning mappings "conventionalized in the speech community and entrenched as language knowledge in the learner's mind" (Ellis, 2007, p. 78).

In Chapter 3, constructions are clearly defined, rendering the connection between Construction Grammar and Pattern Grammar more tangible. Besides, important hypotheses concerning the acquisition of constructions, the generalization hypothesis, and constraints of overgeneralization (e.g. entrenchment, preemption, and semantic constraints) are systematically reviewed by citing representative empirical research. Approaching the end of Chapter 3, research on learning of constructions from the perspective of second language acquisition (SLA) is discussed drawing on theories and studies on first language (L1) acquisition.

Grammar patterns, a concept originating from Corpus Linguistics, are perceived as purely observational phenomena, while constructions are an attempt to model the mental representation of language from the cognitive linguistic perspective (Hunston & Su, 2019). Chapter 4, with a focus on grammar patterns and Pattern Grammar theory exclusively, reviews studies of Corpus Linguistics pertaining to grammar patterns, mainly including discipline variability in the grammar patterns used by expert writers and novice writers. Chapter 4 concludes with pedagogical implications aiming at facilitating the instruction in grammar patterns and multi-word units. Most importantly, Chapter 4 highlights that even though grammar patterns are closely related to learners' language proficiency and empirical studies have facilitated the instruction in grammar patterns, the question of which grammar patterns to be prioritized in practical instruction has yet to be answered. Therefore, this book intends to develop a frequency list of grammar patterns for academic verbs so as to shed light on the teaching of grammar patterns to learners of English for Academic Purposes (EAP). In addition, the methodology proposed for extracting grammar patterns in this book can be used to extract grammar patterns from any corpus and facilitate grammar pattern teaching.

Chapter 5 provides an in-depth description of the rule-based approach to grammar pattern extraction, primarily including materials adopted, detailed procedures, data analysis, and the list of grammar patterns for the 115 most frequent academic verbs developed in this book.

Since Corpus Linguistics and Construction Grammar adopt different signs to symbolize the same patterns / constructions, these signs are presented in this book in a manner consistent with the original sources.

Part of the book has been published in the journal *English for Specific Purposes*.

References

Ellis, N. (2007). The associative-cognitive CREED. In B. Van Patten & J. Williams (eds.), *Theories in second language acquisition*. Mahwah, NJ: Erlbaum, 77-96.

Francis, G., Hunston, S. & Manning, E. (1998). *Collins Cobuild grammar patterns 2: Nouns and adjectives*. London: Collins CoBUILD.

Green, C. (2019). Enriching the academic wordlist and secondary vocabulary lists with lexicogrammar: Toward a Pattern Grammar of academic vocabulary. *System*, 87(1), 1-10.

Green, C. & Lambert, J. (2019). Position vectors, homologous chromosomes and grammar rays: Producing disciplinary literacy through Secondary Phrase Lists. *English for Specific Purposes*, 53, 1-12.

Hunston, S. & Su, H. (2019). Patterns, constructions, and local grammar: A case study of "evaluation". *Applied Linguistics*, 40(4), 567-593.

Jaen, M. M. (2007). A corpus-driven design of a test for assessing the ESL collocational competence of university students. *International Journal of English Studies*, 7(2), 127-147.

Qian, D. & Schedl, M. (2004). Evaluation of an in-depth vocabulary knowledge measure for assessing reading performance. *Language Testing*, 21(1), 28-52.

CHAPTER 2

Frequency Lists and Vocabulary Learning

2.1 Importance of English Vocabulary Knowledge

The importance of vocabulary in English language learning has been widely recognized (Nation, 2001). Teachers and researchers generally view vocabulary knowledge (lexical competence) as the core of communicative competence and a "reliable predictor of learners' proficiency in a second or foreign language" (Stæhr, 2009, p. 577). These claims are well supported by empirical evidence relating to the four basic communicative skills, namely reading, listening, speaking, and writing (e.g. Bonk, 2000; De Jong et al., 2012; Hu & Nation, 2000; Laufer & Ravenhorst-Kalovski, 2010; Olinghouse & Wilson, 2013; Stæhr, 2009). In addition, the impacts of vocabulary knowledge on the four skills have been investigated dichotomously with regard to two dimensions: vocabulary depth (i.e. the amount of information learners know about specific words and the organization of words) and vocabulary breadth (i.e. the amount of words that students can recognize) (Stæhr, 2009).

2.1.1　Vocabulary Knowledge and Reading

Vocabulary has been claimed as crucial to comprehension (Nation, 2006). Ever since Laufer (1988), a substantial body of research has been devoted to establishing the relationship between learners' vocabulary knowledge and reading comprehension ability (Hu & Nation, 2000) by answering two critical research questions: (1) "how much of a text's vocabulary should readers know to reach adequate comprehension?" (2) "how large should the readers' vocabulary be in order to understand the necessary percentage of the texts' words?" (Laufer, 2013, pp. 868–869)

With regard to the first research question, Laufer (1988) specified that only knowledge of over 95% of words in a text could ensure sufficient comprehension, and knowing less than 95% of all words could lead to difficulty of guessing the meaning of unknown words. Similarly, Hu and Nation (2000) investigated what percentage of known words in a text was sufficient for unassisted reading by measuring three levels of densities of unknown vocabulary (95%, 90%, and 80%) and assessing reading comprehension ability through multiple choice questions and written recall questions. Their results indicated that no participants were able to comprehend texts adequately with a lexical coverage of 80% and that a lexical coverage of 98% was required for adequate comprehension. Specific to the comprehension of academic texts, the study of Schmitt et al. (2011), requiring 661 participants to complete a reading comprehension test and a vocabulary measure test, revealed that a vocabulary coverage of 98% was optimal to ensure 70% of comprehension scoring.

The second research question emphasizes on the relationship between students' vocabulary size and their reading comprehension ability. Many researchers have underlined the importance of quantifying the lexical threshold for comprehension, where comprehension improves significantly at a particular vocabulary coverage, since researchers generally believe that reading skills (e.g. distinguishing between main and peripheral information as well as between explicit and implicit information) function most efficiently on the basis that students possess the minimal lexical knowledge required (Hsu, 2019). By adopting a corpus-based approach, Nation (2006) revealed the number of word families that learners need to comprehend texts of different genres, such as novels, news, and short stories. Laufer and Ravenhorst-Kalovski (2010) added learners' vocabulary size to the previously discussed variables, i.e. vocabulary coverage and reading comprehension proficiency. Their finding suggested that with a vocabulary size of 6,000–8,000 word families, students were able to understand 98% of words in texts, while a vocabulary coverage of 95% could be achieved when learners grasped 4,000–5,000 word families. Hsu (2019) measured three variables, including reading comprehension ability, lexical coverage of texts, and students' vocabulary size, and performed a linear regression to show the predicting power of vocabulary scores on reading ability. The results indicated that 64% of reading scores were explained by students' vocabulary size, with a correlation of 0.80 between the two measures. In addition, an increase of 1,000 words yielded 10 more points in reading comprehension. The relationship between students'vocabulary size and their performance in reading comprehension was generally linear. These studies, although different in research design, participants, and textual materials, unanimously underlined the importance of vocabulary knowledge in the development of learners' reading comprehension ability.

2.1.2 Vocabulary Knowledge and Listening

Compared with the large amount of research that identified vocabulary knowledge as a significant predictor of students' reading success, the predicting power of vocabulary knowledge on listening ability is less frequently investigated and reported (Stæhr, 2009). In addition, correlations between vocabulary size and listening comprehension are generally lower than those between vocabulary size and reading comprehension. Nevertheless, the correlations between the former two also tend to be consistently strong (Zhang & Graham, 2020). For example, to testify the predicting power of lexical knowledge on listening proficiency, Bonk (2000) recruited 59 low-intermediate to advanced Japanese learners of English as a Foreign Language (EFL) and required them to complete a dictation test, aiming to measure their familiarity with lexis in the texts, and a comprehension test, which allowed the participants to write a recall protocol in their first language. According to Bonk (2000), familiarity with less than 75% of the lexis in the listening text was associated with comprehension difficulty, while a vocabulary coverage of 90% ensured satisfactory comprehension, regardless of learners' differences in listening proficiency. Even though efficient strategies could promote comprehension to some extent, most learners still relied more on lexical familiarity.

By distinguishing the two different dimensions of vocabulary knowledge, Stæhr (2009) found that both dimensions of depth (measured by the Vocabulary Levels Test) and breadth (measured by the Word Associates Test) of vocabulary knowledge were significantly related to the listening comprehension performances of 115 advanced Danish EFL learners, tested by a listening test of the Cambridge Certificate of Proficiency in English. A lexical coverage of 98% was identified as the threshold of understanding the listening texts, a result very similar to the vocabulary coverage required for reading comprehension.

Through a Pearson correlation coefficiency analysis, Li (2019) also identified a strong positive correlation between 146 college students' receptive vocabulary knowledge, tested by the Listening Vocabulary Levels Test developed and validated by McLean et al. (2015), and listening proficiency, measured by the General English Proficiency Test validated previously (Liao, 2009; Wu & Wu, 2010). It was also clarified in Li's (2019) study that knowledge of the most frequent 3,000 word families was required for a lexical coverage of 98% of the listening texts, which tended to result in sufficient comprehension.

2.1.3　Vocabulary Knowledge and Speaking

Research on the relationship between vocabulary knowledge and speaking is generally scarce, but has gradually received more attention. Appearing comparatively late, empirical endeavors viewed vocabulary knowledge and speaking ability as multi-dimensional, and discovered complex interactions between their multi-dimensional variables (Uchihara & Saito, 2019). For example, according to De Jong et al. (2012), vocabulary knowledge included productive vocabulary, grammatical knowledge, pronunciation quality, and lexical retrieval speed, and they identified productive vocabulary, measured by the Productive Vocabulary Levels Test developed by Laufer and Nation (1999), as a predicting variable significantly associated with students' speaking proficiency.

On the other hand, Uchihara and Saito (2019) operationalized students' spontaneous speech production as a multi-dimensional construct that encompasses comprehensibility (i.e. ease of understanding), accentedness (i.e. linguistic nativelikeness), and fluency (i.e. speech rate), and investigated the association between these dimensions of spontaneous speech production and second language (L2) learners' productive vocabulary knowledge. The JACET8000, an automatic scorer which awards one point for each item not appearing in the first 1,000 most frequent words, was applied in Uchihara and Saito's (2019) research to grade students' speech production. Following the conventions in L2 speech research, students' spontaneous speech samples were elicited by a timed picture description task. However, the results suggested that participants' vocabulary raw scores only correlated moderately with fluency, but not with comprehensibility and accentedness. Uchihara and Saito (2019) explained that a larger vocabulary enabled students to retrieve expression more efficiently in real-time communication. While insignificant relationships between vocabulary raw scores and comprehensibility and accentedness were attributed to the tight link between fluency and other linguistic features, such as pronunciation, vocabulary, and grammar.

With a focus on receptive vocabulary size, Uchihara and Clenton (2020) also reported that test scores of receptive vocabulary size could predict L2 spontaneous speaking performances (elicited through picture description tasks and evaluated analytically in terms of fluency, vocabulary, grammar, and pronunciation). A relatively strong correlational relationship was identified between receptive vocabulary size and students' speaking proficiency. Nevertheless, a large vocabulary size did not ensure production of lexically sophisticated words, tentatively suggesting that the predicting power of vocabulary size on L2 speaking was stronger for advanced learners than for low-proficiency learners.

Mostafa and Ali (2021) probed into the correlation between the two dimensions of lexical knowledge, i.e. vocabulary size or vocabulary breadth and depth, and L2 speaking proficiency (encompassing overall performance, fluency and coherence, and lexical resource). The predictor variables, students' vocabulary breadth and depth were measured respectively by the Word Associates Test, the Vocabulary Levels Test, and Lex30.

The speaking tasks of the International English Language Testing System were employed to elicit students' oral responses. To address the issue of multicollinearity among independent variables and small sample sizes, ridge regression was adopted to plot the predicting relationship without removing any of these predictor variables.

2.1.4　Vocabulary Knowledge and Writing

Vocabulary is perceived as important to the descriptiveness, accuracy, and quality of writing production (Read, 1998). Deficiency in vocabulary knowledge greatly contributes to language learners' difficulty in writing English essays. Compared with studies that identify the predicting relations between vocabulary knowledge and reading comprehension abilities, research that probes into the specific roles of vocabulary knowledge in explaining students' writing proficiency falls short greatly in terms of quantity. Nevertheless, these emerging studies have highlighted the great importance of vocabulary knowledge in shaping one's writing performance (Moon et al., 2019). For example, Olinghouse and Wilson examined the interplay between fifth graders' ($N = 105$) writing performances in three genres (story, persuasive, and informative) and "different vocabulary constructs: diversity, maturity, elaboration, academic words, content words, and register"(2013, p. 45). On the basis of multiple linear regression and commonality analysis, Olinghouse and Wilson (2013) discovered that different vocabulary constructs were associated with the quality of different genres. To be specific, vocabulary diversity was exclusively related to story writing, while the quality of both persuasive writing and informative writing could be explained by content words to some extent. Among the very few studies that investigated the influence of language-and literacy-related constructs on writing performance in an integrated manner, Moon et al. (2019) found that the vocabulary knowledge of advanced South Korean EFL learners exerted indirect effects on their writing performances mediated by reading comprehension.

Another line of research, relying on automated writing analysis, also contributed greatly to explaining the importance of vocabulary to students' writing proficiency. Generally, automatic text analysis techniques and statistical methods, such as structural equation modeling and multiple linear regression, were applied to identify specific linguistic and textual features that predict students' writing qualities significantly (e.g. Aryadoust & Liu, 2015; McNamara et al., 2015). For example, by adopting Coh-Metrix (a computational tool that provides quality indexes for surface-and deep-level features of texts), the situation model, "a higher level of comprehension that goes beyond the explicit meaning of texts and constitutes a conceptual representation of the text" (Aryadoust & Liu, 2015, p. 40), and structural equation modeling, Aryadoust and Liu suggested that measures of the surface level (lexicon and syntax) and textbase (a mental representation of the text that maintains the text meaning) can predict students' writing proficiency. McNamara et al. (2015) first implemented a machine learning modeling technique, a hierarchical classification approach, in a similar endeavor. The corpus, including 1,243 argumentative essays written by pre-college students and college freshmen, was first submitted to three automated text analysis tools, i.e. Coh-Metrix, the Writing Assessment Tool, and the Linguistic Inquiry and Word Count, to obtain quality indexes. Sequentially, a predicting model was constructed with these quality indexes as the predicting variables and essay scores as the dependent variables, and resulted in the ranking of indexes, significantly contributing to the evaluation of students' writing samples. Among these quality indexes, those associated with vocabulary knowledge, such as nominalization and lexical diversity, ranked noticeably high, underlining the importance of vocabulary knowledge in writing production.

Overall, there exists no shortage of empirical evidence supporting the vital importance of lexical knowledge to students' English proficiency. Nevertheless, given the vast amount of English words, the goal of learning all words is not realistic for English language learners (Wang et al., 2008), which accentuates the necessity of prioritizing certain words in accordance with target students' immediate learning needs. In this case, the frequency of words plays a significant role.

2.2 Frequency and Vocabulary Learning

Despite the daunting task of memorizing numerous English words, the fact that "all words are not equally important in different stages of learning" offers the possibility of prioritizing certain words according to learners' immediate vocabulary learning needs (Wang et al., 2008, P. 443). To set a clearer and more realistic vocabulary learning goal for language learners, researchers and scholars in Corpus Linguistics have developed various word lists by (1) organizing the word lists based on the frequency of occurrence of each word in a descending order, and (2) considering learners' purposes of English language learning. The practice of selecting words in teaching English to nonnative speakers has long been based on the frequency of occurrence of words in texts (e.g. West, 1953). Nation and Waring (1997) indicated that the first 2,000 most frequently occurring word families of English in the General Service List (GSL) (West, 1953) could satisfy the learning needs of English beginners sufficiently, while the learning goals of the majority of intermediate and / or advanced learners should be shifted to words with lower frequency of occurrence.

Focusing on English for Academic Purposes (EAP), this book emphasizes on the importance of identifying and prioritizing frequent words in academic discourse. The frequency of academic words is essential to EAP vocabulary pedagogy, because it informs instructional decisions concerning which words are to be prioritized given the limited in-class time and independent study time (Coxhead, 2000). The influences of a frequency-based pedagogy are multifold, including "setting vocabulary goals for language courses, guiding learners in their independent study, and informing course and material designers in selecting texts and developing activities" (Coxhead, 2000, p. 214).

For frequency-based pedagogy, a corpus surely is a valuable resource, where lexical information could be extracted (Biber, 1993). Ever since the occurrence of the GSL, the tradition of forming an appropriate corpus and selecting vocabulary on the basis of frequency has long been inherited and developed. The GSL, although not a word list specific to English academic discourse, exemplifies typical steps in the development of academic vocabulary lists and has been utilized in later endeavors of list development for fundamental considerations. The GSL, developing from a corpus of five million words with the needs of English learners in mind, contains the most widely used 2,000 word families in English. West (1953) used a variety of criteria to select these words, including frequency, ease of learning, coverage of useful concepts, and stylistic level. As early as in 1953, West realized the importance of semantics in word list development, and utilized semantic count (the frequency of occurrence of various meanings and uses of words) as the basic unit for the GSL.

As exemplified in Table 2.1, 9% of the occurrence of the word *game* indicated the meaning of "amusement" or "children's play", while 38% of its occurrence indicated the meaning of "competition".

**Table 2.1　Semantic counts of part of the meanings of the word *game*
(adapted from West, 1953)**

Word	Meaning and example	Percentage of occurrence
game	1. amusement, children's play e.g. It's not serious; it's just a game.	9%
	2. with the idea of competition e.g. A game of football	38%
	3. a particular contest e.g. I played a losing game.	23%

According to the compiler, the above-mentioned statistics yield two important pieces of information: (1) Highly frequent words, usually with many different meanings, impose great burden upon learners. Meanwhile, learners' learning burden can be somewhat reduced by focusing on essential senses of the target words. (2) Learners' energy could be further saved by temporarily excluding much less frequent words. The list, nevertheless, was developed on the basis of printed and written materials, including encyclopedia, magazines, textbooks, novels, essays, biographies, books about science, poetry, and the like, thereby leaving the spoken discourse under-represented (West, 1953).

Since meanings of words were analyzed manually by well-trained personnel, this process was only possible under a generous grant allocated by the Rockefeller Foundation for "Studies of English Usage". Besides the GSL, five other early studies, including Lynn (1973), Ghadessy (1979), and Xue and Nation (1984), also created different versions of academic word lists manually without the assistance of computers. This book, nevertheless, focuses on academic word lists developed on the basis of large corpora and automatic extraction techniques. These academic word lists are inspired by early lists (Coxhead, 2016) and are more closely related to the list of grammar patterns of frequent academic verbs delineated in this book.

It is well acknowledged that the practices of setting vocabulary learning goals, facilitating learners' independent study, and systematizing learning materials should be undergirded by academic word lists (Biber et al., 1999). Thus, the trustworthiness of such a list is vitally important, and is related to a few key considerations / criteria adopted in the development process, including the existence / non-existence of an academic core, the representativeness of texts (Biber, 1993), the organization of the corpus (Biber, 1993; Sinclair, 1991), and statistical criteria used for word selection (Coxhead, 2000). The following sections elaborate on these important considerations of the methodology in developing academic word lists, the associations between these considerations, and the trustworthiness of previously published academic word lists.

2.2.1   The Existence / Non-existence of an Academic Core

For EAP students, technical terms are less a problem compared to those EAP jargons, semi-technical vocabulary or academic vocabulary, since technical terms have always received sufficient attention in classroom discussion and textbook explanation, while academic vocabulary is noticeably less visited in mainstream classes (Wang et al., 2008). Nevertheless, empirical evidence suggests that the knowledge of academic vocabulary is indispensable for EAP learners, given the high frequency of academic words in academic discourse (Coxhead, 2000; Santos, 2010) and the power of academic words to differentiate between well-prepared students and under-prepared students (Kuehn, 1996). According to Santos (2010), approximately 16% of the words in textbooks of different disciplines were academic words. Similarly, in Coxhead's (2000) efforts of developing the Academic Word List (AWL), she found that academic words in this list covered 10% of words in the 3.5-million-word academic corpus, from which the AWL was extracted. As to the distinguishing power of academic vocabulary, Kuehn (1996) reported that limited knowledge of academic vocabulary tended to impede EAP learners' comprehension of the required academic texts (Laufer & Nation, 1999). Nevertheless, the distinction between technical vocabulary and academic / sub-technical vocabulary is not always clear-cut (Chung & Nation, 2003; Mudraya, 2006). Expert judgment is still required to distinguish the two in some cases.

It seems that consensus has been reached concerning the importance of discipline-specific (technical) words to the comprehension and production of academic texts. Nevertheless, the viability of a core academic list consisting of words that occur in different disciplines has been questioned by some experts, given that these words may be used to express different meanings in different disciplines (Hyland & Tse, 2007), and are likely to be highly frequent in both general and academic fields (Hancioğlu et al., 2008; Neufeld et al., 2011). Gardner and Davies (2014) defended the viability of a core academic list by arguing that the issue of word-meaning variation was more salient for more general frequency lists, since highly frequent English content words tended to be polysemous (Ravin & Leacock, 2000). Therefore, before the development of a computer program that can accurately tag distinct meanings of a specific word form, the issue of word-meaning variation cannot be avoided, with academic word lists and generalized word lists alike. According to Gardner and Davies (2014), this issue, nevertheless, could be minimized to some extent by adopting lemmas rather than word families as the counting units.

As to the selection of frequent academic words, Gardner and Davies (2014) positioned that general academic vocabulary knowledge contributed significantly to students' academic achievement (Townsend et al., 2012). In addition, the importance of words appearing in a new high-frequency general list should not be diminished in academic training and research (Eldridge, 2008). The acceptance of a list of academic core vocabulary can be reflected in two comparative new lists: the Billuroğlu—Neufeld List (BNL; Hancioğlu et al., 2008) and the new Academic Vocabulary List (Gardner & Davies, 2014). The BNL, an amalgam of several different lists (e.g. the GSL word families, the AWL word families, the first 2,000 words of the Brown Corpus, and several other well-recognized word lists), has been incorporated into Compleat Lexical Tutor developed by Tom Cobb, a web site that facilitates vocabulary learning. The development of the BNL was based on the underlying conception that the combination of different established lists could reduce the influence of the problems of each list individually. The new AVL, on the other hand, was developed on the basis of large representative corpora and through statistical methods considering both frequency and dispersion to ensure that the new AVL demonstrates a wide coverage of disciplines.

In addition to the distribution issue of general academic word lists across disciplines, another issus is that focusing on the core academic core vocabulary may cause students to ignore the discipline-specific meanings of words (Dang et al., 2017). Nevertheless, Nation (2013) explained that the core meanings and discipline-specific meanings should not be considered as distinctive. Rather, knowledge of the core meaning could facilitate the acquisition of discipline-specific meanings (Crossley et al., 2010). If learners have knowledge of the core / general meaning of an academic word, they may gradually deduce the discipline-specific meanings of this word after a sufficient number of encounters with this word in subject areas. In addition, the conceptualization of a core academic word list also caters to different realistic situations: "(a) learners are more heterogeneous in terms of disciplines that they plan to study, (b) learners have not yet identified their target disciplines, (c) learners plan to study interdisciplinary subject areas, or (d) teachers lack background knowledge of learners' specific disciplines" (Dang et al., 2017, p. 961). In addition, university students tend to take courses of different subject areas, which further justifies the development of general word lists that facilitate students to comprehend academic words appearing in a range of disciplines (Dang et al., 2017; Nation, 2013).

As opposed to a limited number of academic word lists that were developed on the basis of the conceptualization of "academic core", more lists were derived by recognizing the significant contributions of discipline-specific words, such as the Medical Academic Word List (Wang et al., 2008), and the New Medical Academic Word List (Lei & Liu, 2016). Hyland (2016) argued that the assumptions of general and discipline-specific word lists could be better described as a continuum rather than a dichotomy, which indicates that either type of academic word lists could be more appropriate and suitable in a specific context. For example, in EAP programs, students' subject areas are comparatively homogeneous, such as Mathematics, Physics or Chemistry. Discipline-specific word lists should be more appropriate than general academic word lists in highlighting the most frequent words in the target disciplines and reducing students' workload of focusing on less frequent words. Nevertheless, general academic word lists tend to fit learners studying a wider range of disciplines, learners who have not decided on a specific discipline, and learners who study interdisciplinary subject areas (Dang et al., 2017).

2.2.2　Statistical Measures in the Development of Academic Word Lists

After the establishment of a corpus, statistical measures are applied to generate lists of vocabulary in academic discourse. One typical criticism of statistical measures is that

17

word lists developed through statistical measures are deprived of semantic information, ignoring the fact that a specific word may well demonstrate different meanings or functions in different discourse types or academic registers (Dang et al., 2017). Dang et al. (2017), nevertheless, defended the use of statistical methods in the development of word lists by arguing that students' knowledge of the core meanings of words frequently appearing in specific subject areas could facilitate their acquisition of the discipline-specific meanings. In addition, in view of the complexity of language use, Dang et al. (2017) emphasized the importance of the underlying connection between the meaning and use of a word across academic and nonacademic discourse.

General academic vocabulary lists and discipline-specific vocabulary lists differ in statistical methods. For general academic vocabulary lists, high frequency, wide range, and even distribution across different academic areas rank among the major concerns (Gardner & Davies, 2014). These qualities are measured by frequency (frequency of occurrence of a word in the entire academic corpus), range (the number of subject areas where a word appears), and dispersion (even distribution of a word across a number of subject areas) respectively (Coxhead, 2000; Gardner & Davies, 2014; Nation, 2016).

2.2.2.1 *Frequency*

With regard to frequency, two statistical approaches have been used in facilitating the defining of academic vocabulary with reference to two different views concerning the relationship between academic Vocabulary and general vocabulary: (1) Academic vocabulary is related to general vocabulary (Coxhead, 2000). (2) Academic vocabulary is distinct from the most fequent 1,000 words of general vocabulary (Gardner & Davies, 2014).

The first approach adopted in the development of the Academic Word List (Coxhead, 2000) represents the view that academic vocabulary is related to general vocabulary. General vocabulary is divided into several layers, with the first 1,000 words in the General Word List (West, 1953) considered as the most frequent and widely occurred words, while the next 1,000 words are viewed as less frequent and narrowly distributed. It is also worth noticing that researchers, such as Nation (2013) and Schmitt and Schmitt (2014), have not reached a consensus as to the classification of these layers of words. To be specific, Nation (2013) viewed the first 2,000 words as high-frequency general words, while to Schmitt and Schmitt (2014), high-frequency general words referred to the first 3,000 words. The disagreement among researchers and limitations of GSL may render this first approach somewhat arguable.

In practice, Coxhead's (2000) approach excluded the first 1,000 words in the General Word List on the basis of the assumptions that learners had already knew these high-frequency general words and academic word lists should focus on identifying lower-frequency words featuring a wide range and high frequency in academic discourse. Empirical evidence also supports this approach by showing that most first- and second-year college students have demonstrated a sufficient command of the 1,000 and 2,000 most frequently occurring words in the GSL (Barrow et al., 1998; Liu & Han, 2015). In addition, "a view on the role of GSL words in academic texts…suggests that the use of these words as alternatives for words from the AWL would render academic texts less formal and serious" (Martínez et al., 2009, p. 192). As exemplified in Liu and Han (2015), even though some words in the AWL, such as *establish*, *conclude*, and *demonstrate*, and some words in the GSL, such as *show*, *find*, and *report*, have the same rhetorical value, apparently words in the AWL are more formal than those covered in the GSL, thus words included in the AWL are appropriate to be classified as academic words (Farrell, 1990).

The other approach adopted by the development of the new Academic Vocabulary List (Gardner & Davies, 2014) defines academic vocabulary on its own without referring to the GSL. This approach does not assume that EAP students have acquired high-frequency general words. Any words that are used in a wider range at a higher freguency in academic discourse compared with nonacademic discourse are candidates for the new Academic Vocabulary List (Gardner & Davies, 2014).

Dang et al. (2017) perceived both approaches as valuable and meaningful in that the first approach could prevent learners and teachers from repeating words that students are very familiar with, while the second approach recognized the variation of word meanings and uses across different discourse types and avoided the limitations of the GSL. Nevertheless, Dang et al. (2017) pointed out that both approaches shared the same limitation of treating learners homogeneously in terms of vocabulary knowledge.

2.2.2.2 Range

The word selection criteria for "range" is defined as "the number of files in which each word occurs" (Coxhead, 2000, p. 221). A corpus analysis program "Range" was developed by Heatley and Nation and has been frequently used in the practice of word list development to calculate the range of word lists (e.g. Coxhead, 2000; Liu & Han, 2015). As to the selection criteria for range, researchers operationalize the specific index slightly differently. For example, Wang et al. (2008) specified that a word family has to occur at least in 16 out of the 32 subject areas to be selected.

2.2.2.3 Dispersion

Dispersion index signals "an item's distribution across different texts, [indicating] whether that item is commonly used academic word in a particular discipline" (Liu & Han, 2015, p. 5). However, if some words are highly frequent in certain subject areas and unevenly distributed in the complete corpus, dispersion value for these words would be very limited. Due to the low frequency of these words in other subject areas, these words with very low dispersion value may be excluded from the academic word lists. Juilland and Chang-Rodríguez (1964) once proposed a word selection criterion — usage, a more scientific index realized by combining the frequency and distribution of a word. This method was further improved by Liu and Han (2015) and calculated as the following:

$$U_{opt} = D * (F - \text{MAX}(N_1, \dots N_n))$$

Where U_{opt} is optimized usage (the improved version of usage), D is dispersion, F is the total word frequency value in the corpus where the word list is extracted, n is the number of a subject area, N is the word frequency value in a standardized subject area, and MAX (N_1, … N_n) is the highest word frequency value in the subject areas. The cut-off point for optimized usage is generally determined based on the coverage of the tentative word list. For example, Liu and Han (2015) set the optimized usage value at 30.00, since lowering the cut-off point (e.g. at 20.00) led to 78 more words in the list but improving the coverage only by 0.46%, while 61 word families were excluded from the tentative word list and the coverage was lowered by 0.67%, when the cut-off point was set as high as 40 times of the minimum occurrence in most subject areas.

Word lists developed using statistical methods not only are replicable, but also provide possible users (e.g. researchers, teachers, and learners) with precise and useful information concerning the practical use and actual frequency of academic vocabulary (Dang et al., 2017).

2.3 Lists of Academic Words / Multi-word Units

As reviewed previously, frequency provides vital information as to which words / linguistic features to be prioritized in language learning process. Therefore, various lists of words / linguistic features have been created to facilitate learners' different language learning goals. The following sections elaborate on important frequency lists that showcase methodological considerations in developing these lists. With regard to target entities, the lists are generally grouped into lists of words and lists of multi-word units, and each type is further classified into general lists and discipline-specific lists on the basis of acceptance / non-acceptance of the "academic core". Since the majority of the word / multi-word unit lists are extracted from the discourse of academic writing, lists developed from the register of spoken language are attached to the end of each section.

2.3.1 General Academic Word Lists

The AWL developed by Coxhead (2000) ranks among the most widely adopted academic word lists, and has become the new standard of academic vocabulary in English education (Gardner & Davies, 2014). Nation (2011) attributed the widespread use of the AWL to its applicability and availability. The AWL can be freely downloaded and has been incorporated to several corpus-based language learning tools, such as the Compleat Lexical Tutor created by Tom Cobb, the Range Program, the AWL Gapmaker, and the AWL Highlighter created by Sandra Haywood (Coxhead, 2016).

Focusing on the frequency of words not covered in the first 2,000 most frequently occurring words of English proposed by West (1953), Coxhead (2000) developed and evaluated a new academic list on the basis of a 3.5-million-word academic writing corpus. Coxhead argued that "ideal word list would be divided into smaller, frequency-based sublists to aid in the sequencing of teaching and in material development. A word list based on the occurrence of word families in a corpus of texts representing a variety of academic registers can provide information about how words are actually used" (2000, p. 214).

In terms of the development of the academic corpus from which the AWL was extracted, Coxhead (2000) constructed a corpus containing 414 academic writing by more than 400 authors with 3.5 million tokens (running words) and 70,377 types (individual words). The corpus was then divided into four subcorpora: arts, commerce, law, and science, and each subcorpus was further divided into seven subject areas with generally equal amount of running words in each subcorpus and each subject area. This 3.5-million-word corpus included a wide variety of academic texts, such as 158 journal articles, 51 edited academic journal articles from the Internet, 43 university textbooks or course books, 42 texts from the Learned and Scientific section of the Wellington Corpus of Written English (Bauer, 1993), and so forth. The frequency of each word was calculated by using the corpus analysis program "Range", which was able to count the frequency of each word in 32 files simultaneously, record the number of files that each word occurs in, and the total frequency of each word in each file. Words selected for the new AWL were: (1) word families not covered in the first 2,000 most frequent words presented in the GSL; (2) word families that occured at least 10 times in each of the four main sections of the corpus and in above 15 subject areas; (3) word families that occured at least 100 times in the 3.5-million-word academic corpus. Based on the above criteria, Coxhead (2000) developed the AWL, including 570 word families in total.

In view of the methodological issues involved in the development of the AWL (Coxhead, 2000), Gardner and Davies (2014) derived the AVL from the academic subcorpus of the Corpus of Contemporary American English (COCA). Gardner and Davies (2014) pointed out two problematic practices: (1) using word families as units of meaning; (2) excluding the most frequent 2,000 words of the GSL. In the AWL, a word family refers to a stem (headword) and all its inflectional and transparent derivational forms containing the stem. For example, the headword *react* and all its inflections (e.g. *reacted, reacts, reacting*) and derivations (e.g. *reaction, reactions, reactive, reactor*) were united as one item in the AWL. Nevertheless, these different forms related to *react* could be used to express drastically different meanings. For example, *reactor* refers to "a device or apparatus", while *reactionary* means "strongly opposed to social or political change" (Gardner & Davies, 2014, p. 307). Listing these forms with different meanings as one item could be somewhat misleading. In addition, the same form (e.g. *report*) could be used to express different meanings without grammatical identity. When used as a noun, *report* means "an account prepared for the benefits of others", while the verb *report* can be defined as "tell people certain information" (https://www.collinsdictionary.com/dictionary/english/report). In view of these issues with the AWL, Gardner and Davies (2014) explained that using lemmas (a headword and its inflectional forms) attached with parts of speech could solve the aforementioned issues by separating word forms with distinctive meanings while grouping word forms with same meanings. For instance, the noun *proceedings* (meaning "records" or "minutes"), the noun *procedure* (meaning "technique") and the adjective *procedural* (meaning "technical" or "routine") could be counted as distinct items given the differences in meaning. Meanwhile, *procedure* and its plural form *procedures* (meaning "techniques") can be grouped together given their same meaning. In addition, *report* as a noun and *report* as a verb can be listed as separate items to preserve the difference in meaning. Gardner and Davies (2014) also pointed out that students' knowledge of derivational forms has generally been acquired much later than knowledge of inflectional relationship, and derivational analysis only happens on the basis of learners' existing vocabulary knowledge. Thus, for learners at a beginning to intermediate level, organizing word lists on the basis of lemmas attached with grammatical identification can be more useful than on the basis of word families. The close relation between the AWL and the GSL also somewhat undermines the appropriateness of the AWL. The AWL was built on the basis of the GSL by deleting the most frequent 2,000 words to ensure that words covered in the AWL were low-frequency words in the GSL. However, the GSL is outdated and the AWL actually contains the words highly frequent in the British National Corpus (BNC; Nation et al., 2004; Schmitt & Schmitt, 2014).

In the development of the AVL, Gardner and Davies (2014) addressed the above-mentioned issues by (1) using lemmas attached with grammatical identification as the basic units, and (2) drawing upon a large and representative corpus of academic English—the academic subcorpus of COCA. Both academic and nonacademic materials were incorporated in the initial steps of developing the AVL for the purpose of distinguishing academic core words ("those that appear in the vast majority of the various academic disciplines"), high-frequency general words ("those appear with roughly equal and high frequency across all major registers of the large corpus, including the academic register"), and academic technical words ("those that appear in a narrow range of academic disciplines") (Gardner & Davies, 2014, p. 312). Four criteria were applied to obtain the academic core: (1) locating words (lemmas) that occurred above 42% of the time in the academic section of COCA through setting the word-selection ratio threshold; (2) ensuring the wide range of the AVL by selecting words (lemmas) that occur at a frequency of at least 20% in at least 7 out of the 9 academic disciplines; (3) including words (lemmas) that have a dispersion value of at least 0.80, with 0.01 indicating that "the word only occurs in an extremely small part of the corpus", and 1.00 indicating "perfectly even dispersion in all parts of the corpus" (Gardner & Davies, 2014, p. 316); (4) applying discipline measures to exclude words that occur less than 3 times per million words in each discipline.

2.3.2 Discipline-Specific Academic Word Lists

It has been well accepted that words are used differently across academic disciplines, therefore researchers find it necessary to develop discipline-specific academic word lists (Lei & Liu, 2016). Several academic word lists were developed accordingly, mainly including but not restricted to the Engineering Academic Word List (Mudraya, 2006), the Medical Academic Word List (Wang et al., 2008), the Nursing Academic Word List (Yang, 2015), the Environmental Academic Word List (Liu & Han, 2015), and the new Medical Academic Vocabulary List (Lei & Liu, 2016).

The majority of the discipline-specific word lists were generated by excluding the high-frequency general words included in the GSL, a key procedure demonstrated in Coxhead's (2000) development of the AWL, with the development of the new Medical Academic Vocabulary List by Lei and Liu (2016) as an exception. Behind this practice is the assumption that before language learners are proficient enough to learn lower-frequency words and academic words they should have grasped these high-frequency words in the GSL. Lei and Liu (2016) attributed this assumption to Nation's (2001) classification of words: high-frequency words, academic words, technical words, and low-frequency words. It is worth noticing that afterwards Nation (2013) recognized the overlap of high-frequency, academic, and technical words, and reclassified words into (1) high-frequency words, (2) mid-frequency words, (3) low-frequency words, and (4) specialized words (including academic and technical vocabulary).

To facilitate the design of medical course books and help learners of English for Medical Purposes (EMP) know clear their vocabulary learning goals, Wang et al. (2008) developed a Medical Academic Word List (MAWL). A corpus of about 1.1 million words, consisting of 288 medical research articles across 32 subject areas (downloaded from http://www.sciencedirect.com), was first created, since reading and writing medical research articles were the main tasks of learners of EMP. The MAWL was extracted by following the word selection criteria specified by Coxhead (2000), which covered three main aspects: specialized occurrence, range, and frequency. In terms of specialized occurrence, Wang et al. (2008) also excluded the 2,000 most frequent words listed in West's GSL. To ensure the range of the medical word list, Wang et al. (2008) determined that word families could be selected only when they occurred in at least 16 of the 32 subject areas. In addition, the threshold of frequency was set as 30 times in the corpus of medical research articles. Given the unclear distinction between technical and academic vocabulary, two experienced professors of English for Medical Purposes were employed to make final decisions when a concern was raised as to the computer-generated tentative list.

In 2016, a new Medical Academic Vocabulary List (Lei & Liu, 2016) was compiled to better serve the needs of the target group—medical English learners. According to Lei and Liu (2016), the new Medical Academic Vocabulary List (MAVL) they created was 53% shorter than the existing Medical Academic Word List generated by Wang et al. (2008), and demonstrated a wider coverage of medical English. Furthermore, the highlight of Lei and Liu's research also lies in its enhanced methodology realized by combining somewhat contradictory methods and procedures presented in Coxhead (2000) and Gardner and Davies (2014). Almost all discipline-specific word lists before the MAVL adopted the key procedure demonstrated in Coxhead (2000), namely excluding the top frequent words in the GSL. However, Lei and Liu (2016) acknowledged the viewpoint of Gardner and Davies (2014) that many general high-frequency words occurred more frequently in academic English than in general English and were attached with special meanings in academic English. Lei and Liu (2016) derived the new MAVL by lemmatizing and POS-tagging words of the raw texts using the Stanford CoreNLP, a tool frequently used for natural language processing. A list based on lemmas rather than word families was set as the research goal, since lemma-based lists tended to be more effective in excluding others items in a word family that rarely appear in the target field—medical English (Lei & Liu, 2016). A Python script was then created to extract lemmas from the corpus data. Six aspects were considered to finalize the new MAVL: minimum frequency (excluding words with a high frequency ratio but a low overall frequency), frequency ratio (to avoid including or excluding too many high-frequency general words), range ratio (including lemmas occurring at a frequency of 20% in at least 12 out of 21 subfields in medical English), dispersion (with Juilland's D value of at least 0.50 indicating of even distribution of a lemma in the corpora), discipline measure (excluding discipline-specific and technical words), and special criterion for high-frequency general words (High-frequency lemmas obeying the previous five measures can be included when they have special medical meanings.).

Besides the methodology, Lei and Liu (2016) also intended to distinguish from the MAWL developed by Wang et al. (2008) in many other aspects. First, the corpus from which Wang et al. (2008) derived their word list mainly consisted of medical English academic articles, while Lei and Liu (2016) used two different data sets to extract the new MAVL: a 2.7-million-word corpus of medical journal articles (MAEC) and a 3.5-million-word corpus of medical English textbooks (MTEC). Lei and Liu (2016) emphasized the indispensability of including medical English textbook data by stating that the target users of the new MAVL were mainly medical students or prospective medical students, who inevitably read medical textbooks, and there might exist linguistic and discourse differences between medical English textbooks and published medical English articles. Therefore, Lei and Liu (2016) found it imperative to include a medical textbook corpus as a cross-check source. Meanwhile, MAEC was used as the primary corpus, since medical English research articles were accessed and read by both medical students and medical professionals. The MAEC also differed from the corpus used in Wang et al. (2008) in that the MAEC included both research articles and review articles, while Wang et al.'s (2008) corpus was composed of research articles only. Lei and Liu (2016) explained that some of the journals they selected only published review articles, and that they viewed review articles and research articles as equally important to students and professionals in medicine. Second, different from Wang et al. (2008), who excluded published articles produced by nonnative speakers, Lei and Liu (2016) sided with Lee and Chen (2009), and included both native and nonnative speakers' articles, since all published articles, by native and nonnative speakers alike, have been carefully reviewed and revised. Lei and Liu (2016) also pointed out that the significantly larger size of MAEC used in their study ensured a higher representativeness of their data.

Even though developers of the academic core word lists have examined the validity of these lists by using a reference corpus, the development of discipline / field-specific academic word lists have rarely incorporated validating corpora, or examined the coverage of academic word lists in the original corpora (Liu & Han, 2015). Therefore, Liu and Han (2015) not only developed the Environmental Academic Word List (EAWL), but also examined its validity by comparing the coverage of EAWL and AWL in the validating corpus. The development of this EAWL was inspired by the observation that some high-frequency words in the Environmental Science corpus did not appear in the AWL or the GSL, indicating that the AWL did not reflect words used in Environmental Science discipline. In this study, the Environmental Science corpus was built by following a few principles related to the specialty of the texts, size, representativeness, and date of publication. Nevertheless, in terms of the discourse genre included in the corpus, only research articles were covered, since the researchers identified reading and writing research articles as the fundamental concerns for the majority of students studying Environmental Science. Textbooks were not included in the Environmental Science corpus, leaving the representativeness of this corpus somewhat questionable. Similar to the development of the AWL (Coxhead, 2000), the first 2,000 most frequent word families in the GSL were also excluded by Liu and Han

(2015), since these words were considered as prerequisites for EAP students. Words were selected and included into the EAWL by following three criteria: words not ranking among the first 2,000 most frequent words in the GSL, word families with an optimized usage of 30 (an improved version of Julliland's usage statistics), and words occurring in at least 8 out of the 10 subject areas. This EAWL was then validated by examining whether its coverage was higher than that of the AWL in the validating corpus, which was built by following the same criteria of the original corpus.

2.3.3 Register-Specific Academic Word Lists

With a dominant number of academic word lists focusing on academic written English, Dang et al. (2017) developed and validated an Academic Spoken Word List (ASWL) with the purpose of aiding L2 learners in comprehending academic speech in English-medium universities. The development of this ASWL was supported by the realization that there exists a great difference between the coverage of words in academic speech (4%) and that in academic writing (10%) in the AWL (Dang & Webb, 2014; Thompson, 2006; Dang et al., 2017), indicating that lists of academic written words cannot represent academic spoken vocabulary. The distinctive differences in linguistic features between academic speech and writing have also been identified in lexicogrammar research (Biber, 2006; Biber et al., 2002).

In reality, L2 learners' ability of comprehending reading materials, lectures, seminars, labs and tutorials is strongly associated with their academic achievement (Becker, 2016; Biber, 2006), and these tasks are generally essential but challenging for L2 learners (Flowerdew & Miller, 1992; Lynch, 2011; Mulligan & Kirkpatrick, 2000). Researchers have attributed L2 learners' difficulty to their limited vocabulary knowledge in academic spoken discourse, since vocabulary knowledge and listening comprehension proficiency are closely related (Van Zeeland & Schmitt, 2013). Therefore, the ASWL developed by Dang et al. (2017) can sufficiently contribute to EAP learners' development of vocabulary knowledge in spoken discourse and academic success.

The ASWL was developed on the basic of the existence of an academic core list. Four corpora were adopted by Dang et al. (2017): (1) an academic spoken corpus used for the development of the ASWL; (2) an academic spoken corpus used to determine whether the ASWL reflects the vocabulary in academic spoken discourse; (3) a cademic written corpus used for examining whether the ASWL represents spoken vocabulary; (4) a nonacademic spoken corpus used for examining whether the ASWL represents academic vocabulary. The representativeness of the two academic spoken corpora was achieved by following Biber's (1993) and Coxhead's (2000) guidelines. To be more specific, the two corpora consisted of spoken discourse from the four disciplines (i.e. hard pure, hard applied, soft pure, and soft applied) specified in Becher and Trowler (1989). The subcorpus was further divided into different subject areas to avoid bias toward specific discipline or subject area. In addition, the two spoken corpora consisted of four kinds of speech events: lectures, seminars, labs and tutorials. Similar to some previous studies (Gardner & Davies, 2014; Lei & Liu, 2016), the lemma was determined as the basic unit for calculation. Four aspects were consideved in the development of the Academic Spoken Word List, including size and coverage (containing a smaller number of word families with greater coverage), word families (focusing on word families not covered in the BNC / COCA 2,000), distribution across the four subcorpora (selecting words equally distributed in the subcorpora of the first academic spoken corpus), and adaptability to learners' levels (including words belonging to four different levels according to Nation's BNC / COCA lists to serve learners with different levels of proficiency). The list was further validated from three different aspects: range (only including word families that occurred in all four discipline subcorpora: hard pure, hard applied, soft pure, and soft applied), frequency (including word families that occurred at least 350 times in the first academic spoken corpus), and dispersion (indicating an even distribution of the words across the majority of the 24 subjects).

2.3.4 Multi-word Unit Frequency Lists

As reviewed in the previous sections, various types of academic word lists have been developed and evaluated to facilitate the teaching and learning of academic discourse. Nevertheless, the prevalent multi-word units for meaning-making are not considered in the design of these lists (Durrant, 2009). The scope of the list development research is further expanded to lists of various types of constructions / multi-word units (i.e. form-meaning mappings), since Functional and Cognitive Linguistics and usage-based theories of language recognized that multi-word units, basic units for meaning-making, are "conventionalized in the speech community, and entrenched speakers' mind" (Simpson-Vlach & Ellis, 2010, p. 488). Even though these multi-word units are significant in terms of their semantic, pragmatic, and discourse functions (Simpson-Vlach & Ellis, 2010), and empirical evidence suggests that knowledge of multi-word units is highly associated with language learners' proficiency (Howarth, 1998; Liu, 2012), acquisition of linguistic features can be very challenging since "they are often language-specific and enormous in number" (Liu, 2012, p. 25). Since these multi-word units are difficult to learn by referring to dictionaries, the development of a list is therefore necessary to allocate learners' attention systematically (Ackermann & Chen, 2013).

With the shift of research interest in Corpus Linguistics towards multi-word units as the basic units for meaning-making, an increasing number of empirical studies have begun to examine multi-word units in academic discourse by adopting similar statistical measures adopted in developing word lists, such as frequency and dispersion (e.g. Biber et al., 2004; Chen & Baker, 2010; Hyland, 2008), and developing frequency lists for different variations of multi-word units (Ackermann & Chen, 2013; Simpson-Vlach & Ellis, 2010). Different from traditional approaches that rely on expert judgment to identify multi-word units, the corpus-driven approach to the development of lists for multi-word units is realized through various statistical methods, such as using statistics to represent the strength of word co-occurrence, and automatic extraction of certain variations of multi-word units (Ackermann & Chen, 2013).

The methods in Moon (1998), probably one of the first studies in Corpus Linguistics that focused on multi-word units, were not advanced enough to use automatic extraction. Rather, a reference list of multi-word units selected from dictionaries and reference materials was adopted as a guide. Only fixed / non-compositional / idiomatic expressions were included in Moon's (1998) list of multi-word units, leaving some highly frequent ones, such as the lexical bundles identified by Biber and his colleagues (Biber et al., 1999), neglected.

The criteria used to define and identify multi-word units vary from perceptual salience to frequency criteria. Biber et al. (2004) focused on lexical bundles, presented a frequency-driven approach to multi-word units, and compared the use of lexical bundles in classroom teaching and textbooks with those in conversation and academic prose. Lexical bundles are defined as "the most frequent recurring lexical sequences in a register" (Biber et al., 2004, p. 376). Lexical bundles are "recurrent expressions, regardless of their idiomaticity, and regardless of their structural status" (Biber et al., 1999, p. 990). The statistical threshold for identifying lexical bundles varied from 10 to 40 per million words (PMWs). The corpus adopted in this study was the TOEFL 2,000 Spoken and Written Academic Language Corpus (T2K-SWAL) (Biber et al., 2004), which efficiently represented the spoken and written registers that EAP students had access to, such as classroom teaching, office hours, study groups, textbooks and other written materials. Lists of the most frequent lexical bundles with four to six words were successfully extracted by drawing upon an automated extraction method. These lexical bundles were carefully classified according to the functional categories, including stance expressions, discourse organizers and referential expressions.

Liu (2012) claimed that before his extraction of the most frequently occurring multi-word constructions in academic written English, Biber and his colleagues' approach that relied solely on frequency was the most widely used. Their approach, nevertheless, was problematic in prioritizing recurrent word sequences that were less psycholinguistically salient (Liu, 2012; Simpson-Vlach & Ellis, 2010). For example, even though formulaic sequences *on the other hand* and *at the same time* were more psycholinguistically salient than *to do with the* or *I think it was*, they might be presented as equivalents in terms of frequency. This phenomenon was attributed to the structural incompleteness of the majority of lexical bundles (Carter & McCarthy, 2006; Liu, 2012). According to Biber and Conrad (1999), only 15% of lexical bundles identified in conversation and 5% in academic writing were complete structures. In addition, many lexical bundles seemed to be "neither terribly functional nor pedagogically completing" (Simpson-Vlach & Ellis, 2012, p. 493).

To address this problem, Simpson-Vlach and Ellis (2012) adopted an innovative measure of utility, called formula teaching worth (FTW), for extracting meaningful lexical bundles, which took both frequency and mutual information (MI) score (a statistic that indicates the likelihood that the components in a multi-word unit co-occur) into consideration. Even though Simpson-Vlach and Ellis' (2012) approach reduced the number of lexical bundles ending with *a / the* noticeably, such lexical bundles were not eliminated, and 18% of written academic lexical bundles still ended with *a / the*. Simpson-Vlach and Ellis (2010) derived a list of formulaic expressions that used an innovative combination of quantitative and qualitative criteria, corpus statistics and linguistic analysis, psycholinguistic processing metrics, and instructor insights. A 2.1-million-word academic writing corpus and a 2.1-million-word academic speech corpus were adopted to extract the target academic formulas list. One nonacademic speech corpus and one nonacademic writing corpus were used for comparison and validation. In the development process, three-, four-, and five-word sequences were extracted from the above-mentioned four corpora by using the program Collocate developed by Michael Barlow in 2004, and the cutoff range of frequency was set as at least 10 times per million in more than 4 out of 5 of the academic disciplines (e.g. Humanities and Arts, Social Sciences, Biological and Health Science, Physical Sciences, and Engineering). To obtain a list that include formulas more frequent in the academic corpora than in nonacademic discourse, the log-likelihood was adopted to compare the frequency of the formulas across the academic corpora and their nonacademic counterparts. Formulas that demonstrated a significant p value (a significance level of $p = 0.01$) were identified as those that occurred statistically more frequent in academic discourse. Nevertheless, solely relying on frequency could be problematic, since a n-gram could be very frequent due to the high frequency of their component words or grammatical functions (e.g. *and this is*, *this is the*), and some less frequent but useful formulas (e.g. *we're interested in*, *think about how*) could be neglected. The MI index was also not a highly reliable statistics in extracting formulas, since it privileged low-frequency items (Simpson-Vlach & Ellis, 2010). Finally, the FTW score, a combination of MI and frequency, was used as an innovative approach to selecting academic formulas, since "it allows for a prioritization based on statistical and psycholinguistic measures, which a purely frequency-based ordering does not" (Simpson-Vlach & Ellis, 2010, p. 497). To further facilitate pedagogical decisions, the finalized list was classified according to major discourse-pragmatic functions, generally including referential expressions, stance expressions, and discourse organizing functions.

Even though the above-mentioned studies contributed greatly to the methodology of developing lists of multi-word units, there still existed some limitations. Corpora adopted in these studies only had five million words or fewer. Many multi-word units yielded from these studies were "incomplete structures with functionality" (Liu, 2012, p. 25), with Simpson-Vlach and Ellis (2010) being an exception. Liu (2012), therefore, intended to further examine the issue by adopting a larger database, namely the academic writing sub-corpora of the 400-million-word Corpus of Contemporary American English and the 100-million-word British National Corpus. Liu (2012) pointed out that using abstract representation of language structures could address the issue with structural completeness and functionality. For example, *this is the* seems to be structural incomplete. However, this lexical bundle can be structural complete after it is described as "this is determiner + noun phrase". The academic writing sub-corpora in COCA and BNC were adopted in Liu's (2012) study for their large size, wide coverage of academic disciplines, and contemporariness. Liu (2012) extracted multi-word units, including lexical bundles, idioms, and phrasal / prepositional verbs from the academic writing sub-corpora in COCA and BNC by searching these multi-word units through the supplied search functions (e.g. the pats of speech query and the lemma sorting function). Similar to Moon (1998), Liu (2012) based his candidate queries on multi-word units derived from a series of previous studies, such as Biber et al. (1999), Carter and McCarthy (2006), and Simpson-Vlach and Ellis (2010), Biber et al. (1999); Gardner and Davies (2007), Liu (2003, 2008); and dictionaries, such as *Cambridge International Dictionary of Idioms* (1998), *Cambridge International Dictionary of Phrasal Verbs* (2001), *Oxford Idioms Dictionary* (2001), *Oxford Phrasal Verbs Dictionary* (2001). An item occurring 20 times per million words in either 6 out of 8 academic disciplines in COCA academic writing sub-corpus or 5 out of 6 academic disciplines in BNC was included in Liu's (2012) list. The 228 most frequently occurring academic written English multi-word units in the finalized list were further categorized according to sematic functions, including referential / ideational phrases, stance / interpersonal expressions, and discourse / textual organizers. According to Liu (2012), limitations of this study included: (1) relying heavily on previous research for candidate multi-word units; (2) questionable classification of these multi-word units in accordance with semantic functions; (3) unsystematic notation method for representing the multi-word units.

Being aware of the existence of an academic core, Ackermann and Chen (2013) developed the Academic Collocation List. Their database was the written curricular component (25.6 million words) of the Pearson International Corpus of Academic English, which consists of over 37 million words of academic texts, such as lectures, seminars, textbooks, and journal articles. The development of the Academic Collocation List was conducted by following four steps: Firstly, computational methods was practiced to extract the frequent collocation candidates. Secondly, the data-driven list was then polished through manual analysis. Thirdly, expert judgments were applied to ensure that the collocations included in the list were pedagogically relevant. In this book, collocations are defined as words that co-occur within the +3 span of reference words at least five times across at least five different texts within a MI score of three and higher and a *t* score of two and higher. In terms of the automatic extraction of collocations, a list of content words was first obtained by using MonoConc Pro 2.2 and then words occurring more than five times per million words in more than five different texts were compiled. Function words, proper nouns, personal names, non-words, and words included in the GSL were removed from the contend word list. Collocates of these finalized contend words were then extracted by calculating the MI score, indicating the strength of association between the elements within a collocation, and *t* score, measuring the certainty of a collocation. A high MI score suggests a fixed phrase, while a high *t* score is associated with collocates with high frequency (Ackermann & Chen, 2013). The list then underwent a very strict refining process, including filtering (decision on the cut-off value of MI score and *t* score to balance the inclusion of unsuitable combinations and exclusion of real collocations), POS tagging (facilitating the extraction of four POS combinations: verb + noun, adjective + noun, adverb + adjective, and adverb + verb), manual vetting (Each item was reviewed by the researchers to include appropriate collocations, while excluding inappropriate ones.), and expert review (expert judgments on the appropriateness and relevance of each item). Lastly, this list was validated by being compared with collocations extracted from nonacademic registers (imaginative writings and informative writings).

2.3.5　Discipline-Specific Lists of Academic Multi-word Units

Academic written discourse covering a variety of disciplines was actually heterogeneous per se (Durrant, 2009). Nevertheless, researchers also discovered that generic discourse and discipline-specific discourse were not distinctively different in terms of vocabulary use (Hyland & Tse, 2007; Durrant, 2014). The academic corpus employed in Hyland and Tse (2007) included a variety of writing texts in a wide range of academic disciplines, including Biology, Physics, Computer Science, Mechanical and Electronic Engineering, Sociology, Business Studies, and Applied Linguistics. From each of the above-mentioned disciplines, 30 research articles, 7 textbook chapters, and 20 academic book reviews were collected. In addition, 45 scientific letters were extracted from Physics and Biology, thus representing the academic discourse that EAP students tend to read in academic context. To represent language / vocabulary produced by L2 students, Hyland and Tse (2007) also added eight Master's theses, six doctoral dissertations, and eight final-year undergraduate project theses by L2 students from each of the disciplines. The methodology adopted to compile this corpus was an improvement of Coxhead's methodology, which was considered to be opportunistic from Hyland and Tse's (2007) perspective, since Coxhead's corpus included (1) unequal numbers of texts in each field, (2) texts from dated sources (Lancaster-Oslo / Bergen Corpus and Brown Corpus and Wellington Corpus), and (3) no students' writing production. The corpus was then organized based on disciplines and fields via Corpus Builder developed by Tom Cobb, and further processed via Range created by Paul Nation, a software that shows the frequency and range of each item in a given corpus.

In spite that the previous research on word / multi-word unit list development could be generally classified into generic and discipline-specific lists, Durrant (2014) suggested that this dichotomy might not be well-grounded. To empirically examine the variations between disciplines, Durrant (2014) used texts selected from the British Academic Written English corpus, consisting of the assignments of students in British univeristies, as the main data source so as to investigate texts that students tend to write rather than read. Each written text was tagged with discipline and level of study. This corpus included about 5.8 million words, approximately equally distributed across different disciplines and study levels. Words appearing more than 100 times per million words in each discipline level and occurring in more than 10% of texts were extracted as frequent words. It is worth noticing that this standard of extracting frequent words is fundamentally different from that used by Paquot (2007) and Simpson-Vlach and Ellis (2010), which extracted words that were significantly more frequent in academic discourse than in a reference corpus of general English. Durrant (2014) defended his method of extracting frequent words by stating that words frequent in both academic and general English could have special use in academic discourse. By adopting cluster analysis, Durrant (2014) identified the overlaps of various disciplines in terms of frequent words, further challenging the dichotomy of generic and discipline-specific word lists.

Since collocations are generally less frequent than individual words, a large corpus is required to reflect the distribution and use of these multi-word units. To ensure that the list of collocations derived was not specific to particular subject areas, Durrant (2009) constructed his corpus by balancing written discourses from a wide range of academic disciplines. Five million words were collected for multiple disciplines, including Arts, Humanities, Engineering, Medicine and Health Sciences, Education, etc. Keywords for each discipline were obtained and a matrix was presented to show the percentage of overlapping keywords of each pair of disciplines. A cluster analysis was applied afterwards to reveal the linguistic connection and distinction between different disciplines, and the constitution of the corpus was modified based on the results of the cluster analysis. Collocation, in this study, was defined as "word pairs which co-occur with at least moderate frequency across a wide range of academic disciplines, but which are not often found in nonacademic language" (Durrant, 2009, pp.161–162). By using the word list function in WordSmith Tools developed by Mike Scott, Durrant (2009) generated a list of word pairs co-occuring within a four-word span of each at least once per million word. To select collocations that were more frequent in academic fields than in nonacademic fields, another list of collocations was generated from the BNC via the same method to function as a reference. Log-likelihood ratios were calculated to facilitate the identification of exclusively frequent academic collocations, with the value higher than 82.00 indicating that collocations occurred more frequently in academic fields. Nevertheless, Durrant (2009) pointed out that the list of lexical collocations somewhat disappointing and misguiding, since an exclusive focus on lexical collocations was contradictory to the fundamental linguistic framework that viewed lexis and grammar as highly associated. Most importantly, Durrant (2009) pointed out the importance and usefulness of having learners focus on a list of grammatical collocations (i.e. grammar patterns) and combine lexis and grammar as a whole, underlining the necessity of developing a frequency list of grammar patterns.

2.4 Summary

Chapter 2 emphasizes the importance of developing word / multi-word unit lists by presenting the association between lexical knowledge and English language proficiency and the necessity of prioritizing certain lexical entities in light of the limited learning and instruction time. The review of previous research on the development of word / multi-word lists centers around fundamental considerations, including the existence / non-existence of an academic core and the statistical criterion in selecting frequent words / multi-word units. Specific empirical studies are reviewed afterwards by following the order of general word lists, general multi-word lists, academic word lists, and academic multi-word lists. Nevertheless, some researchers have questioned the distinction between generic and discipline-specific word lists by empirically identifying the overlaps of different disciplines in word use.

References

Ackermann, K. & Chen, Y. (2013). Developing the academic collocation list (ACL)— A corpus-driven and expert-judged approach. *Journal of English for Academic Purposes*, 12, 235-247.

Aryadoust, V. & Liu, S. (2015). Predicting EFL writing ability from levels of mental representation measured by Coh-Metrix: A structural equation modeling study. *Assessing Writing*, 24, 35-58.

Barrow, J., Nakanishi, Y. & Ishino, H. (1998). Assessing Japanese college students' vocabulary knowledge with a self-checking familiarity survey. *System*, 27, 223-247.

Bauer, L. (1993). *Manual of information to accompany the Wellington Corpus of Written New Zealand English*. Wellington, New Zealand: Victoria University of Wellington.

Becher, T. & Trowler, P. R. (1989). *Academic tribes and territories: Intellectual enquiry and the culture of disciplines*. 2nd ed. Buckingham: Open University Press.

Becker, A. (2016). L2 students' performance on listening comprehension items targeting local and global information. *Journal of English for Academic Purposes*, 24, 1-13.

Biber, D. (1993). Representativeness in corpus design. *Literary and Linguistic Computing*, 8, 243-257.

Biber, D. (2006). *University language: A corpus-based study of spoken and written registers*. Amsterdam: John Benjamins.

Biber, D. & Conrad, S. (1999). Lexical bundles in conversation and academic prose. In H. Hasselgard & S. Oksfjell (eds.), *Out of corpora: Studies in honor of Stig Johansson*. Amsterdam: Rodopi, 181-190.

Biber, D., Conrad, S. & Cortes, V. (2004). If you look at…: Lexical bundles in university teaching and textbooks. *Applied Linguistics*, 25(3), 371-405.

Biber, D., Conrad, S., Reppen, R., Byrd, P. & Helt, M. (2002). Speaking and writing in the university: A multi-dimensional comparison. *TESOL Quarterly*, 36, 9-48.

Biber, D., Johansson, S., Leech, G., Conrad, S. & Finegan, E. (1999). *Longman grammar of spoken and written English*. London: Longman.

Bonk, W. (2000). Second language lexical knowledge and listening comprehension. *International Journal of Listening*, 14(1), 14-31.

Cambridge international dictionary of idioms (1998). Cambridge: Cambridge University Press.

Cambridge international dictionary of phrasal verbs (2001). Cambridge: Cambridge University Press.

Carter, R. & McCarthy, M. (2006). This that and the other: Multi-word clusters in spoken English as visible patterns of interaction. In M. McCarthy (ed.),

Explorations in Corpus Linguistics. Cambridge: Cambridge University Press, 7-26.

Chen, Y. H. & Baker, P. (2010). Lexical bundles in native and non-native academic writing. *Language Learning and Technology*, 14(2), 30-49.

Chung, T. M. & Nation, P. (2003). Technical vocabulary in specialized texts. *Reading in a Foreign Language*, 15(2), 103-116.

Coxhead, A. (2000). A new Academic Word List. *TESOL Quarterly*, 34(2), 213-238.

Coxhead, A. (2016). Reflecting on Coxhead (2000), "A new Academic Word List". *TESOL Quarterly*, 50(1), 181-185.

Crossley, S., Salsbury, T. & McNamara, D. (2010). The development of polysemy and frequency use in English Second Language speakers. *Language Learning*, 60, 573-605.

Dang, T. N. Y. & Webb, S. (2014). The lexical profile of academic spoken English. *English for Specific Purposes*, 33, 66-76.

Dang, T. N. Y., Coxhead, A. & Webb, S. (2017). The academic spoken word list. *Language Learning*, 67(4), 959-997.

De Jong, N. H., Steinel, M. P., Florijn, A. F., Schoonen, R. & Hulstijn, J. H. (2012). Facets of speaking proficiency. *Studies in Second Language Acquisition*, 34(1), 5-34.

Durrant, P. (2009). Investigating the viability of a collocation list for students of English for Academic Purposes. *English for Specific Purposes*, 28(3), 157-159.

Durrant, P. (2014). Discipline and level specificity in university students' written vocabulary. *Applied Linguistics*, 35, 328-356.

Eldridge, J. (2008). "No, there isn't an 'academic vocabulary', but..." A reader responds to K. Hyland and P. Tse's "Is there an 'academic vocabulary'?". *TESOL Quarterly*, 42, 109-113.

Farrell, P. (1990). *Vocabulary in ESP: A lexical analysis of the English of Electronics and a study of semi-technical vocabulary* (ERIC No. ED332551). Retrieved from Institute of Education Sciences: https://eric.ed.gov/?id=ED332551.

Flowerdew, J. & Miller, L. (1992). Student perceptions, problems and strategies in second language lecture comprehension. *RELC Journal*, 23, 60-80.

Gardner, D. & Davies, M. (2007). Pointing out frequent phrasal verbs: A corpus analysis. *TESOL Quarterly*, 41, 339-359.

Gardner, D. & Davies, M. (2014). A new Academic Vocabulary List. *Applied Linguistics*, 35(3), 305-327.

Ghadessy, P. (1979). Frequency counts, word lists, and materials preparation: A new approach. *English Teaching Forum*, 17, 24-27.

Hancioğlu, N., Neufeld, S. & Eldridge, J. (2008). Through the looking glass and into the land of lexico-grammar. *English for Specific Purposes*, 27, 459-479.

Howarth, P. (1998). Phraseology and second language proficiency. *Applied Linguistics*, 19(1), 24-44.

Hsu, W. (2014). Measuring the vocabulary load of Engineering textbooks for EFL undergraduates. *English for Specific Purposes*, 33, 53-64.

Hsu, W. (2019). Voice of America news as voluminous reading material for mid-frequency vocabulary learning. *RELC Journal*, 50(3), 408-421.

Hu, M. & Nation, I. S. P. (2000). Unknown vocabulary density and reading comprehension. *Reading in a Foreign Language*, 13, 403-430.

Hyland, K. (2002). Specificity revisited: How far should we go now?. *English for Specific Purposes*, 21(4), 385-95.

Hyland, K. (2008). Academic clusters: Text patterning in published and postgraduate writing. *International Journal of Applied Linguistics*, 18(1), 41-62.

Hyland, K. (2016). General and specific EAP. In K. Hyland & P. Shaw (eds.), *The Routledge handbook of English for Academic Purposes*. London: Routledge, 17-29.

Hyland, K. & Tse, P. (2007). Is there an "academic vocabulary"?. *TESOL Quarterly*, 41, 235-253.

Juilland, A. & Chang-Rodríguez, E. (1964). *Frequency dictionary of Spanish words*. Berlin: De Gruyter Mouton.

Kuehn, P. (1996). *Assessment of academic literacy skills: Preparing minority and LEP (limited English proficient) Students for the postsecondary education* (ERIC No. ED415498). Retrieved from Institute of Education Sciences: https://eric.ed.gov/?id=ED415498

Laufer, B. (1988). What percentage of lexis is necessary for comprehension? In C. Lauren & M. Norman (eds.), *Special language: From humans to thinking machines*. Clevedon: Multilingual Matters, 316-323.

Laufer, B. (2013). Lexical thresholds for reading comprehension: What they are and how they can be used for teaching purposes. *TESOL Quarterly*, 47(4), 867-872.

Laufer, B. & Nation, P. (1999). A vocabulary-size test of controlled productive ability. *Language Testing*, 16(1), 33-51.

Laufer, B. & Ravenhorst-Kalovski, G. (2010). Lexical threshold revisited: Lexical text coverage, learners' vocabulary size and reading comprehension. *Reading in a Foreign Language*, 22(1), 15-30.

Lee, D. Y. W. & Chen, S. X. (2009). Making a bigger deal of the smaller words: Function words and other key items in research writing by Chinese learners. *Journal of Second Language Writing*, 18, 149-165.

Lei, L. & Liu, D. (2016). A new Medical Academic Word List: A corpus-based study with enhanced methodology. *Journal of English for Academic Purposes*, 22, 42-51.

Li, C. (2019). Using a listening vocabulary levels test to explore the effect of vocabulary knowledge on GEPT listening comprehension performance. *Language Assessment Quarterly*, 16(3), 328-344.

Liao, Y. F. (2009). *A construct validation study of the GEPT reading and listening sections: Re-examining the models of L2 reading and listening abilities and their relations to lexico-grammatical knowledge.* (Doctoral dissertation, Columbia University). Retrieved from https://scholars.lib.ntu.edu.tw/handle/123456789/565472.

Liu, D. (2003). The most frequently used idioms in American spoken English: A corpus analysis and its implications. *TESOL Quarterly*, 37, 671-700.

Liu, D. (2008). Linking adverbials: An across-register study and its implications. *International Journal of Corpus Linguistics*, 13, 491-518.

Liu, D. (2012). The most frequently-used multi-word constructions in academic written English: A multi-corpus study. *English for Specific Purposes*, 31, 25-35.

Liu, J. & Han, L. (2015). A corpus-based Environmental Academic Word List building and its validity test. *English for Specific Purposes*, 39, 1-11.

Lynch, T. (2011). Academic listening in the 21st century: Reviewing a decade of research. *Journal of English for Academic Purposes*, 10, 79-88.

Lynn, R. W. (1973). Preparing word lists: A suggested method. *RELC Journal*, 4(1), 25-32.

Martínez, I. A., Beck, S. C. & Panza, C. B. (2009). Academic vocabulary in agricultural research articles: A corpus-based study. *English for Specific Purposes*, 28, 183-198.

McLean, S., Kramer, B. & Beglar, D. (2015). The creation and validation of a listening vocabulary levels test. *Language Teaching Research*, 19(6), 741-760.

McNamara, D., Crossley, S. A., Roscoe, R. D., Allen, L. K. & Dai, J. (2015). A hierarchical classification approach to automated essay scoring. *Assessing Writing*, 23, 35-59.

Meara, P. & Wolter, B. (2004). V-links: Beyond vocabulary depth. *Angles on the English-Speaking World*, 4, 129-140.

Moon, R. (1998). *Fixed expressions and idioms in English: A corpus-based approach.* Oxford: Oxford University Press.

Moon, Y., Choi, J. & Kang, Y. (2019). Does reading and vocabulary knowledge of advanced Korean EFL learners facilitate their writing performance. *The Journal of Asia TEFL*, 16(1), 149-162.

Mostafa, J. E. & Ali, D. (2021). Vocabulary size and depth as predictors of second language speaking ability. *System*, 99, 1-15.

Mudraya, O. (2006). Engineering English: A lexical frequency instructional model. *English for Specific Purposes*, 25(2), 235-256.

Mulligan, D. & Kirkpatrick, A. (2000). How much do they understand? Lectures, students and comprehension. *Higher Education Research & Development*, 19, 311-335.

Nation, I. S. P. (2001). *Learning vocabulary in another language.* Cambridge: Cambridge University Press.

Nation, I. S. P. (2006). How large a vocabulary is needed for reading and listening?. *Canadian Modern Language Review*, 63, 59-82.

Nation, I. S. P. (2011). Research into practice: Vocabulary. *Language Teaching*, 44, 529-539.

Nation, I. S. P. (2013). *Learning vocabulary in another language.* 2nd ed. Cambridge: Cambridge University Press.

Nation, I. S. P. (2016). *Making and using word lists for language learning and testing.* Amsterdam: John Benjamins.

Nation, I. S. P., Bogaards, P. & Laufer, B. (2004). A study of the most frequent word families in the British National Corpus. In P. Bogaards & B. Laufer (eds.), *Vocabulary in a second language: Selection, acquisition, and testing.* Amsterdam: John Benjamins, 3-13.

Nation, P. & Waring, R. (1997). Vocabulary size, text coverage and word lists. In N. Schmitt & M. McCarthy (eds.), *Vocabulary: Description, acquisition and pedagogy.* Cambridge: Cambridge University Press, 6-19.

Neufeld, S., Hancioğlu, N. & Eldridge, J. (2011). Beware the range in RANGE, and the academic in AWL. *System*, 39, 533-538.

Olinghouse, N. & Wilson, J. (2013). The relationship between vocabulary and writing quality in three genres. *Reading & Writing*, 26(1), 45-65.

Oxford idioms dictionary. (2001). Oxford: Oxford University Press.

Oxford phrasal verbs dictionary. (2001). Oxford: Oxford University Press.

Paquot, M. (2007). Towards a productively-oriented academic word list. In J. Walinski, K. Kredens & S. Gozdz-Roszkowski (eds.), *Practical applications in language and computers.* Frankfurt am Main, Germany: Peter Lang, 127-140.

Ravin, Y. & Leacock, C. (2000). Polysemy: An overview. In Y. Raven & C. Leacock (eds.), *Polysemy: Theoretical and computational approaches*. Oxford: Oxford University Press, 1-29.

Read, J. (1998). Validating a test to measure depth of vocabulary knowledge. In A. J. Kunnan (ed.), *Validation in language assessment*. New York: Routledge, 41-60.

Santos, M. (2010). Depth of academic vocabulary knowledge: Investigating depth of academic vocabulary knowledge among language-minority community college students. *Reflections on English Language Teaching*, 9(1), 19-42.

Schmitt, N. & Schmitt, D. (2014). A reassessment of frequency and vocabulary size in L2 vocabulary teaching. *Language Teaching*, 47(4), 484-503.

Schmitt, N., Grabe, W. & Jiang, X. (2011). The percentage of words known in a text and reading comprehension. *The Modern Language Journal*, 95, 26-43.

Simpson-Vlach, R. & Ellis, N. C. (2010). An academic formulas list: New methods in phraseology research. *Applied Linguistics*, 31(4), 487-512.

Sinclair, J. (1991). *Corpus, concordance and collocation*. Oxford: Oxford University Press.

Stæhr, L. S. (2009). Vocabulary knowledge and advanced listening comprehension in English as a Foreign Language. *Studies in Second Language Acquisition*, 31(4), 577-607.

Thompson, P. (2006). A corpus perspective on the lexis of lectures, with a focus on economics lectures. In K. Hyland & M. Bondi (eds.), *Academic discourse across disciplines*. New York: Peter Lang, 253-270.

Townsend, D., Filippini, A., Collins, P. & Biancarosa, G. (2012). Evidence for the importance of academic word knowledge for the academic achievement of diverse middle school students. *The Elementary School Journal*, 112, 497-518.

Uchihara, T. & Clenton, J. (2020). Investigating the role of vocabulary size in second language speaking ability. *Language Teaching Research*, 24(4), 540-556.

Uchihara, T. & Saito, K. (2019). Exploring the relationship between productive vocabulary knowledge and second language oral ability. *The Language Learning*

Journal, 47(1), 64-75.

Van Zeeland, H. & Schmitt, N. (2013). Lexical coverage in L1 and L2 listening comprehension: The same or different from reading comprehension?. *Applied Linguistics*, 34, 457-479.

Wang, J., Liang, S. & Ge, G. (2008). Establishment of a Medical Academic Word List. *English for Specific Purposes*, 27(4), 442-458.

West, M. (1953). *A General Service List of English words*. London: Longman, Green & Co.

Wu, J. R.W. & Wu, R. Y. F. (2010). Relating the GEPT reading comprehension tests to the CEFR. In W. Martyniuk (ed.), *Aligning tests with the CEFR: Reflections on using the Council of Europe's draft manual*. Cambridge: Cambridge University Press, 204-224.

Xue, G. & Nation, I. S. P. (1984). A university word list. *Language Learning and Communication*, 3, 215-229.

Yang, M. (2015). A Nursing Academic Word List. *English for Specific Purposes*, 37, 27-38.

Zhang, P. & Graham, S. (2020). Learning vocabulary through listening: The role of vocabulary knowledge and listening proficiency. *Language Learning*, 70(4), 1017-1053.

CHAPTER 3

Construction Grammar

3.1 Definition of Constructions

Constructions refer to the form and meaning / function pairs entrenched in speakers' mind and conventionalized in the speech community (Bybee, 2010; Goldberg, 1995, 2003; Trousdale & Hoffmann, 2013), including morphemes, words, idioms, partially lexically filled patterns (e.g. *the more...*, *the more...*) and general linguistic patterns (e.g. passive) (see Table 3.1) (Goldberg, 2003, 2006; Goldberg & Suttle, 2010). Constructions are operationalized as a multi-level construct, ranging from constructions with very specific meanings (e.g. "accident waiting to happen" construction) to constructions with general meanings (e.g. the "interrogative" construction) (Stefanowitsch & Gries, 2003). Since the specific meanings of constructions can vary, it is impossible to calculate the number of potential constructions by introducing the variable of how specific the constructions are (Hunston & Su, 2019).

Table 3.1   Examples of constructions at varying levels of size and complexity
(adapted from Goldberg & Suttle, 2010, p. 469)

Construction	Form / Example
Word	Example: ornithology or ornery
Partially filled word (aka morpheme)	Example: anti-N, pre-N, V-ing
Complex word	Example: daredevil, shoo-in
Idiom (filled)	Example: trip the light fantastic
Idiom (partially filled)	Example: jog someone's memory
Covariational-conditional construction	Form: the X-er, the Y-er (e.g. The more you think about it, the less you understand.)
Ditransitive (double-object) construction	Form: Subj V Obj_1 Obj_2 (e.g. He baked her a muffin.)
Passive construction	Form: Subj Aux PP (by) (e.g. The hedgehog was struck by lightning.)

Discussion on constructions has often been related to three factors, including schematicity, productivity, and compositionality.

Schematicity refers to the gradual abstraction procedure manifested in categorization. "A schema is a taxonomic generalization of categories, whether linguistic or not" (Traugott & Trousdale, 2013, p. 13). Linguistic schemas are semantically general / abstract groups of constructions with more concrete sub-level linguistic entities nested under (i.e. subschemas). For example, *fruit* is more abstract / general / inclusive than *apple*, while *apple* can be further divided into *fuji*, *gala*, *honeycrisp*. A construction may consist of abstract / schematic components or a combination of schematic and concrete components (Goldberg, 2006). According to Goldberg (2006), speakers accumulate item-specific knowledge about particular expressions through interactions and are able to generalize to construct schematic knowledge about various expressions. For instance, speakers can generalize individual construction type (e.g. X give Y Z) by encountering expressions, such as *I gave him a book* / *I baked him a cake*, and finally reach schematic constructions (e.g. [Subj V Obj_1 Obj_2]) through generalizing mechanism (Traugott & Trousdale, 2013).

Productivity indicates "i) the extent to which they sanction other less schematic constructions, and ii) the extent to which they are constrained" (Traugott & Trousdale,

2013, p. 17). With reference to morphology, the formula of creating nouns [Adj + th] is less productive than [Adj + ness], since the schema [Adj + ness] (e.g. *helplessness, trustworthiness, forgiveness*) is used to construct more nouns than [Adj + th]. Discussion on productivity of constructions has to be related to type / construction frequency (i.e. the freguency of different forms of a particular construction in texts) and token / construct frequency (i.e. the frequency of a specific form occurring in texts). The concept of "frequency of use" approximates "construct frequency" more.

Compositionality pertains to the transparency / predictability of the connection between form and meaning (Traugott & Trousdale, 2013). "Syntax is compositional in that it builds more complex well- formed expressions recursively, on the basis of smaller ones, while semantics is compositional in that it constructs the meanings of larger expressions on the basis of the meanings of smaller ones (ultimately words, or rather morphemes)" (Hinzen et al., 2012, p. 3). The meaning of constructions can be predictable (e.g. transitive, ditransitive, and intransitve constructions) or unpredictable (e.g. idioms or covariational-conditional constructions) from the component lexis, lending support to the argument that meaning belongs to the construction rather than to the individual lexis (Stefanowitsch & Gries, 2003; Goldberg, 2006, 2013; Gries & Stefanowitsch, 2004). When the meaning of a construction is unpredictable, the construction is termed as "unusal pattern". Hearers or readers can comprehend semantically unpredictable / non-compositional constructions only when they are in conventional forms.

Much of our knowledge of language consists of a network of general constructions (e.g. relative clauses, various exclamatives, questions, topicalization), with more specific constructions inherited from general ones (Fillmore et al., 1988; Goldberg, 1995; Lakoff, 1987). Argument structure constructions are constructions "that relate abstract meanings with arrays of grammatical relations" (Goldberg, 2013, p. 437), e.g. transitive, intransitive, and ditransitive constructions. The ditransitive construction, for example, has two object complements (without preposition between the two object complements) and is reliably associated with the actual or potential transfer (Goldberg,

2013). "Arguments" refer to the complements associated with the key word (the verb in this construction) in a construction. For example, *give* is a three-argument verb with three complements, including the agent (the giver), the recipient (the receiver), and theme (the entity being passed).

Construction Grammar offers two alternative perspectives in describing the relationship between form and meaning in verb-argument constructions (VAC$_s$): the construction-oriented interpretation and the verb-oriented interpretation.

The construction-oriented interpretation of form-meaning relation suggests that constructions, regardless of the main verbs, bear meaning. For example, people tend to interpret *moop* (a nonsense verb) in the sentence *She mooped him something* as either *give* or verbs indicating literal or metaphorical transfer (Ahren, 2003; Goldberg, 1995). Empirical efforts have also been made to clarify the relationship between constructions and sentence meaning. For example, by adopting the research paradigm of having students sort sentences based on meaning, Bencini and Goldberg (2000) found that constructions had a greater effect on the perception of sentence meaning than the morphological forms of verbs. The data collection materials included sixteen English sentences of four verbs (*throw, slice, get,* and *take*) in four constructions (ditransitive, caused motion, resultative, and transitive constructions). Participants were required to (1) paraphrase each sentence to ensure that they processed the meaning of the whole sentence, and (2) sort these sentences according to the meaning. The researchers also reminded the participants that the same words could be used to convey different meanings. Inconsistent with the verb-centered perspective, the result showed that 7 out of 17 participants completed the task, and the rest 10 participants mixed verb-oriented and construction-oriented standards in the sorting process. This result suggested that participants sorted or classified meanings according to construction, challenging the once dominant view that subjects grouped sentences with the same verbs together.

Kaschak and Glenberg (2000) also provided supportive evidence for the construction-oriented interpretation by examing the Indexical Hypothesis proposed by Glenberg and Roberbson (1999). This hypothesis postulates that three processes are involved in sentence comprehension, including "mapping / indexing words and phrases to referents, deriving affordances (Gibson, 1979) from these referents, and meshing (Glenberg, 1997) these affordances under the guidance of intrinsic biological and physical constraints" (Kaschak & Glenberg, 2000, p. 508). "Mapping / indexing" is related to the comprehension of who / what is being discussed. "Affordances" refers to ways that individuals interact with things in the environment. For example, a person can interact with books by reading them or using them as decorations. "Meshing", the third process, combines interactions between individuals and coherent actions that contribute to a goal. Kaschak and Glenberg (2000) empirically tested the third process and found that the interaction between syntax (i.e. constructions) and semantics (rather than verbs) contributed to understanding. Kaschak and Glenberg built up the final conclusion by drawing upon three findings of four consecutive experiments: (1) The meanings of innovative verbs (e.g. denominal verb *crutch*) are influenced by different syntactic constructions. (2) The possible interactions between individuals and the objects (i.e. the affordances of the objects) are considered for meaning construction. (3) The interactions between individuals and the objects are interpreted with reference to "situation-specific actions needed to complete the goal specified by the syntactic construction" (Kaschak & Glenberg, 2000, p. 508).

Generally, many argument structure constructions are associated with meanings independent from the verbs that can be used in these constructions (Goldberg, 2013). The verb-oriented interpretation suggests that the general interpretation of a sentence is determined by semantic and / or syntactic information specified by the main verb (Levin & Hovav, 1994; Pinker, 1989). Many verbs can appear with several different complement configurations, with the most frequent case as the prototype. Take the verb *sneeze* as an example. It is frequently used with an intransitive construction. The sentence *I sneezed* can, therefore, be viewed as the prototypical argument structure of the verb *sneeze*. However, it is still possible to see *sneeze* used in a three-argument construction (e.g. *He sneezed his tooth right across town.*). From the verb-oriented interpretation, the main verb *sneeze* determines the argument structures it can appear in. Verbs that can be used in multiple argument structures often statistically favor one argument structure over others. The crucial role of the main verb in restricting argument structures that they can be used in also manifest its peculiarity in resisting some patterns that other semantically or phonologically similar verbs appear in (Goldberg, 2013).

In the field of Linguistic Theory and psycholinguistic models, the relationship among verbs, constructions, and sentence meanings has been thoroughly investigated (Chomsky, 1965; Levin & Hovav, 1994; Pinker, 1989). Compared with other words, verbs are more tight to overall sentence meanings. From theoretical perspective, the dominant view since Chomsky (1965) suggested that the main verb specified / projected "the number and types of arguments corresponding to the participants in the event described by verbs" (Bencini & Goldberg, 2000, p. 640). Empirically, Healy and Miller (1970) had the participants sort 25 sentences with 5 verbs (*sold*, *wrote*, *criticized*, *studied*, and *published*) according to meanings of the sentences. They found that the participants tended to sort sentences based on the main verb. Nevertheless, this view is somewhat weakened by two observations (Bencini & Goldberg, 2000). First, a verb can appear in more multiple argument structures than generally expected. For example, *kick*, a prototypical transitive verb, can occur in around seven other argument structures (e.g. *Pat kicked Bob black and blue.* / *Horses kick.* / *Pat kicked his way out of the operating room.*) (see more examples in Bencini & Goldberg, 2000, p. 641). The variability of the meanings of *kick* associated with argument structures definitely undermines the predicting power of the main verb. The second observation is that even though some argument structures of a verb are transformations of the dominant one (i.e. transitivity), they convey different meanings. For example, the ditransitivity of *bring* requires that the goal be animate (e.g. *I brought Pat a glass of water.* *[1] *I brought the table a glass of water.*), while

---

1 The symbol * indicates a problematic sentence.

its alternative with reposition *to* does not have the same requirement (e.g. *I brought a glass of water to the table.*) (Bencini & Goldberg, 2000; Partee, 1965).

Given that the two alternative ways accounting for constructions have been supported by empirical evidence, researchers reach a compromise. Namely, verbs contribute more to subtle aspects of meanings than complete constructions, since constructions indicate general meanings rather than specific meanings. Therefore, to achieve the event-level interpretation (who did what to whom) of a sentence, grasping the general meaning of a construction is necessary. However, a full interpretation of a sentence requires knowledge of the specific meanings contributed by the verb. Therefore, verb-argument constructions (VACs) form the core of meanings, and have been attached greater importance in theoretical and empirical studies (Römer & Berger, 2019).

3.2 Acquisition of Constructions

Construction Grammar, or constructionist approaches, can be understood with reference to the mainstream generative grammar theory, which argues that language is learned by familiarizing oneself with language-specific grammar (universal grammar). Both theories view language as a cognitive (mental) system, and productivity of utterances is realized through combining structures. However, Construction Grammar contrasts drastically with Generative Grammar in that it recognizes inductive learning through general cognitive mechanisms and emphasizes the detailed semantics of structures at various levels (Goldberg, 2013), while the latter prioritizes studying formal structures, and views structures as independent from semantic or discourse functions.

To capture the unpredictable and predictable aspects of language, a usage-based approach to Construction Grammar speculates that language is learned through both the input and general cognitive mechanisms that make genenalizations based on the input (Goldberg, 2006). Both unpredictable words / patterns and predictable ones that are sufficiently frequent are stored as constructions (Bybee, 1995; Byee & Hopper, 2001; Pinker & Jackendoff, 2005). An actual expression typically involves the combination of several different constructions.

The core of emergentist and usage-based approaches to language acquisition is the assumption that language can be learned from language input through generalizations (Behrens, 2009), which include semantic generalizations and generalizations of information structure, i.e. "speakers' awareness of the hearers' state of mind / knowledge" (Goldberg, 2006, p. 10) that is reflected in the surface form of language. The surface generalization hypothesis states that between the same surface form and a distinct form (which is the hypothesis derived from the surface form syntactically or semantically), there exist broader syntactic and semantic generalizations associated with a surface argument form (Goldberg, 2006, p. 25).

As summarized by Behrens (2009), entrenchment, i.e. repeated encounters of a particular construction, functions as the core psychological process of language learning from the usage-based linguistic perspective. Through entrenchment, constructions are stored as prefabricated linguistic chunks. However, simple repetition cannot develop into more general information without applying the generalization mechanism, which happens when speakers actively categorize new units according to similarities and dissimilarities between new units and established units that speakers detect. In the process of generalization, speakers form schemas. A schema defined as a "semantic, phonological, or symbolic structure that, relative to another representation of the same entity, is characterized with lesser specificity and detail" (Langacker, 1987, p. 492). Larger units (e.g. sentences) can be constructed through composing schemas. When schemas are combined together, new qualities emerge (Behren, 2009). "New and more complex structures can emerge from simpler basic facts" (Behren, 2009, p. 387). Emergentism suggests that emergence is central to language learning and linguistic knowledge emerges from interactions.

The "poverty of the stimulus" argument (Pinker, 1994) suggests that children are entitled to innate ability of acquiring language while making little errors given the limited input for making generalizations. In view of this argument, researchers of Construction Grammar have gathered various types of evidence to testify that at least certain patterns can be learned through general categorization strategies (Bybee & Slobin, 1982; Jackendoff, 2002; Scholz & Pullum, 2002). For example, the findings related to transitional probabilities have explained how children pick up the boundaries between various levels of constructions. Generally, the transitional probabilities between syllables provide children clues to discover word boundaries (Hauser et al., 2001), syntactic regularities (Marcus et al., 1995), and phonological paradigms (Gerken et al., 2005) from continuous speech (Saffran et al., 1996). More related empirical studies that investigate the learnability of constructions focus on distributional properties of the input (skewed input) and general categorization strategies.

3.2.1   Skewed Input and the General Verbs

To shed light on the learning of constructions through language input and generalization strategies, a lot of research investigated the statistical distribution of constructions in natural language by adopting a corpus linguistic methodology (e.g. Bates et al., 1988; Goldberg et al., 2004). The corpus used was Bates et al.'s corpus (1988) consisting of transcripts of 27 children's (20–28 months old) daily conversations with their mother. These studies identified Zipfian distribution of verbs appearing in each construction, with one verb occurring visibly more frequently than other verbs in the constructions examined. Zipfian distribution of language input is thus termed as "skewed input" to capture its statistical characteristic. Bates et al. (1988) found that 39% of the occurrence of the construction [Subj V Obj] was associated with the verb *go*, while a significantly lower percentage of the occurrence of this specific construction was associated with other verbs. This tendency was also observed in other constructions examined, including [Subj V Oblique$_{path}$] and [Subj V Obj$_1$ Obj$_2$]. To quantify the frequency of these particular verbs in specific constructions while considering the overall frequencies of the verbs in the language, Stefanowitsch and

Gries (2003) suggested applying measures of association (e.g. Fisher's Exact Test).

The Zipfian distribution of input was also observed in children's early speech (Goldberg et al., 2004). In speeches produced by mothers and children, the verbs—*go*, *put*, and *give*—were the most frequent. Researchers attributed this phenomenon to the following reasons: (1) These verbs could be attached with a wider range of arguments (Heine, 1993); (2) Constructions involving these verbs were paired with meanings readily accessible to the children (Slobin, 1985).

These highly frequent general verbs appearing in mothers / children's speech were regarded as important aids / basis for children to generalize patterns from the input (Goldberg, 1996). Goldberg (1995) observed that the meaning of the most frequent verb in each construction was identical to the meaning independently posited for that specific construction.

Empirical evidence suggests that when acquiring a verb argument structure construction, children often master constructions used with the most frequent verbs initially, and then learn constructions appearing with other verbs. Drawing upon the longitudinal data of language production by 16 children during the period when they gradually grew from the single-word stage to the multi-word stage, Ninio (1999) investigated verbs that these children gradually incorporated in [V Obj] and [Subj V Obj] constructions, and mapped the development procedure along the temporal parameters. The results suggested that these children learned these two constructions for a few verbs in a "piecemeal" manner, and tended to use the early learned general verbs for a longer period of time than other verbs. Once they were secured with these first "pathbreaking" verbs, their learning process accelerated and an increasing number of verbs gradually participated into the two constructions under investigation. This learning process suggests that children generalize the syntactic pattern on the basis of early general verbs. The generalization then facilitates children in incorporating new verbs that bear semantic resemblance to the early general-purpose verbs semantically in this syntactic pattern (Goldberg, 2006). Therefore, the early use of general-purpose verbs facilitates the acquisition of form and meaning correspondences (i.e. constructions) by preparing children for both initial syntactic and semantic generalizations.

3.2.2 Generalization Strategies

The corpus data demonstrates that a single verb accounts for the lion's share of tokens for all of the constructions, i.e. Zipfian distribution. However, the evidence based on corpus analysis is limited in demonstrating that the Zipfian distribution of tokens facilitates the acquisition of constructions (Goldberg et al., 2004). The claim that general-purpose verbs should be learned early motivated researchers to empirically test the association between skewed input (i.e. Zipfian distribution of input) in language learning and learners' process of acquiring constructions. Studies reviewed in this section showcase the methodologies that psycholinguistic researchers adopted to experimentally establish the causal relation between skewed input and subjects' learning gains by controlling other variables.

Goldberg et al. (2004) provided supportive evidence for the learnability of constructions realized through the skewedness of input and learners' generalization strategies. In the experimental design, 81 university undergraduates were required to learn a novel construction—[Subj Obj V]—with the main verb being a pseudo word attached with morphological mark -*o* under three conditions: (1) the control condition (directly to the test phase without watching either video); (2) the balanced condition (frequency of the pseudo verbs involved: 4-4-4-2-2); (3) the high-token frequency condition (skewed frequency of pseudo verbs involved: 8-2-2-2-2). The comprehension of each sentence including the target construction embedded in was facilitated by a video clip. The most frequent pseudo verb was allocated the most general meaning appearing (without specifying a manner) in the experiment, to be consistent with the repeatedly verified finding that the most frequent verb had a very general meaning. Subjects' learning gains were tested through a comprehension task, which required subjects to choose one from two simultaneously appearing sentences that matched the meanings of the sentences they heard. The result showed that the students assigned to the high-token-frequenay condition scored significantly higher than those assigned to the balanced condition, lending supportive evidence to the hypothesis that skewed input facilitates the acquisition of constructional knowledge.

With Goldberg et al. (2004) as a precedent focusing on adult learners, Casenhiser and Goldberg (2005) are claimed to be the first researchers that investigated how children establish the association between novel phrasal forms and novel meanings. Casenhiser and Goldberg (2005) conducted two experiments, answering two questions respectively: (1) whether skewed input facilitates children's acquisition of a non-English word order construction with the main verbs being pseudo words; (2) how children manage to learn the mapping between a non-English word order construction and the novel meaning it carries.

In the first experiment, 51 children were randomly assigned to three conditions: the skewed frequency condition (frequency of five pseudo verbs: 4-1-1-1-1), the balanced frequency condition (frequency of five pseudo verbs: 1-1-2-2-2) and the control condition (watching video clips without hearing any language). The comparison between children's performance on a comprehension task (i.e. picking one from two video clips that matched the sentence heard) showed that students assigned to the skewed input condition outperformed those assigned to other conditions, a finding consistent with the research of Goldberg et al. (2004) on adult learners.

The second experiment further explained: (1) whether children are able to learn the novel construction without a morphological cue (i.e. -o, which was provided in the first experiment); (2) how differently children react to a novel construction and a known construction (e.g. transitive construction). In the second experiment, 48 children were randomly assigned to two conditions: the training condition (the same task conducted by the skewed input group in the first experiment) and the control condition (watching video clips without hearing any language). In the comprehension test, children heard three new instances of the novel construction and three new instances of the transitive construction with novel verbs. The results showed that for the novel construction, children assigned to the skewed input condition significantly outperformed children assigned to the control condition, indicating that children after receiving skewed input were able to acquire the novel construction and associate it with its meaning even when no morphological cue was present. In terms of the transitive construction, both groups demonstrated a similar level of familiarity, and the skewed input did not improve accuracy of the high-token frequenry group on transitive construction.

In view of the results obtained through non-linguistic learning experiments on category learning (Elio & Anderson, 1984), Cashenhiser and Goldberg (2005) concluded that the general categorization strategies demonstrated in non-linguistic tasks also applied to linguistic learning, and these strategies were most powerful when the input was skewed with the most prototypical item being the most frequent. Non-linguistic learning experiments indicated the existence of children's general categorization strategies by showing that (1) input presented in a skewed manner led to more accurate category learning than that presented in a balanced manner, and (2) children trained with more similar items to the prototype were more likely to identify low-similarity items than those trained with items less similar to the prototype (Gentner et al., 2007).

3.2.3 Constraints of Overgeneralization

The previous section uncovers generalizations made by learners to acquire constructions, while this section focuses on how learners constrain overgeneralization while incorporating new verbs into constructions. To explain the mechanism learners adopt to avoid or recover / retreat from overgeneralization in language production, some theorists have argued that sufficient frequency may play a role (Braine & Brooks, 1995; Brooks & Tomasello, 1999; Goldberg, 2006; Ambridge et al., 2018). Goldberg (2006) summarized that at least four factors were likely to be associated with the productivity of constructions: (1) the token frequency of an item, i.e. degree of entrenchment (Ambridge et al., 2015; Braine & Brooks, 1995; Brooks et al., 1999); (2) statistical preemption, i.e. the frequency of a word appearing in a competing construction (Brooks & Tomasello, 1999; Goldberg, 1993, 1995); (3) type frequency of a construction (Bybee, 1985; Goldberg, 1995; MacWhinney, 1978; Plunkett & Marchman, 1991; 1993); (4) the variability of items that occur in a construction, i.e. semantic constraints or a construction's degree of openness (Bowerman & Choi, 2001; Bybee, 1995; Gropen & Goldberg, R., 1991; Osherson et al., 1990; Pinker, 1989).

The entrenchment hypothesis (e.g. Braine & Brooks, 1995) states that learners gradually realize that the probability of a verb appearing in a non-attested construction is low through repeated exposure to the speacific verb in various appropriate / attested constructions (Ambridge et al., 2018). Statistical preemption (Goldberg, 1995, 2006), also a learning process averting overgeneralization through probability inference, postulates that possible overgeneralizations are constrained by constructions that can be used as a close paraphrase, rather than constructions that the key verb appears with. While statistical preemption provides indirect negative evidence, it does not "account fully for children's lack of overgeneralizations" (Goldberg, 2006, p. 98). Type frequency has also been considered to be correlated with productivity (Bybee 1985, 1995; Clausner & Croft, 1997; Goldberg, 1995). Compared to constructions appearing with a few types, constructions appearing with many different types are more likely to appear with new types. For example, argument structure constructions used with many different verbs are more likely to be extended by learners to incorporate additional verbs (Goldberg, 2006, p. 99). The semantic constraints apply to situations when learners use alternate constructions of a novel verb. Pinker (1989) postulated that learners were more likely to use novel verbs in alternating constructions if these novel verbs were semantically similar to verbs that they had encountered in specific constructions.

A substantial body of empirical research has been conducted to test the effects of these factors on language learning. Researchers have been particularly interested in entrenchment and preemption (Abbot-Smith & Tomasello, 2010; Ambridge et al., 2018; Ambridge et al., 2012; Ambridge et al., 2014; Brooks & Tomasello, 1999; Gropen & Goldberg, 1991). Generally, entrenchment is robust across a range of argument structure overgeneralizations and across learners at different proficiency levels, while preemption is identified with older children sufficiently exposed to input (Brooks & Tomasello, 1999; Ambridge et al., 2015), since less proficient L2 learners may lack the knowledge of semantically relating alternatives to the novel construction. Ambridge et al. (2015) suggested that positioning preemption as a special type of entrenchment rather than a rival factor might provide a more reasonable explanation for the observation concerning the effects of entrenchment and preemption. Ambridge and Blything (2016) further emphasized the importance of incorporating entrenchment, preemption, and semantic constraints into a comprehensive model when examining the effects of these factors across argument structures and participants' language proficiency levels.

The empirical studies investigating how entrenchment, preemeption, and semantic constraints influence language acquisition have witnessed great evolution in terms of scope and methodology. Generally speaking, early studies focusing on single constructions viewed entrenchment, preemption, and semantic constraints as discrete constructs (Braine & Brooks, 1995; Brooks et al., 1999; Brooks & Tomasello, 1999; Gropen & Goldberg, 1991). Participants at different ages were equally divided into different groups with controlled intervention. Data mainly included participants' performances in grammaticality judgment tasks or language production tasks. More recent research aims at incorporating a wider variety of argument structures to promote the generalizability of the findings (Ambridge et al., 2012; Ambridge et al., 2014; Ambridge, 2013; Blything et al., 2014; Ambridge et al., 2015). This goal has led to several improvements in methodology: (1) Factors many children adopted to avoid overgeneralizability are operationalized as statistical measures, and frequency information is extracted from reference corpora to calculate these statistical measures. (2) Statistical methods used for data analysis have evolved from traditional statistical methods to computational methods to solve the issue of collinearity to some extent.

The following section reviews important empirical studies that contribute to our knowledge of how L1 learners avoid making overgeneralization errors and learn novel constructions through generalizations. As aforementioned, related empirical endeavors have evolved greatly. The following review focuses on early research on single constructions and recent research demonstrating a considerably higher degree of generalization.

3.3 Research on Construction Acquisition

The factors used to avoid overgeneralizations are not mutually exclusive in the process of language acquisition. Rather, they are intertwined. Brooks et al. (1999) proposed that children were less likely to say or write *A big bird disappeared it* if they had (1) witnessed *disappear* used in an intransitive construction a sufficient number of times, but never in a transitive construction (entrenchment); (2) noticed *disappear* in sentences like *He made it disappear* many times (preemption); (3) formed the semantic class of verbs used in intransitive construction, and none of the verbs in this semantic class can be used in transitive construction. The following review focuses on the factors under discussion, i.e. entrenchment, preemption, and semantic constrains. A clear definition of each factor precedes the review of studies that focus on that specific factor.

3.3.1 Entrenchment

Entrenchment, "the establishment of a linguistic structure via repeated occurrences" (Zhang & Mai, 2018, p. 414), has been considered as an equivalent to the token frequency of an item (Goldberg, 2006). Entrenchment has been associated with first language learning, since repeated use of a linguistic form in one structure is likely to prevent overgeneralization. For example, the repeated occurrence of *I / you fall* and *she / he falls* help people infer that *I / you falls* and *she / he fall* are less acceptable. Braine and Brooks' (1995) theory of "unique argument-structure preference" exemplified the notion of entrenchment in constraining overgeneralizations. According to Braine and Brooks (1995), the initial learning of constructions happens by establishing association between form and meaning through repeated encounters with exemplars of a particular construction. Overgeneralizations are very occasional. The theory of "unique argument-structure preference" speculates that "once an argument-structure (e.g. a transitivity status) has been solidly learned for a verb, this learning tends to block usage of another argument structure unless the other argument structure has been independently learned" (Braine & Brooks, 1995, p. 367).

The study of Brooks et al. (1999) provided supportive evidence for this hypothesis by examining children's tendency to make overgeneralization errors in terms of transitivity / intransitivity. Three groups of children were presented with four pairs of verbs with each pair consisting of an early age of acquisition (AOA) verb and a late AOA verb. The meaning of each verb was presented by a puppet performing denoted actions. After the training, researchers interacted with the children to elicit their responses with the usage of verbs overgeneralized. Researchers reported that all the children tended not to use a verb in other constructions once they were very familiar with the verb used in a specific construction (e.g. transitivity / intransivity), suggesting that the effect of entrenchment impacted even very young children's acquisition of argument structures.

By adding generalization tests that targeted verbs not covered in the training session, Abbot-Smith and Tomasello (2010) investigated the possibility of children extending their newly acquired constructions to untrained verbs. In this study, sixteen five-year-old German children with no prior exposure to English were trained on two grammatical constructions (caused-motion and psychological state) by watching puppets act out the actions denoted by these two constructions. These two grammatical constructions were heard in the two forms respectively: "X was V-ing" (used with cause-motion verbs) and "X got V-ed" (used with psychological verbs). As shown in Table 3.2, the verbs were presented to the children with skewed frequency. This design, similar to Casenhiser and Goldberg's (2005) study, included two untrained verbs for each semantic condition (shown in the bottom row of Table 3.2). The result demonstrated significant effect of verb frequency. These children tended not to overgeneralize, which demonstrated the effect of entrenchment in language acquisition. For untrained verbs, a majority of children used one or both verb argument structures with these novel verbs. This finding suggests that children successfully extracted the morphological paradigms and were able to apply these paradigms with untrained verbs.

Table 3.2   The frequency of the verb types heard during training and testing (adapted from Abbot-Smith & Tomasello, 2010, p. 86)

Training & Testing	Semantic condition 1: caused motion (always heard in intransitive "NOUN was __ing")	Semantic condition 2: psychological state (always heard in passive "NOUN got __ed")
Training: Stories 1 & 3	swing (x 4 items) bend (x 2) slide (x 2) topple (x 2)	annoy (x 4 items) surprise (x 2) bore (x 2) tempt (x 2)
Training: Stories 2 & 4 / 5	swing (x 4 items) turn (x 2) bounce (x 2)	annoy (x 4 items) scare (x 2) embarrass (x 2)
Generalization testing	twist (x 2), drop (x 2)	worry (x 2), grieve (x 2)

3.3.2 Preemption

Even though the association between entrenchment and overgeneralization is supported by some empirical evidence (Brooks et al., 1999; Brooks & Tomasello, 1999), it fails to explain cases where verbs appearing dominantly in one argument structure pattern are also used creatively and appropriately in new argument structure patterns (Goldberg, 2006). Even though entrenchment and preemption are theoretically independent, Brooks et al. (1999) stated that these two factors actually worked simultaneously, and the strength of preemption varied. The important assumption behind preemption is that no constructions are identical. There only exist paraphrasable constructions that preempt / block overgeneralizations.

To account for the creative use of verbs in new argument structure patterns, researchers pointed out that "more specific knowledge always preempts general knowledge in production, as long as either would satisfy the functional demands of the context equally well" (Goldberg, 2006, p. 94). Therefore, more specific constructions (e.g. *She sneezed the foam off the cappuccino.*) are preferred in production to the more general and frequent constructions involving the target verbs (e.g. *She sneezed.*). With reference to morphological preemption (or blocking), one of the generalizations is adding the suffix *-er* for the agents (e.g. *driver, writer, teacher...*), while this generalization is suppressed / preempted by the long-existing agentive nominal counterparts of some words (e.g. *referee, architect, cook*) (Clark, 1988).

Some verb argument patterns preempt other possible alternatives, while many other verbs freely appear in other constructions (e.g. transitive, passive, intransitive), causing Pinker (1989) to argue for a statistical charateristic of preemption. The message that can be inferred is that a person chooses to use one construction over its alternatives for a reason. Empirical evidence has supported the claim that "statistical (statistically based) preemption, involving related but non-synonymous constructions, plays a role in avoiding overgeneralizations" (Goldberg, 2006, p. 96). Meanwhile, frequency is also related to preemption, because learners can successfully infer the principles underlying preemption only when the frequency of a given pattern passes the threshold of sufficiency. Theorists and researchers believe that the process of statistical preemption exposes learners to indirect negative evidence to constrain possible overgeneralizations (Brooks et al., 1999; Goldberg, 2006). For example, the child, who has heard or used *disappear* in an intransitive construction (e.g. *He made it disappear.*) for many times, is less likely to use *disappear* in a transitive form (e.g. *They disappeared it.*) (Brooks et al., 1999). However, there do exist constructions, the overgeneralizations of which may not be effectively preempted, since these constructions are extremely infrequent or semantically or pragmatically specialized with a few paraphrases (Goldberg, 1995; Goldberg, 2006).

Brooks and Tomasello (1999) investigated how English-speaking children learned to avoid making argument structure errors (e.g. *Don't giggle me.*) by using alternative constructions (e.g. a passive construction being an alternative to a simple transitive construction). These alternative constructions can be viewed as indirect negative evidence that preempts tendencies to overgeneralization. The preemption group, 32 children at the age of 2.5, 4.5, 6 and 7, were presented with preempting alternatives of the two target pseudo verbs: *meek* meaning "make go up" and *tam* meaning "swing", a manner of motion. For example, children in the preemption group heard the verb *meek* in transitive construction (e.g. *Ernie's meeking the car.*) and passive construction afterwards (e.g. *The car is meeked.*). Even though Brooks and Tomasello (1999) empirically verified the effects of preemption with elder children, no evidence of preemption effect was identified with the two-year-old, indicating that preemption started to function on the basis of considerable exposure to English verbs used in constructions that these verbs are canonically associated with (i.e. entrenchment). Specific to the acquisition of transitivity, preemption happens when children are aware that a passive construction and a simple transitive construction share the same transitivity status, and that a periphrastic causative construction and an intransitive construction share the same transitivity status (Brooks et al., 1999).

3.3.3 Semantic Constraints

Learners productive use of constructions is not solely based on type frequency. Rather, learners tend to incorporate a new verb into a familiar pattern when the new verb bears semantic resemblance to verbs that they have witnessed being used with a particular construction (Goldberg, 2006). Pinker's (1989) theory provides systematic explanation for semantic constraints that language learners adopt to avert overgeneralizations. From Pinker's (1989) perspective, children are conservative in nature when learning constructions, and only use novel verbs in alternate constructions if these novel verbs are semantically similar to verbs that they have encountered in those specific constructions. These semantic constraints are classified as broad and narrow constraints. The broad ones constrain the selection of appropriate argument structure, while the narrow ones distinguish verb semantic classes (Joo, 2003).

"Broad constraints convey the meaning of a syntactic construction as a whole and define the semantic roles of each of its arguments" (Brooks & Tomasello, 1999, p. 721). For example, constructions that can be used with verbs denoting the manner of changing or location of a substance belong to this category (Gropen & Goldberg, 1991). This type of constraints, nevertheless, are too broad to specify the class of verbs appropriate for particular constraints. "Compatibility with the broad-range rules (BBR) is only a necessary, not a sufficient, condition for a verb to alternate" (Inagaki, 1997, p. 639). Even though *give* and *donate* refer to the transference of possession, this semantic observation is not sufficient to explain why *He donated the library a book* is unacceptable, while *He gave the library a book* is acceptable (Brooks & Tomasello, 1999). Therefore, to use constructions with verbs denoting appropriate and conventionalized meaning, children must familiarize themselves with narrow semantic constraints that prescribe nuances helping children clearly distinguish between appropriate / inappropriate verbs relating to a particular construction. The semantic differences between verbs with fixed transitivity and verbs with flexible transitivity can be subtle to some extent (Brooks & Tomasello, 1999).

Pinker (1989) attributed children's overgeneralization errors to their partial knowledge of a verb's meaning. When children's understanding of a verb is incomplete, they may attach the verb to a construction that they heard or used. This generalization process can be adventurous, since the novel verb and verbs appropriately used in the construction may not belong to the same narrow semantic class. These errors can gradually disappear with children acquiring the narrow semantic constraints and polishing their knowledge of specific verbs (Brooks & Tomasello, 1999).

With a focus on broad semantic constraints on verb productivity, Gropen and Goldberg's (1991) research provided supportive evidence for Pinker's (1989) hypothesis by underlining the association between children's semantic knowledge of the target locative verbs and errors elicited from the children's speech. Their results showed that children who misinterpreted verbs' meanings also tended to use verbs with incorrect forms of constructions. In this study, subjects were grouped according to age (including both children and adults) and trained with two pairs of verbs (*pour* & *fill*, *dump* & *empty*), with the former of each pair denoting the manner of location changing of a substance and the latter specifying the resulting state of the container. Knowledge of verb meanings was tested by forcing the subjects to choose from two pictures the one that matched the sentence presented. To fulfill this task, the subjects needed to distinguish between manner and state. The subjects' productive use of these verbs was elicited by a syntax test to test their syntactic knowledge of constructions involving the target verbs. Even though many subjects of different age groups successfully related *fill* and *empty* to the find state as the most important meaning, a great number of young children understood the pouring manner as the most important meaning of *fill* and *empty*.

Based on the above findings, Gropen and Goldberg (1991) proposed a universal linking rule—object affectedness—which speculated that children tended to assign the direct object role to an argument when the argument was affected by the action denoted by the verb. It is, therefore, more likely for children to misuse endstatus verbs, the direct object of which is not the argument being affected by the action. For example, children may produce sentences like *I filled the water* instead of *I filled the cup*. Older children and adults' outstanding performance in this study further supports the claim that the syntactic errors gradually disappear with increasing input.

As reviewed in chapter 3, Brooks and Tomasello positioned their study as "the first study to demonstrate the constraining effect of the narrow-range semantic classes that are at the heart of Pinker's theory" (1999, p. 733), by suggesting that children demonstrated higher accuracy in novel verbs introduced with a fixed transitivity status than in those presented with both transitivity classes. Similar to their findings concerning preemption, semantic constraints were observed among older children. The cross-sectional analysis suggested that it took 2.5 to 4.5 years for children to internalize the narrow semantic constraints. Brooks and Tomasello explained that "to construct narrow semantic verb classes, children need to identify regularities in the constructions in which familiar verbs occur and note semantic similarities among different verbs that appear in the same constructions" (1999, p. 733). Therefore, only older children with sufficient input can establish the appropriate narrow-range semantic classes.

3.3.4 Research with Higher Generalization

Nevertheless, the generalizability of abovementioned experimental findings is very limited, since conclusions are usually drawn on the basis of observations concerning a single construction pair. The narrow scope of these studies makes one wonder whether the mechanism learners adopt to avoid overgeneralizations in acquiring these specific types of constructions also applies to a wider range of constructions. Clark (1988) emphasized the necessity of extending the constructions under investigation to include words, sentences, and other language materials. Research has gradually incorporated a wide variety of constructions, and becomes more cautious in drawing conclusions (Ambridge & Blything, 2016; Ambridge et al., 2012; Ambridge et al., 2015; Harmon & Kapatsinski, 2017).

Studies investigating a comparatively wider range of constructions mainly rely on a grammaticality judgment paradigm, where participants rate acceptability of sentences using a Likert scale (Ambridge et al., 2018). Even though participants' introspective judgments can be unreliable, possible alternatives are also problematic. For example, the production paradigm asking participants to produce target constructions without priming was unable to differentiate levels of acceptability (Ambridge, 2017; Harmon & Kapatsinski, 2017). Studies focusing on a range of constructions did not adopt the production paradigm (Ambridge et al., 2018). In addition, different from early studies that divided participants into different groups (e.g. the entrenchment group, the preemption group, and the semantic constraint group) based on different ways of input, more research (Ambridge et al., 2012; Ambridge et al., 2014; Ambridge, 2013; Blything et al., 2014; Ambridge et al., 2015) operationalized these conceptualizations as statistical measures and entered these measures into statistical models to predict difference scores (i.e. the degree of preference for one construction to another), which were calculated by subtracting the acceptability rating of one construction from that of its alternative. The overall frequency of a verb extracted from a reference corpus was adopted as the measure of entrenchment, while the frequency of the verb in a specific competing construction was adopted as the measure of preemption. Semantic constraints were operationalized as "the frequency-weighted average of the semantics of each item which appeared in that position in the input utterances that gave rise to the construction" (Ambridge & Blything, 2016, p. 1248).

Ambridge et al. (2018), nevertheless, found the statistical measures of entrenchment and preemption unsound theoretically and statistically for two reasons: (1) Entrenchment and preemption were probabilities in nature, and they did not determine a single choice of usage. (2) When entrenchment and preemption scores were zero (indicating a verb alternated between two constructions), the statistical model could simply assign a difference score of zero for these related verbs. However, the preference for alternating constructions varied greatly (Ambridge et al., 2014). In addition, Ambridge et al. (2018) pointed out that corpus frequency of the target verb in the alternative construction (the measure of preemption) was a subset of the overall frequency of the target verb (the measure of entrenchment), probably resulting in the disentanglement of these two factors. To address these issues, Ambridge et al. (2018) advocated using Stefanowitsch's (2008) measures of contingency to quantify entrenchment and preemption. Besides, Ambridge et al. (2018) also found the measure of dependent variable in previous analysis somewhat deficient. The utilization of difference scores: (1) biased for preemption against entrenchment or vice versa; (2) was unable to distinguish judgments as highly grammatical or ungrammatical; (3) failed to recognize the possibly increased acceptability of both constructions (e.g. *Bart gave a present to Lisa*; *Bart gave Lisa a present.*); (4) blocked information concerning preference for one construction to another. Therefore, Ambridge et al. (2018) adopted raw acceptability judgment ratings as the dependent variable.

To ensure the generalizability of results concerning a variety of constructions, empirical studies adopted mixed-effects models (Ambridge et al., 2012; Ambridge et al., 2015; Blything et al., 2014). However, the attempt to "address the problem of collinearity by residualizing predictor variables against one another" (Wurm & Fisicaro, 2014, p. 7) was not appropriate, since contributions by each individual predictor could not be assessed through residualization. Thereafter, Ambridge et al. (2018) suggested using a computational approach, a Bayesian mixed-effects model. Small corpus size could also weaken the generalizability of some empirical studies. For example, Ambridge et al. (2012) used a one-million-word corpus to extract the frequency of verbs and constructions, rendering many verbs not attested. To illustrate the methodological improvement and evolution happened in studies focusing on a wide range of constructions, the following section presents exemplars of research in this category.

Ambridge et al. (2015) tested the preemption and entrenchment hypotheses by including nine sentence-level verb argument structure constructions selected from four different categories: Dative (PO-dative, DO-dative), Causative (Intransitive inchoative, Transitive causative, Periphrastic causative), Locative (Figure locative, Ground locative) and Passive (Active, Passive). To generalize across these constructions, mixed-effect models with crossed random effects for participants (aged 5–6, 9–10 and 18–22) and items (including verbs and constructions) were adopted. The researchers cautioned that results based on such analysis only indicated whether entrenchment and preemption effects were identified across these constructions, not whether these effects influenced any particular constructions. The dependent variable of the analysis was participants' ratings of overgeneralization errors involving the nine verb argument structures. In this case, preemption and entrenchment were operationalized as (1) the log frequency of each verb in the most synonymous construction, (2) the log frequency of the total occurrence of that specific verb. The frequency counts were extracted from SUBTLEX-UK which includes 200-million-word subtitles from British TV programs. This study identified the entrenchment effect for children aged 9–10 and adults and null effect for the preemption predictor across age groups, leaving the researchers to consider it a mistake to view preemption and entrenchment dichotomously. According to Ambridge et al. (2015), the reason for preemption effects being only associated with certain constructions (as shown in previously discussed studies) was that preemption was a special subtype of entrenchment and only emerged when the preempting construction was "particularly frequent relative to the error construction and particularly closely synonymous with the error construction" (Am bridge et al., 2015, p. 17).

Due to the complexity of the relation between entrenchment and preemption, Ambridge and Blything (2016) intended to propose one integral learning mechanism that encompassed all the three effects that gathered substantial supportive empirical evidence: entrenchment, preemption, and semantic verb class hypotheses. The underlying assumption of this model is that argument structure constructions stored in speakers' mind compete to express speakers' intended information, and the competition process is influenced by four factors: verb-in-construction frequency (entrenchment), relevance (preemption), fit (semantic properties), and overall construction frequency. The computational model adopted by Ambridge and Blything (2016) served to simulate the mechanism in learning verb argument structure constraints, since children learn probabilistic links between verbs and constructions through semantic and statistical information embedded in input data. In the process of model comparison, the most comprehensive model, the lexeme-based Semantics + Entrenchment + Preemption model, was the most robust in simulating the mechanism in retreating from overgeneralization and predicting correct argument structure for verbs, indicating that the traditional perspective viewing entrenchment, preemption and semantic constraints as rival effects is problematic. Rather, all three are intertwined in a learning mechanism and bear probabilistic association with particular verbs and argument structure constructions.

Based on an insightful review of five previous studies, Ambridge et al. (2018) made several important adjustments in their new study of un- prefixation: (1) using contingency statistics for predictor variables (entrenchment and preemption);

(2) using raw acceptability judgment ratings as the dependent variable; (3) adopting of the comprehensive Bayians mixed effects model presented in Ambridge and Blything (2016); (4) relying on the large corpus British National Corpus for frequency counts. By synthesizing findings from the aforementioned studies, Ambridge et al. (2018) concluded that when entrenchment and preemption were appropriately operationalized, both of them could be observed as independent of each other through model comparison. No evidence was found in terms of whether these effects varied with different constructions investigated in these studies.

The increasingly sophisticated methodological design has gradually deepened our understanding of the factors related to language learners' acquisition of new constructions while averting overgeneralizations. Meanwhile, methodological improvements are still possible. For example, Ambridge et al. (2018) suggested using a discriminative learning model for further research to explain the effects of entrenchment, preemption, and semantic constraints.

3.4 Constructions and Second Language Acquisition

Investigations into the effects of preemption, entrenchment, and the semantics of target constructions in L2 learning have been comparatively rare. Several topics regarding L2 construction learning and representation emerge from an extensive review of literature: (1) whether learners know L2 constructions (e.g. Gries & Wulff, 2005, 2009; Shin, 2010); (2) how learners acquire the semantic constraints of L2 constructions (e.g. Bley-Vroman & Joo, 2001; Bley-Vroman & Yoshinaga, 1992; Inagaki, 1997; Joo, 2003); (3) how effects of preemption, entrenchment, and the semantics constrain L2 learners' overgeneralizations (Zhang, 2017; Zhang & Mai, 2018; Zhang & Wen, 2019); (4) how L2 learners interact with their target language construction representation (Römer et al., 2014a; Römer et al., 2017; Römer & Berger, 2019); (5) how learners develop L2 constructional knowledge (Bley-Vroman & Joo, 2001; Joo, 2003; Römer et al., 2014a; Römer et al., 2017; Römer & Berger,

2019). The following sections revolve around the methodologies and findings of these empirical studies to clarify how these studies contribute to our understanding of the development of L2 constructional knowledge.

3.4.1 Learners' Knowledge of L2 Constructions

Research exploring whether learners know L2 constructions relied on sentence completion tasks (priming) as the major data elicitation method (e.g. Gries & Wulff, 2005, 2009). Sentence sorting and grammaticality judgment tasks were also adopted to complement the data elicited through priming tasks (Gries & Wulff, 2005, 2009). The majority of these studies succeeded in identifying learners' L2 constructional knowledge with little contradictory findings.

Following Pickering and Branigan's (1998) paradigm of sentence completion task, Gries and Wulff (2005) probed into this issue by conducting a syntactic priming study of German English learners' mental representation of constructions. Subjects were required to complete two types of incomplete sentences (the primes): (1) most naturally continued as a ditransitve (e.g. *The racing driver showed the helpful mechanic* ___.); (2) most naturally continued as a prepositional dative (e.g. *The racing driver showed the torn overall* ___.). Researchers found that there existed similarities between L2 learners and native speakers in terms of preferences of verbs used in each argument structure constructions, suggesting that L2 learners have stored formal aspect of argument structure constructions in a native-like manner. This syntactic priming task was also followed by a semantic sorting task, where another twenty-two L2 English learners sorted sixteen cards, with one sentence on each card, into four piles (four cards each pair) according to the meaning of these sentences. The sixteen sentences exemplified four different verbs (*cut, get, take* and *throw*) and each verb was used in four different argument structure constructions (caused-motion, ditransitive, resultative, and transitive). The results showed that subjects relied more on the semantics of complementation configurations than on lexical similarities of the main verbs for assorting sentences. According to Pickering and Branigan (1998), the findings from the sentence-completion and sentence-sorting tasks testified the existence of L2 learners' constructional knowledge.

The research paradigm of syntactic priming was afterwards applied to investigate whether L2 learners stored gerunds (e.g. *She tried rocking the baby.*) and infinitives (e.g. *She tried to rock the baby.*) as constructions (Gries & Wulff, 2009). Verbs that are distinctively associated with the target constructions were identified through a computational method, the distinctive collexeme analysis. In this study, learners' knowledge of the target constructions was demonstrated by the finding that the verbs preferred in these constructions cast the strongest influence over students' sentence completion. In addition, sentences including the preferred collexem of the main verbs tended to receive higher acceptability ratings.

3.4.2 Acquisition of the Semantic Constraints

Research in this regard empirically examined whether learners acquired the broad-range rules and narrow-range rules that constrain overgeneralizations in construction use with little "negative feedback" (Pinker, 1989). The broad-range rules govern the selection of appropriate argument structures for the intended general meaning. For example, locative verbs "denote a transfer of a substance or a set of objects (the theme, content, or figure) into a container or onto a surface (the goal, container, location or ground)" (Pinker, 1989, p. 49). These locative verbs can be used with two different argument structures, namely figure-object frame (e.g. *Kim loaded hayfigure onto the wagonground.*) and ground-object frame (e.g. *Kim loaded the wagonground with hayfigure.*). However, the broad-range rules are not useful in ruling out the issues involved in these sentences: e.g. **John poured the glassground with waterfigure. *John filled waterfigure into the glassground* (Joo, 2003). Namely, the locative verbs frequently registered with one of the locative argument structures are used wrongly with the other argument structure. L2 research has, to date, investigated dative and locative verbs, and concludes that L2 learners are generally successful in learning the broad-range rules, but the narrow-range rules are only acquired for some verb classes. Three different hypotheses have been employed to explain the findings: the fundamental difference hypothesis (similarities and differences between L1 and L2), the selective access to universal grammar (UG), and frequency. However, none is sufficient to fully explain the findings. The following review unfolds the details of learners' knowledge of broad and narrow semantic constraints.

Inagaki (1997) investigated the acquisition of narrow-range rules governing the dative alternation, including (1) prepositional datives (PD), e.g. *John threw a ball to Mary*; (2) double object datives (DOD), e.g. *John threw Mary a ball*. According to Pinker (1989), four narrow-range verb classes exist in dative verbs and the verb classes differ in terms of the dative alternations that they are associated with (shown in the parentheses): the throw class (PD & DOD), the push class (PD) (e.g. *John pushed a ball to Mary. * John pushed Mary a ball.*), the tell class (PD & DOD) (e.g. *John told a secret to Mary. John told Mary a secret.*), and the whisper class (DOD) (e.g. *John whispered a secret to Mary. *John whispered Mary a secret.*). Participants rated the acceptablity of prepositional and double object datives containing both pseudo and real verbs. In the training session, pictures and descriptive words were used to denote the meaning of the pseudo verbs. Each desriptive paragraph was followed by two sentences using the target pseudo verb in the PD construction and the DOD construction respectively. Three groups of participants' (native speakers of English, Chinese and Japanese learners of English) ratings of the acceptability of these sentences were analyzed and compared. The underlying reasoning of this design is that knowledge of narrow-range constraints of a novel verb occurring in the PD construction will result in low ratings in the acceptability of the DOD construction, and vice versa, unless the novel verb is witnessed in both alternations. The results showed that both Japanese and Chinese speakers were able to distinguish tell class verbs from those with whisper class verbs in terms of the constructions they associated with, but failed to achieve the same understanding of the difference between throw class verbs and push class verbs.

Inagaki (1997) intended to explain his findings relating to the three different hypotheses. The fundamental difference hypothesis generally attributes learners' learning gains to the similarities between their L1s and the target language, and their incompetence to the differences between their L1s and the target language. However, this hypothesis can only explain part of the findings. The Chinese learners' successfulness in identifying the difference between tell class verbs and whisper class verbs may due to the reason that such a distinction also exists in Chinese. However, Japanese failed to distinguish throw class verbs and push class verbs, contradicting to the fundamental hypothesis. The selective access to UG suggests that "some properties of UG are more or less easy for adult L2 learners to access than others" (Inagaki, 1997, p. 659). As suggested by the current empirical finding, the distinction between the tell class and the whipser class verbs seems to be more accessible than the distinction between the throw class and the push class verbs. Nevertheless, Inagaki (1997) stated that explanation adopting UG is ad hoc, thus not powerful in predicting the empirical results. Frequency is also not sufficient to explain why both groups still were able to distinguish the pseudo tell class verbs from the pseudo whisper class verbs used in DODs, when the frequency effect was controlled by using pseudo verbs. Inagaki (1997) concluded by suggesting future research incorporate more detailed comparison between L1 and L2's grammatical subsystems and recruits learners at lower proficiency levels (less exposure to English) to further probe L1 and frequency influences.

Similar findings were also obtained in Bley-Vroman & Joo's (2001) research on locatives. To understand their research, a review of Pinker's (1989) semantic typology of locative verbs is fundamental. According to Pinker (1989), two constructions are associated with locative verbs (the broad-range rule): figure-object frame (e.g. *Kim loaded hayfigure onto the wagonground.*) and ground-oriented frame (e.g. *Kim loaded the wagonground with hayfigure.*). Some verbs (e.g. *load*) can be used with both constructions, while other verbs are stably registered with one of these constructions. For example, *pour* can only be used with figure-object frame (e.g. *John poured waterfigure into the glassground.*), and *fill* is used with ground-object frame exclusively (e.g. *John filled the glassground with waterfigure.*). South Korean English learners' knowledge of broad and narrow classes of 12 locative verbs (4 from each category) were investigated through a forced-choice picture-desription task, where subjects were presented with figure-object or ground-object sentences and asked to choose the picture that appropriately describe the meaning of the target sentence. By comparing native speakers' and South Korean English learners' performances, the researcher concluded that the subjects learned the broad properties of constructional meaning but not the narrow class constraints, indicating that South Korean L2 learners were not able to discern specific semantics underlying the occurrences of verbs in particular constructions. Still, there are some cases where learners make correct judgments in terms of appropriate constructions for specific verbs.

Relying on a more specific typology of locative verbs (Pinker, 1989), Joo (2003) reconfirmed this finding concerning whether L2 (South Korean) learners can acquire native-like knowledge of broad-range classes and narrow-range classes. Pinker (1989) divided English locative verbs into four semantic classes: pour class, spray class, cover class, and load class. The association between constructions and semantic classes of locative verbs was specified by Pinker as follows:

Pour class (figure-oriented non-alternating): A mass is enabled to move via the force of gravity. Examples include dribble, drip, drizzle, dump, ladle, pour, shake, slop, slosh, spill.

Spray class (figure-oriented alternating): Force is imparted to a mass, causing ballistic motion in a specified spatial distribution along a trajectory. Examples include inject, spatter, splash, splatter, spray, sprinkle, squirt.

Cover class (ground-oriented non-alternating): A layer completely covers a surface. Examples include cover, encrust, face, inlay, pave; fill is also similar, with one more dimension.

Load class (ground-oriented alternating): A mass of a size, shape, or type defined by the intended use of a container is put into the container, enabling it to accomplish its function. Examples include load, pack, stock (Pinker, 1989, pp. 126-127).

Following Pinker's (1989) typology, 12 English locative verbs were included for examination. South Korean college learners' knowledge of the locative verbs was probed through a force-choice picture-description task and a forced-choice sentence selection task. Similar to Bley–Vroman and Joo (2001), Joo (2003) found that the subjects successfully acquired the broad-range constraint. However, it is not clear whether their learning gains were due to learners' interlanguage system or L1 transfer, since Korean has the equivalent of locative constructions. As to the narrow-range constraints, the subjects demonstrated great difficulty even with English locative verb classes that have equivalent verbs in Korean.

3.4.3   Preemption, Entrenchment, and Semantics

Similar to first language acquisition, the acquisition of a second language has also been viewed as a statistically driven process where learners generalize abstract construction schemata by witnessing specific instances (Bybee, 2008; Ellis, 2012; Ellis & Larsen-Freeman, 2009; Zhang, 2017). Even though L2 learners' knowledge of English constructions is characterized with mismatches between lexical items and constructions (e.g. *He untied his laces.*), similar to L1 learners, L2 learners can also gradually realize the issues in their interlanguage and retreat from overgeneralizations with an increasing exposure to the target language (Zhang, 2017). In the field of L1 acquisition, cognitive mechanisms including entrenchment, preemption and construction semantics have been studied intensively. However, investigation into these effects in L2 development has been comparatively scarce (Zhang, 2017; Zhang & Mai, 2018; Zhang & Wen, 2019), and mostly followed the Ambridge's paradigm that operationalizes related constructs (e.g. entrenchment and preemption) as statistical measures and builds prediction models (Ambridge, 2017; Ambridge et al., 2018; Ambridge et al., 2015; Ambridge & Blything, 2016).

Zhang (2017) focused on the negative *un-* prefixes used for expressing the undoing of an action or reversible actions. Since Chinese and English differ greatly in terms of lexicalizing the meaning of reversible actions, Chinese learners have to re-establish the semantic associations between *un-* prefixation and intended meaning. In this study, the effects of entrenchment, preemption, and verb semantics were tested using linear mixed-effects models. The dependent variable was the acceptability of each *un-* form rated by the participants using a 5-point scale. The predictor variables were measures of entrenchment, preemption, and verb semantics. Entrenchment was operationalized as the raw frequencies of all inflected forms of each verb in the BNC. Since the frequencies for each bare verb were not normally distributed, the data was logistically transformed. The frequencies of competing verbs (the two competing verbs were suggested by 13 additional Chinese English teachers) were obtained similarly as preemption statistics. As to verb semantics, *un-* prefixation verbs were divided into several categories (Zhang, 2017) based on Whorf (1956) and Ambridge's (2013) framework. The controlled variables include: reversibility (the reversibility of the action denoted by the bare verb rated by 13 Chinese English teachers), acceptability of the bare form (rated by the participants on a 5-point scale), and frequency of the *un-* prefixation (log transformed frequency of each *un-* form in the BNC). Results suggested that entrenchment and verb semantics affected Chinese learners' cognitive mechanism in avoiding overgeneralization errors, while preemption demonstrated no effect.

Zhang and Mai (2018) investigated the effects of entrenchment and preemption in L2 learners' acceptance of English denominal verbs (DVs). The participants, two groups of Chinese learners of English (20 fourth-year English major students and 20 teachers of English), judged the acceptability of 75 English locatum and 75 location DVs. Locatum DVs were used to replace the phrase describing the location of one thing with respect to another (e.g. *They watered the flowers* replaces *They poured water on the flowers.*), while location DVs were used to replace the phrase referring to the place where an action happens (e.g. *Lisa boxed the apples* replaces *Lisa put the apples into the box*.). The data analysis adopted the linear mixed-effects models with ratings of the acceptability for each DV as the dependent variable and predictor variables were measures of entrenchment and preemption. Entrenchment was measured by applying natural log-transformation to the frequency of each noun in the BNC and another 10 teachers' introspective judgment of the frequency. Preemption was operationalized by having the 10 teachers propose as many competing words for the target DVs, and obtaining the frequency of these competing verbs through corpus search. Results suggested that both entrenchment and preemption play a role in restricting L2 learners' acceptance of English DVs.

To investigate the factors that constrain Chinese English learners' development of polysemous phrasal verbs (PVs), Zhang and Wen (2019) introduced more factors in their mixed-effects model, including frequency of polysemous senses, interference from high-frequency meaning sense, semantic transparency (judged by another 10 participants using a 5-point scale), exposure of English (obtained through questionnaire), and L2 proficiency, in addition to entrenchment (total frequency of verbs) and preemption (frequency of competing verbs suggested by eight English native speakers). The results suggested that the advanced learners' knowledge of the high-frequency senses is associated with PV frequency, semantic transparency, and the time spent reading books and watching films / TV, while their knowledge of the low-frequency senses can be predicted by PV frequency and preemption. For the intermediate learners, their mastery of the high-frequency senses can be predicated by semantic transparency, PV frequency, and preemption. The intermediate learners' mastery of low-frequency senses are affected by semantic transparency, frequency of high-frequency senses, and preemption.

3.5　First Language and Semantic Constraints

In the field of second language acquisition, learners' interlanguage has long been related to their first language (Bley-Vroman & Joo, 2001; Inagaki, 1997; Joo, 2003; Römer et al., 2014a; Römer et al., 2017). Specific to constructional knowledge, studies investigating L2 learners' acquisition of semantic constraints intend to attribute successfully acquired narrow-range rules to the similarities between learners' first language and the target language, and the unlearned ones to the differences between the two, as stated by the fundamental difference hypothesis (Bley-Vroman & Joo, 2001; Inagaki, 1997; Joo, 2003). However, as previously reviewed in Chapter 3, the fundamental differences can only lend partial support to their findings. This section, nevertheless, focuses on cross-linguistic transfer effects of L2 learners' first language on learners' verb-argument structure mental representations (Cifuentes-Férez & Gentner, 2006; Römer et al., 2014b; Römer et al., 2017).

Researchers believed that the typological distinction of learners' first language is one of the most significant factors that influence the degree to which learners' knowledge of English verb argument structures resembles that of native speakers' (Römer et al., 2014a). The discussion of leaners' first language is based on language typology introduced by Talmy (1985, 1991, 2000). Language typology divides the world's languages into two categories according to whether the core schema (the expression of the path of motion) is expressed by the main verb or by the satellite (i.e. a combination of verbs followed by preposition or particle): (1) verb-framed languages that express path of motion by the main verb include Romance and Semitic languages, Japanese, and Tamil; (2) satellite-framed languages that express manner in the main verb and path of motion include Germanic, Slavic, Finno-Ugric languages, and Chinese.

The differences among L2 learners' mental representations of English VACs have been identified as closely associated with the closeness of their first language to the target language in terms of Talmy's typological distinction (Cifuentes-Férez & Gentner, 2006; Römer et al., 2014a; Römer et al., 2017). Learners' first language that received extensive attention include Spanish (a verb-framed language) (Römer et al., 2017; Römer & Berger, 2019), German (Römer et al., 2017; Römer & Berger,

2019), and Czech (two satellite-framed languages) (Römer et al., 2014a). Compared to speakers of verb-framed languages (e.g. Spanish), English speakers tend to utilize manner verbs to express motion and have more linguistic choices to achieve this goal (Slobin, 2003). For example, the Spanish motion verb *saltar* can be translated into to several different English equivalents including *jump (over, up), leap, climb, skip, spurt,* and *hop.* Therefore, the conclusion can be drawn that manner of motion is less commonly expressed in verb-framed languages. Cifuentes-Férez and Gentner's (2006) study lend support to this assumption by finding out that in a word mapping task, Spanish speakers were more likely to interpret a novel motion verb as a path of motion than a verb expressing manner. English speakers, on the other hand, favored manner over path interpretations (Slobin, 2003). It is worth noticing that even though Slavic Languages are generally identified as satellite-framed languages (Slobin, 2003), Czech is less prototypical (Gehrke, 2008, p. 203). In Czech, its quality of being a satellite-framed language has manifested that motion and manner are encoded in the main verb. However, in Czech, paths of motion is expressed through not only the verb and / or a directional preposition (a typical case for the satellite-framed language), but also the verb itself (a typical case for the verb-framed language).

Relying on language typology proposed by Talmy (1985, 1991, 2000), empirical studies provide supportive evidence for cross-linguistic transfer by suggesting that L1 German and L1 Czech learners (i.e. speakers of languages that share the same typological pattern as English—satellite-framed languages) have demonstrated more similar patterns to the native speaker group than L1 Spanish learners in the mappings of VACs (i.e. speakers of a language that is typologically different from English—a verb-framed language) (Römer & Berger, 2019). These studies collocated data mainly through verbal fluency tasks, which require native speakers of English and English learners complete VAC frames (i.e. *She ___ about the ...*) with the verbs coming to mind. Research has gradually adopted corpus analysis to complement the psycholinguistic data (Römer et al., 2017). The differences between different groups' learners' VAC production are compared and discussed with relating to their first language. For instance, Römer et al. (2014) found that compared to German and Czech learners, Spanish learners produced the highest numbers of non-target-like verbs in response to VACs that express a path of motion using satellite structures (e.g. "V over N" and "V against N"). In addition, Spanish learners produced more general motion verbs in their survey responses than German and Czech learners and avoided specific motion verbs. These findings suggest that manner of motion is a less entrenched concept in the minds of speakers whose L1 is verb-framed (e.g. Spanish). Römer et al. (2017) also observed that German learners produced more tokens than their Spanish counterparts for 20 out of 34 English VACs investigated. A dominant number of these VACs include satellite structures indicating path (e.g. "V after N" and "V between N"). Effects of learners' L1 background underlines the necessity of clarifying which meanings are typically related to specific constructions and drawing learners' attention to less target-like constructions, especially for those whose L1 is satellite-framed as with English.

Besides L1 background, research on VACs in L2 learners' language production has also investigated its relationship with learners' proficiency levels. A substantial number of studies have contributed to this issue by suggesting that advanced learners' VAC knowledge differs from that of native speakers systematically (Gries & Wulff, 2005; Römer et al., 2014a; Römer et al., 2017; Römer et al., 2014b; Römer & Berger, 2019).

These studies mainly relied on psycholinguistic experiments (i.e. verbal fluency tasks) to elicit language learners'(with different L1 backgrounds) and native speakers' mental representation of VACs. An increasing number of studies have also adopted corpus analysis to complement the data collected through psycholinguistic experiments (Römer et al., 2014a; Römer et al., 2017; Römer et al., 2014b; Römer & Berger, 2019), since researchers considered corpus as a more natural source of linguistic data than responses elicited through psycholinguistic experiments (Römer et al., 2014a; Römer et al., 2017; Römer et al., 2014b; Römer & Berger, 2019). However, corpora of learners' language production are less natural than that of native speakers, since learner corpora usually consist of texts produced for language practice or assessment rather than fulfilling authentic communicative purposes. Another issue of adopting corpus data is that data retrieved from corpora tended to be comparatively scarce due to the Zipfian distribution of verb tokens in VACs. With a few verbs accounting for the lion's share of VACs, other verbs may only appear a few times or even be absent (Ellis et al., 2016), suggesting that a considerable larger token numbers are necessary for more verbs to emerge. The verbal fluency task, even though less natural, is able to elicit more tokens for all VACs, and produce "datasets robust enough for quantitative and semantic analysis" (Römer et al., 2017, p. 24).

By comparing different groups of language learners' (e.g. Czech, German, Spanish L1 learners) responses and their native speaker counterparts' responses to verbal fluency tasks, researchers identified considerable overlaps between verbs associated with VACs that were produced by native speakers and advanced language learners, indicating that these common VACs are deeply entrenched in the minds of advanced English learners (Römer et al., 2014b; Römer et al., 2017). Despite the similarities between advanced learners' and native speakers' mental representation of VACs, it was equally noticeable that learners provided more general verbs (e.g. *be, come, do*), while native speakers yielded more specific verbs (e.g. *slip, reach, crawl*) (Römer, et al., 2014b) in verbal fluency tasks. In addition, learners tended to associate VACs with meanings that are different from native speakers' semantic mapping. For example, learners associated "V against N" with verbs indicating a reaction or argument (e.g. *fight, argue, speak*), while native speakers tended to associate this VAC with verbs referring to physical contact of collision (e.g. *lean, push, bump*) (Römer et al., 2014b). For VACs that are entrenched as polysemous in native speakers' mind (e.g. "V about N" elicits verbs indicating communication or directed motion), learners tended to recognize these VACs as monosemous concepts (Römer et al., 2017). Another observation concerning L2 learners' constructional knowledge that learners formed less idiomatic VACs by providing verbs that are simply related to core verbs semantically (e.g. *complain about* and *speak about*) (Römer et al., 2017).

However, with focus on constructional knowledge of advanced language learners, these studies are very limited in uncovering of the emergency and development of learners' constructional knowledge. Researchers have also realized the necessity of tracking the development of linguistic features from morphology, tense forms, and phonology to constructional knowledge at the interface of lexis and grammar (Ortega & Byrnes, 2008; Ortega & Iberri-Shea, 2005). Due to the difficulties involved in collecting cross-sectional and longitudinal L2 learner data, research on the development of L2 constructions has generally been sparse (Meunier, 2015). Several earlier usage-based studies reached to their conclusions through corpus data collected from a small number of learners (Eskildsen, 2012, 2014, 2017; Roehr-Brackin, 2014; Tode & Sakai, 2016). These studies view construction learning as "the collaboration of the memories of all of the utterances in a learner's entire history of language use and the frequency-biased abstraction of regularities within them" (Ellis & Larsen-Freeman, 2009, p. 92), and provide in-depth information concerning the emergence of L2 learners' constructional knowledge.

Eskildsen (2009) investigated the emergence of the *can*-pattern in L2 learners' language production by drawing upon a small longitudinal corpus of one L1 Spanish learners' classroom speech. He identified an increasing of type (i.e. *can*-pattern) and token (verbs used for specific *can*-pattern) ratio through five years of observation, suggesting that *can*-pattern become increasingly varied. Even though the hypothesized movement towards fully abstract constructions did not emerge in this data set, the usage-based language path of acquisition was successfully identified with negation construction (Eskildsen & Cadierno, 2007; Eskildsen, 2012). By analyzing a Mexican learner's *do*-negation use, Eskildsen and Cadierno (2007) found that more verbs and pronouns were gradually incorporated into the *do*-negation construction with the underlying knowledge becoming increasingly abstract. Two longitudinal studies focusing on the negation-pattern in classroom speech produced by two adult Mexican Spanish-speaking learners was reported in Eskildsen and Cadierno (2012). An increase of token, type frequencies and type-token ratios were observed in both studies, indicating the gradual abstraction of the negation construction. The similar developmental pattern of learners' constructional knowledge was also further testified in the studies of Li et al. (2014) and Eskildsen et al. (2015) on learners' developing inventory of motion constructions. Even though Ellis and Ferreira-Junior (2009) have expanded the constructions under discussion to include verb locative, verb object locative, and verb ditransitive constructions, these studies were very limited in terms of generalizability due to a small number of participants involved (Eskildsen, 2014, 2017) or a small number of constructions covered (Ellis & Ferreira-Junior, 2009; Eskildsen, 2009; Eskildsen & Cadierno, 2007; Eskildsen, 2012).

Given the small number of participants involved, the generalizability of these studies needs to be further testified by adopting a larger data set. Römer and Berger (2019) investigated the emergence of L2 learners' constructional knowledge drawing upon a corpus consisting of language produced by a large number of language learners. Adopting the usage-based approach, Römer and Berger (2019) investigated the development of German and Spanish learners' knowledge of 19 English verb-argument constructions (e.g. "V across N", "V among N", and "V off N"). The data included writing samples extracted from the EF-Cambridge Open Language Database produced by learners in Germany (dominant / official L1 German) and learners in Mexico (dominant / official L1 Spanish) across the five proficiency levels (A1, A2, B1, B2, C1 and C2 in an ascending order) specified in the *Common European framework of reference for languages: Learning, teaching, assessment—companion volume* (Council of Europe, 2020). Similar to previous studies on longitudinal development of L2 learners' constructional knowledge (Eskildsen, 2009, 2012; Eskildsen & Cadierno, 2007; Li et al., 2014), these findings suggested that with proficiency levels increasing, learners produced a wider range of VACs and used more varieties of verbs (Römer & Berger, 2019; Römer et al., 2014b; Römer et al., 2017). In addition, VACs used by learners at the higher proficiency levels bear a higher degree of resemblance to the native norm. With regard to learners' L1 background, more similar use of verb-VAC associations appeared at lower proficiency levels between L1 German and L1 Spanish learners compared to their higher proficiency level counterparts.

The significant progress in the research on L2 learners' acquisition of constructional knowledge has prepared researchers for future improvements. First, future research could consider increasing the number of VACs examined in each empirical endeavor (Römer & Berger, 2019; Römer et al., 2014b). Even though a large number of constructions have been investigated, including *can*-pattern, negation, and most "V preposition N" constructions, there exist an even larger body of constructions that have yet to be investigated. For example, a large number of constructions identified in *Cobuild Grammar Patterns 1: Verbs* (Francis et al., 1996) have not been investigated from the usage-based linguistic / psycholinguistic perspective, let alone noun, adjective, and adverb patterns covered in *Cobuild Grammar Patterns 2: Nouns* and *Adjectives*, and constructions at other levels. The inclusion of language produced by learners from more diverse L1 backgrounds could also enrich the agenda of research on L2 learners' acquisition of constructions. The data could be adopted to further validate the influence of language typology (Tamly, 1985, 1991, 2000) over, the acquisition of constructional knowledge, and shed light on language pedagogy that takes learners' L1 background into consideration. Besides, the availability of a significantly larger learner corpus could yield more information, especially for verbs that appeared only a few times due to Zipfian distribution of tokens in VACs. If the large learner corpus could be designed and compiled to include production by the same learners throughout a long period of time, namely a longitudinal rather than a pseudo-longitudinal corpus, the conclusions could be more safely drawn.

Despite of the above-mentioned aspects that require improvements, the current findings have yielded valuable implications for language teaching and second language acquisition (SLA) research (Römer et al., 2014b). Findings of these studies emphasized the importance and pervasiveness of constructions. Nevertheless, most textbooks, developed based on models that view lexis and grammar as separate entities, failed to convey this information to L2 English learners. Therefore, future teaching materials should be designed to forge the connection between grammar, lexis, and constructions. Second language instruction could consider teaching semantically related constructions (e.g. VACs indicating a reaction or argument) simultaneously, so that learners could infer meanings of new constructions on the basis of their existing knowledge (Littlemore, 2011).

3.6 Cognitive Linguistics and Language Teaching

Cognitive linguistic research has yielded many theories, including Frame Semantics (Fillmore, 1976), Conceptual Metaphor Theory (Lakoff & Johnson, 1980), Conceptual Semantics (Talmy, 1985), Cognitive Grammar (Langacker, 1987), Construction Grammar (Goldberg, 1995), and Conceptual Integration Blending (Fauconnier & Turner, 1996). These theories share two main foundational principles: (1) Language is "an integral part of cognition, not in isolation but in relation to other cognitive abilities, such as memory, attention, and categorization"; (2) "Language is perceived as usage-based rather than as a standalone human ability" (Hijazo-Gascón & Llopis-García, 2019, p. 2). Recent years have witnessed an emerging interest in extending Cognitive Linguistics (CL) to L2 learning, especially acquisition of prepositions (Ansari, 2016; Tyler et al., 2011; Hijazo-Gascón & Llopis-García, 2019). These studies approached linguistic knowledge from the cognitive linguistic perspective without clearly identifying the specific theories involved. Even though not directly utilizing findings in Construction Grammar, these studies are still related to Construction Grammar to some extent for two shared groundings. First, the instructional strategies and materials presented in these studies set examples for further research and teaching in terms of how to transform theoretical notions into linguistic knowledge that is available and accessible to L2 language learners and teachers (Tyler et al., 2011). Second, cognitive linguistic research on (spatial / oriental) prepositions offers a systematic and principled explanation of distinct meanings of prepositions (e.g. Tyler & Evans, 2001, 2003; Vandeloise, 1991, 1994).

Relying on cognitive analysis of English prepositions (*to*, *for*, *at*) as instructional content, Tyler et al. (2011) conducted a quasi-experimental study investigating the effectiveness of teaching English prepositions to 14 advanced Italian English learners by applying a cognitive linguistic approach. The comparison of the subjects' performances before and after the test demonstrated significant improvement, indicating that instruction adopting the cognitive linguistic perspective was effective in promoting L2 learners' knowledge of the semantics of the three prepositions. Following Norris and Ortega's (2000) suggestion, the instruction in the study of Tyler et al. (2011) included explicit instruction and communicative tasks. The teacher-dominated instruction was conducted through explicit explanation of the prepositions from a cognitive linguistic perspective, introduction to related networks of meanings, and emphasis on the central meaning of each preposition. Meanwhile, numerous visuals and diagrams were employed to demonstrate the meaning of each preposition used in various sentences. Two interactive tasks happened afterwards to have the participants work in pairs filling in the correct labels accompanying each visual.

With a focus on prepositions (e.g. *across*, *up*, *down*, *off*, *in*, and *out*), the quasi-experiment by Ansari (2016) investigated the impact of the Cognitive Linguistics on the acquisition of phrasal verbs by college EFL learners at intermediate level. Compared with the research design of Tyler et al. (2011), the research design of Ansari (2016) was more rigorous. Ansari (2016) recruited a control group, who were provided with the translation of the orientational particles appearing with concrete verbs and a treatment group, who were provided instruction in the same particles from the perspective of Cognitive Linguistics facilitated with visual aids. The positive impact of the instruction inspired by Cognitive Linguistics was successfully recognized, given that the treatment group outperformed the control group in both the exposed (i.e. prepositions and their collocating verbs that appeared in the treatment) and unexposed items (i.e. trained prepositions appearing with verbs not covered in the treatment). The treatment group was provided with explanations of the prepositions derived on the basis of the semantic classification of the particles. Meanwhile, visual aids were presented to facilitate students' understanding of these phrasal verbs, and promote vigorous learning.

As can be deduced from the review, studies on language teaching informed by Cognitive Linguistics relied on explicit instruction in semantics (semantic classification) and visual aids. The positive evidence concerning the effectiveness of these strategies has lent support to this pedagogy, even though experimental / quasi-experimental designs of these studies still need improvement in terms of the control of variables. Nevertheless, the wide adoption of this pedagogy is still difficult to achieve given the unavailability of teaching materials. In these empirical studies, teachers were also linguistic researchers, who had deep understanding and thorough knowledge of cognitive linguistic theories and findings. However, in real language teaching contexts, teachers are not very likely to command related knowledge and may rely heavily on textbooks. Therefore, a call for the development of language teaching materials is indispensable for the systematic instruction from the cognitive linguistic perspective. The list of grammar patterns that we create in this book may well facilitate the design of such a systematic teaching material.

3.7 Summary

Chapter 3 focuses on theoretical and empirical research on Construction Grammar from the perspective of Cognitive Linguistis. Important hypotheses concerning the acquisition of constructions reviewed include the generalization hypothesis and constrains of overgeneralization (e.g. entrenchment, preemption, and semantic constraints). In addition, the research on the learning of constructions from the perspective of second language acquisition is discussed with reference to theories and studies on first language acquisition.

References

Abbot-Smith, K. & Tomasello, M. (2010). The influence of frequency and semantic similarity on how children learn grammar. *First Language*, 30(1), 79-101.

Ahren, K. (2003). Verbal integration: The interaction of participant roles and sentential argument structure. *Journal of Psycholinguistic Research*, 32(5), 497-516.

Ambridge, B. (2013). How do children restrict their linguistic generalizations? an (un-) grammaticality judgment study. *Cognitive Science*, 37(3), 508-543.

Ambridge. B. (2017). Horses for courses: When acceptability judgments are more suitable than structural priming (and vice versa). *Behavioral and Brain Sciences*, 40, 256-284.

Ambridge, B. & Blything, R. (2016). A connectionist model of the retreat from verb argument structure overgeneralization. *Journal of Child Language*, 43(6), 1245-1276.

Ambridge, B., Pine, J. M. & Rowland, C. F. (2012). Semantics versus statistics in the retreat from locative overgeneralization errors. *Cognition*, 123(2), 260-279.

Ambridge, B., Barak, L., Wonnacott, E., Bannard, C. & Sala, G. (2018). Effects of both preemption and entrenchment in the retreat from verb overgeneralization errors: Four reanalyzes, and extended republication, and a meta-analytic synthesis. *Collabra: Psychology*, 4(1), 23-59.

Ambridge, B., Pine, J. M., Rowland, C. F., Freudenthal, D. & Chang, F. (2014). Avoiding dative overgeneralization errors: semantics, statistics or both?. *Language, Cognition and Neuroscience*, 29(2), 218-243.

Ambridge, B., Bidgood, A., Twomey, K., Pine, J., Rowland, C. & Freudenthal, D. (2015). Preemption versus entrenchment: Towards a construction-general solution to the problem of the retreat from verb argument structure overgeneralization. *PLOS ONE*, 10(4), 1-20.

Ansari, M. (2016). The acquisition of phrasal verbs through cognitive linguistic approach: The case of Iranian EFL learners. *Advances in Languages and Literary Studies*, 7(1), 185-194.

Bates, E., Bretherton, I. & Synder, L. (1988). *From first words to grammar: Individual differences and dissociable mechanisms*. New York: Cambridge University Press.

Behrens, H. (2009). Usage-based and emergentist approaches to language acquisition.

Linguistics, 47(2), 383-411.

Bencini, G. M. L. & Goldberg, A. E. (2000). The contribution of argument structure constructions to sentence meaning. *Journal of Memory and Language*, 43, 640-651.

Bley-Vroman, R. & Yoshinaga, N. (1992). Broad and narrow constraints on the English dative alternation. Some fundamental differences between native speakers and foreign language learners. *University of Hawai'i Working Papers in ESL*, 11(1), 157-199.

Bley-Vroman, R. & Joo, H. (2001). The acquisition and interpretation of English locative constructions by native speakers of Korean. *Studies in Second Language Acquisition*, 23, 207-219.

Blything, R. P., Ambridge, B. & Lieven, E. V. M. (2014). Children use statistics and semantics in the retreat from overgeneralization. *PLOS ONE*, 9(10), 1-11.

Bowerman, M. & Choi, S. (2001). Shaping meanings for language: Universal and learning specific in the acquisition of spatial semantic categories. In M. Bowerman & S. C. Levinson (eds.), *Language acquisition and conceptual development*. Cambridge: Cambridge University Press, 475-511.

Braine, M. & Brooks, P. (1995). Verb argument structure and the problem of avoiding an overgeneral grammar. In M. Tomasello & W. Merriman (eds.), *Beyond names for things: Young children's acquisition of verbs*. Hillsdale, NJ: Lawrence Erlbaum Associates, 353-376.

Brooks, P. & Tomasello, M. (1999). How children constrain their argument structure constructions. *Language*, 75(4), 720-738.

Brooks, P., Tomasello, M., Dodson, K. & Lewis, L. (1999). Young children's overgeneralizations with fixed transitivity verbs. *Child Development*, 70(6), 1325-1337.

Bybee, J. L. (1985). *Morphology: A study of the relation between meaning and form*. Amsterdam: John Benjamins.

Bybee, J. L. (1995). Regular morphology and the lexicon. *Language and Cognitive Processes*, 10, 425-455.

Bybee, J. L. (2008). Usage-based grammar and second language acquisition. In P. Robinson & N. C. Ellis (eds.), *Handbook of Cognitive Linguistics and second language acquisition*. New York: Routledge, 216-236.

Bybee, J. L. (2010). *Language, usage and cognition*. Cambridge: Cambridge University Press.

Bybee, J. L. & Hopper, P. (eds.). (2001). *Frequency and the emergency of linguistic structure*. Amsterdam: John Benjamins.

Bybee, J. L. & Slobin, D. I. (1982). Rules and schemas in the development and use of the English past tense. *Language*, 58, 165-289.

Casenhiser, D. & Goldberg, A. (2005). Fast mapping between a phrasal form and meaning. *Developmental Science*, 8(6), 500-508.

Chomsky, N. (1965). *Aspects of the theory of syntax*. Cambridge, MA: MIT Press.

Cifuentes-Férez, P. & Gentner, D. (2006). Naming motion events in Spanish and English. *Cognitive Linguistics*, 17, 443-462.

Clark, E. V. (1988). On the logic of contrast. *Journal of Child Language*, 15(2), 317-335.

Clausner, T. C. & Croft, W. (1997). Productivity and schematicity in metaphors. *Cognitive Science*, 21, 247-282.

Council of Europe. 2020. *Common European framework of reference for languages: Learning, teaching, assessment—companion volume*. Strasbourg: Council of Europe Publishing.

Elio, R. & Anderson, J. R. (1984). The effects of information order and learning mode on schema abstraction. *Memory and Cognition*, 12, 20-30.

Ellis, N. C. (2012). Frequency effects. In P. Robinson (ed.), *The Routledge encyclopedia of SLA*. New York: Routledge, 260-265.

Ellis, N. C. & Ferreira-Junior, F. (2009). Constructions and their acquisition: Island and the distinctiveness of their occupancy. *Annual Review of Cognitive Linguistics*, 7, 188-221.

Ellis, N. C. & Larsen-Freeman, D. (2009). Constructing second language: Analyses and computational simulations of the emergence of linguistic constructions from usage. *Language Learning*, 59 (S1), 90-125.

Ellis, N. C., Römer, U. & O'Connell, M. B. (2016). Chapter 1: Constructions and usaged-based approaches to language acquisition. *Language Learning*, 66(1), 23-44.

Ellis, P. B., Hunston, S. & Manning, E. (1996). *Collins Cobuild grammar patterns 1: Verbs*. London: Collins CoBUILD.

Eskildsen, S. W. (2009). Constructing another language: Usage-Based Linguistics in second language acquisition. *Applied Linguistics*, 30, 335-357.

Eskildsen, S. W. (2012). L2 negation constructions at work. *Language Learning*, 62, 335-372.

Eskildsen, S. W. (2014). What's new? A usage-based classroom study of linguistic routines and creativity in L2 learning. *International Review of Applied Linguistics*, 52, 1-30.

Eskildsen, S. W. (2017). The emergence of creativity in L2 English: A usage-based case study. In N. Bell (ed.), *Multiple perspectives on language play*. Berlin, Germany: De Gruyter, 281-316.

Eskildsen, S. W. & Cadierno, T. (2007). Are recurring multi-word expressions really syntactic freezes? Second language acquisition from the perspective of Usage-Based Linguistics. In M. Nenonen & S. Niemi (eds.), *Collocations and idioms 1: Papers from the first Nordic conference on syntactic freezes*. Joensuu, Finland: Joensuu University Press, 86-99.

Eskildsen, S. W., Cadiemo, T. & Li, P. (2015). On the development of motion constructions in four learners of L2 English. In T. Cadierno & S. W. Eskildsen (eds.), *Usage-based perspectives on second language learning*. Berlin, Germany: De Gruyter, 207-232.

Fauconnier, G. & Turner, M. (1996). Blending as a central process of grammar. In Adele E. Goldberg (ed.), *Conceptual structure and discourse*. Stanford: CSLI Publications, 113-130.

Fillmore, C. (1976). Frame semantics and the nature of language. *Annals of the*

New York Academy of Sciences: Conference on the Origin and Development of Language and Speech, 280, 20-32.

Fillmore, C. J., Kay, P. & O'Connor, M. C. (1988). Regularity and idiomaticity in grammatical constructions: The case of let alone. *Language*, 64, 501-138.

Gehrke, B. (2008). *Ps in motion: On the semantics and syntax of P elements and motion events*. Utrecht, Netherlands: LOT Publications.

Gentner, D., Loewenstein, J. & Hung, B. (2007). Comparison facilitates learning part names. *Journal of Cognition and Development*, 8(3), 285-307.

Gerken, L., Wilson, R. & Lewis, W. (2005). Infant can use distributional cues to form syntactic categories. *Journal of Child Language*, 32(2), 249-268.

Gibson, J. J. (1979). *The ecological approach to visual perception*. New York: Houghton Mifflin.

Glenberg, A. M. (1997). What memory is for. *Behavioral and Brain Sciences*, 20, 1-19.

Glenberg, A. M. & Robertson, D. A. (1999). Indexical understanding of instructions. *Discourse Processes*, 28, 1-26.

Goldberg, A. E. (1993). Another look at some learnability paradoxes. In E. Clark (ed.), *Proceedings of the 25the Annual Stanford Child Language Research Rofums*. Standford, CA: CSLI Publications, 60-75.

Goldberg, A. E. (1995). *Constructions: A Construction Grammar approach to argument structure*. Chicago: Chicago University Press.

Goldberg, A. E. (1996). Optimizing constraints and the Persian complex predicate. *Berkeley Linguistic Society*, 22, 132-146.

Goldberg, A. E. (2003). Constructions: A new theoretical approach to language. *TRENDS in Cognitive Sciences*, 7(5), 219-224.

Goldberg, A. E. (2006). *Constructions at work: The nature of generalization in language*. Oxford: Oxford University Press.

Goldberg, A. E. (2013). Argument structure constructions versus lexical rules or derivational verb templates. *Mind & Language*, 28(4), 435-465.

Goldberg, A. E. & Suttle, L. (2010). Construction Grammar. *WIREs Cognitive*

Science, 1(4), 468-477.

Goldberg, A. E., Casenhiser, D. M. & Sethuraman, N. (2004). Learning argument structure generalizations. *Cognitive Linguistics*, 15, 289-316.

Gries, S. T. & Stefanowitsch, A. (2004). Extending collostructional analysis: A corpus-based perspective on "alternations". *International Journal of Corpus Linguistics*, 9(1), 97-129.

Gries, S. T. & Wulff, S. (2005). Do foreign language learners also have constructions? Evidence from priming, sorting, and corpora. *Annual Review of Cognitive Linguistics*, 3, 182-200.

Gries, S. T. & Wulff, S. (2009). Psycholinguistic and corpus-linguistic evidence for L2 constructions. *Annual Review of Cognitive Linguistics*, 7, 163-186.

Gropen, J. & Goldberg, R. (1991). Syntax and semantics in the acquisition of locative verbs. *Journal of Child Language*, 18, 115-151.

Harmon, Z. & Kapatsinski, V. (2017). Putting old tools to novel uses: The role of form accessibility in semantic extension. *Cognitive Psychology*, 98, 22-44.

Hauser, M. D., Newport, E. L. & Aslin, R. N. (2001). Segmentation of the speech stream in a non-human primate: Statistical learning in cotton-top tamarins. *Cognition*, 78, 41-52.

Healy, A. & Mill, G. (1970). The verb as the main determinant of sentence meaning. *Psychonomic Science*, 20, 372.

Heine, B. (1993). *Auxiliaries: Cognitive forces and grammaticalization*. New York: Oxford University Press.

Hijazo-Gascón, A. & Llopis-García, R. (2019). Applied Cognitive Linguistics and foreign language learning. Introduction to the special issue. *International Review of Applied Linguistics in Language*, 57(1), 1-20.

Hunston, S. & Su, H. (2019). Pattern, constructions, and local grammar: A case study of "evaluation". *Applied Linguistics*, 40(4), 567-593.

Inagaki, S. (1997). Japanese and Chinese learners' acquisition of the narrow-range rules for the dative alternation in English. *Language Learning*, 47(4), 637-669.

Jackendoff, R. (2002). *Foundations of language*. Oxford: Oxford University Press.

Joo, H. (2003). Second language learnability and the acquisition of the argument structure of English locative verbs by Korean. *Second Language Research*, 19(4), 305-328.

Kaschak, M. P. & Glenberg, A. M. (2000). Constructing meaning: The role of affordances and grammatical constructions in sentence comprehension. *Journal of Memory and Language*, 43(3), 508-529.

Lakoff, G. (1987). *Women, fire and dangerous things: What categories reveal about the mind*. Chicago: University of Chicago Press.

Lakoff, G. & Johnson, M. (1980). *Metaphors we live by*. Chicago: University of Chicago Press.

Langacker, R. (1987). *Foundations of Cognitive Grammar, vol.1: Theoretical prerequisites*. Stanford: Stanford University Press.

Levin, B. & Hovav, M. R. (1994). A preliminary analysis of causative verbs in English. *Lingua*, 92, 35-77.

Li, P., Eskildsen, S. W. & Cadierno, T. (2014). Tracing an L2 learners' motion constructions over time: A usage-based classroom investigation. *The Modern Language Journal*, 98, 612-628.

Littlemore, J. (2011). *Applying Cognitive Linguistics to second language learning and teaching*. Basingstoke, UK: Palgrave Macmillan.

MacWhinney, B. (1978). *The acquisition of morphophonology, vol. 43*. Chicago: University of Chicago Press.

Marcus, G. F., Brinkmann, U., Clahsen, H., Wiese, R. & Pinker, S. (1995). German inflection: The exception that proves the rule. *Cognitive Psychology*, 29, 189-256.

Meunier, F. (2015). Developmental patterns in learner corpora. In S. Granger, G. Gilquin & F. Meunier (eds.), *The Cambridge handbook of learner corpus research*. Cambridge: Cambridge University Press, 379-400.

Ninio, A. (1999). Pathbreaking verbs in syntactic development and the question of prototypical transitivity. *Journal of Child Language*, 26, 619-653.

Norris, J. M. & Ortega, L. (2000). Effectiveness of L2 instruction: A research synthesis and quantitative meta-analysis. *Language Learning*, 50(3), 417-528.

Ortega, L. & Byrnes, H. (2008). The longitudinal study of advanced L2 capacities: An introduction. In L. Ortega & H. Byrnes (eds.), *The longitudinal study of advanced L2 capacities*. New York: Routledge, 3-20.

Ortega, L. & Iberri-Shea, G. (2005). Longitudinal research in second language acquisition: Recent trends and future directions. *Annual Review of Applied Linguistics*, 25, 26-45.

Osherson, D., Wilkie, O., Smith, E. & Lópze, A. (1990). Category-Based induction. *Psychological Review*, 97(2), 185-200.

Partee, B. H. (1965). *Subject and object in modern English*. New York: Garland.

Pickering, M. J. & Branigan, H. P. (1998). The representation of verbs: Evidence from syntactic priming in language production. *Journal of Memory and Language*, 39(4), 633-651.

Pinker, S. (1989). *Learnability and cognition: The acquisition of argument structure*. Cambridge, MA: MIT Press.

Pinker, S. (1994). *Words and rules: The ingredients of language*. New York: Basic Books.

Pinker, S. & Jackendoff, R. (2005). The faculty of language: What's special about it? *Cognition*, 95, 201-236.

Plunkett, K. & Marchman, V. (1991). U-shaped learning and frequency effects in a multilayered perceptron: Implications for child language acquisition. *Cognition*, 38, 43-102.

Plunkett, K. & Marchman, V. (1993). From rote learning to system building: Acquiring verb morphology in children and connectionist nets. *Cognition*, 48, 21-69.

Roehr-Brackin, K. (2014). Explicit knowledge and processes from a usage-based perspective: The development trajectory of an instructed L2 learner. *Language Learning*, 64, 771-808.

Römer, U. & Berger, C. M. (2019). Observing the emergence of constructional knowledge: Verb patterns in German and Spanish learners of English at different proficiency levels. *Studies in Second Language Acquisition*, 41, 1089-1110.

Römer, U., O'Donnell, M. B. & Ellis, N. C. (2014a). Second language learner knowledge of verb-argument constructions: Effects of language transfer and typology. *The Modern Language Journal*, 98, 952-975.

Römer, U., Roberson, A., O'Donnell, M. B. & Ellis, N. C. (2014b). Linking learner corpus and experimental data in studying second language learners' knowledge of verb-argument constructions. *ICAME Journal*, 38, 59-79

Römer, U., Skalicky, S. & Ellis, N. C. (2017). Verb-Argument constructions in advanced L2 English learner production: Insights from corpora and verbal fluency tasks. *Corpus Linguistics and Linguistic Theory*, 1-27.

Saffran, J. R., Aslin, R. & Newport, E. (1996). Statistical learning by 8-month-old infants. *Science*, 274, 1926-1928.

Scholz, B. C. & Pullum, G. K. (2002). Searching for arguments to support linguistic nativism. *Linguistic Review*, 19, 185-224.

Shin, G. (2010). On the contribution of argument structure constructions to sentence meaning for Korean learners of English. *English Teaching*, 65, 263-282.

Slobin, D. I. (1985). Crosslinguistic evidence for the language-making capacity. In D. I. Slobin (ed.), *A crosslinguistic study of language acquisition, vol. 2: Theoretical issues*. Hillsdale, NJ: Lawrence Erlbaum, 1157-1256.

Slobin, D. I. (2003). Language and thought online: Cognitive consequences of linguistic relativity. In D. Gentner & S. Goldin-Meadow (eds.), *Language in mind: Advances in the study of language and thought*. Cambridge, MA: MIT Press, 157-192.

Stefanowitsch, A. (2008). Negative evidence and preemption: A constructional approach to ungrammaticality. *Cognitive Linguistics*, 19(3), 513-531.

Stefanowitsch, A. & Gries, S. T. (2003). Collostructions: Investigating the interaction between words and constructions. *International Journal of Corpus Linguistic*, 8, 209-243.

Talmy, L. (1985). Lexicalization patterns: Semantic structure in lexical form. In T. Shopen (ed.), *Language typology and syntactic description: Grammatical categories and the lexicon*. Cambridge: Cambridge University Press, 57-149.

Talmy, L. (1991). Path to realization: A typology of event conflation. *Proceedings of the Seventeenth Annual Meeting of the Berkeley Linguistics Society*, 480-520. doi: https://doi.org/10.3765/bls.v17i0.1620.

Talmy, L. (2000). *Towards a cognitive semantics, vol. 2: Typology and process in concept structuring*. Cambridge, MA: MIT Press.

Tode, T. & Sakai, H. (2016). Exemplar-based instructed second language development and classroom experience. *International Journal of Applied Linguistics*, 167, 210-234.

Traugott, C. E. & Trousdale, G. (2013). *Constructionalization and constructional changes*. Oxford: Oxford University Press.

Trousdale, G. & Hoffmann, T. (eds.). (2013). *Oxford handbook of Construction Grammar*. Oxford: Oxford University Press.

Tyler, A. & Evans, V. (2001). Reconsidering prepositional polysemy networks: The case of *over*. *Language*, 77(4), 724-765.

Tyler, A. & Evans, V. (2003). *The semantics of English prepositions: Spatial scenes, embodied meaning and cognition*. Cambridge: Cambridge University Press.

Tyler, A., Mueller, C. & Ho, V. (2011). Applying Cognitive Linguistics to learning the semantics of English prepositions *to*, *for*, and *at*: An experimental investigation. *Vigo International Journal of Applied Linguistics*, 8, 180-206.

Vandeloise, C. (1991). *Spatial prepositions: A case study in French*. Chicago: University of Chicago Press.

Vandeloise, C. (1994). Methodology and analyses of the preposition *in*. *Cognitive Linguistics*, 5, 157-184.

Werning, M., Hinzen, W. & Machery, E. (2012). *The Oxford handbook of compositionality*. New York: Oxford University Press.

Whorf, B. L. (1956). *Language, thought, and reality*. Cambridge, MA: MIT Press.

Wurm, L. H. & Fisicaro, S. A. (2014). What residualizing predictors in regression analyses does (and what it does not do). *Journal of Memory and Language*, 72(1), 37-48.

Zhang, X. (2017). Second language users' restriction of linguistic generalization errors: The case of English *un-* prefixation development. *Language Learning*, 67(3), 569-598.

Zhang, X. & Mai, C. (2018). Effects of entrenchment and preemption in second language learners' acceptance of English denominal verbs. *Applied Psycholinguistics*, 39(2), 413-436.

Zhang, X. & Wen, J. (2019). Exploring multiple constraints on second language development of English polysemous phrasal verbs. *Applied Psycholinguistics*, 40, 1073-1101.

CHAPTER 4

Phraseology and Pattern Grammar

4.1 Defining Phraseology

From the perspective of Corpus Linguistics, grammar patterns have been recognized as an important phraseological feature / aspect. To understand grammar patterns and related research, it is important to review the theoretical development and empirical research on phraseology, a field that studies "structure, meaning, and use of word combinations / multi-word units" (Cowie, 1994, p. 3168).

Phraseology, previously presented as a subfield of lexicology, focuses on word combinations rather than single words. Ever since the publication of Pawley and Syder's (1983) seminal article, phraseology has gradually developed into a central aspect in a variety of fields, including natural language processing (NLP), foreign language teaching, and Construction Grammar. Corpus linguists have also come to understand that language consists of not only individual words, but also multi-word sequences as semantic units (Martinez & Schmitt, 2012). The centrality of phraseology was established by the articulation of the idiom principle by Sinclair (1991), which states that "a language user has available to him or her a larger number of semi-preconstructed phrases that constitute single choices, even though they might appear to be analyzable into segments" (Sinclair, 1991, p. 110). Knowledge of phraseological features generally includes three aspects: form, meaning, and use. Each of these aspects can be further divided into several sub-dimensions (see Table 4.1).

Table 4.1 What are involved in knowing phraseological features (adapted from Webb, newton & Chang, 2013, p.97)

Dimension	Aspect	Receptive vs. productive	Question addressed
Form	Spoken	R	What does the collocation sound like?
		P	How is the collocation pronounced?
	Written	R	What does the collocation look like?
		P	How is the collocation written and spelled?
	Word Parts	R	What words are recognizable in this collocation?
		P	What words are needed to express the meaning?
Meaning	Form and Meaning	R	What meaning does this collocation signal?
		P	What collocation can be used to express this meaning?
	Concept and Referents	R	What is included in the concept?
		P	What items can the concept refer to?
	Associations	R	What other words or collocations does this make us think of?
		P	What other words or collocations could we use instead of this one?
Use	Grammatical Functions	R	In what patterns does the collocation occur?
		P	In what patterns must we use this collocation?
	Collocations	R	What words, collocations, or types of collocations occur with this one?
		P	What words, collocations, or types of collocations must we use with this one?
	Constraints on Use (Register, Frequency...)	R	Where, when, and how often would we expect to meet this collocation?
		P	Where, when, and how often can we use this collocation?

Note: R = receptive; P = productive.

A comprehensive definition of phraseological features might be difficult to achieve given their diversity (Schmitt & Carter, 2004). Schmitt and Carter's (2004) discussion on the characteristics of phraseological features, including length, transparency /

opaqueness, fixedness, and semantic prosody, could facilitate the understanding of phraseology, a somewhat all-inclusive term. Phraseological features can be either long or short. Wray (2002) argued that even though single words and morphemes could be regarded as phraseological features, the majority of literature revolved around multi-word sequences as units of analysis. Some phraseological features are fixed (e.g. *ladies and gentlemen*), while others allow slot(s) to be filled with semantically appropriate words or strings of words. Schmitt and Carter (2004) postulated that fixedness sometimes was an advantage, given that more conventionalized warnings (e.g. *Watch out!*) were more effective than creative expressions (e.g. *Watch the car coming behind you!*). Meanwhile, Schmitt and Carter (2004) acknowledged that allowing more flexibility in meaning was also advantageous, because flexibility contributed to language fluency by adapting to various contexts. Phraseological features also vary in terms of transparency / opaqueness, with idioms (e.g. *the elephant in the room*) at the opaque end, and other phraseological features approaching the transparent end (e.g. *my point is that ...*) (Schmitt & Carter, 2004). The slots in phraseological features, nevertheless, are not completely open. Rather, there exist semantic constraints that dictate the choice of words that can be used in the slots. Schmitt and Carter (2004) cited the sentence *Diane thinks nothing of running 5 miles before breakfast* as an example to illustrate the concept of semantic constraints. The basic structure underlying this sentence is "_____ thinks nothing of _____". Even though the second slot allows for a variety of entities, the semantic constraint of this basic structure specifies that the second slot has to be something usual or unexpected. Otherwise, this sentence would be somewhat bizarre (e.g. *She thinks nothing of sleeping 8 hours per night.*). Another observation concerning phraseological features is that they have semantic prosody, referring to the negative or positive evaluation suggested by a phraseological feature (Sinclair, 2004). For example, the word *rife* tends to be used for negative evaluation of the situation or denoting negative meaning. It is usually embedded in the structure "Something undesirable is / are rife in location / time", e.g. "*Male chauvinism was rife in medicine in those days*" or "*Fears are now rife that the price could plunge well below 30p by the end of the year*" (Schmitt & Cartner, 2004, p. 8).

Phraseology is an umbrella term, which encompasses heterogeneous word combinations that linguists naturally feel necessary to subcategorize and disentangle (Ackerley, 2017; Granger & Meunier, 2008). To serve different purposes, e.g. lexicological or lexicographic, pedagogical, and psycholinguistic purposes, different features are selected to categorize multi-word units, resulting in a proliferation of typologies (Granger & Meunier, 2008). These features mainly include: internal structure (e.g. verb + noun, verb + preposition), extent (phrase vs. sentence), degree of semantic compositionality, degree of syntactic flexibility and collocability, and discourse function (Granger & Paquot, 2008). Generally, the multi-word units have been classified into a range of subtypes according to their degree of semantic compositionality / non-compositionality, syntactic fixedness, lexical restrictions, and institutionalization (Granger & Meunier, 2008). As a result, phraseological features have been used in literature somewhat interchangeably with a variety of terms, including lexical patterns (Coxhead et al., 2017), lexical phrases, formulas, fixed expressions, prefabricated patterns (Biber et al., 2004), formulaic sequences (Schmitt & Carter, 2004), lexical bundles (Biber & Barbieri, 2006; Biber et al., 2004), lexical chunks (Schmitt, 2000), and collocations (Sinclair, 1991).

The classification methods of phraseological features have developed from linguistic analysis to the inclusion of automated extraction and neurological evidence. Traditionally, fine-grained linguistic analysis is adopted to develop typologies of phraseological terms by adopting different standards aforementioned (e.g. semantic non-compositionality, syntactic fixedness, lexical restrictions, and institutionalization). Cowie's (1998) phraseological continuum and Mel'cuk's (1998) typology model rank among the most influential typologies deeply rooted in lexicology and lexicography. According to Cowie (1998), phraseological features are divided into composites and formulae. Composites are further classified into restricted collocations, figurative idioms, and pure idioms. Formulae are divided into routine formulae and speech formulae. Mel'cuk's (1998) typology categorizes phraseological features into semantic and pragmatic phrasemes. Semantic phrasemes are divided into semi-phrasemes (i.e. collocations), quasi-phrasemes (i.e. quasi-idioms), and full phrasemes (i.e. idioms).

More recently, researchers have also pointed out that empirical evidence is needed to testify the classification of phraseology and to provide neurological evidence in terms of the processing of phraseological features (Van Lancker-Sidtis, 2004), since not all phraseological features provide the same processing advantages (Columbus, 2010, 2012). Empirically, Columbus (2013) intended to explore whether traditional categories of phraseological features (e.g. idioms, restricted collocations, and lexical bundles) could also be identified through neurological evidence by administering a magnitude estimation survey adapted from Wulff's (2008, 2009) idiomaticity rating questionnaire. The participants (English native speakers) were required to rate the semantic transparency and familiarity of phraseological features randomly embedded in 150 sentences.

Despite the substantial number of phraseological terms proposed, idioms, lexical bundles, (restricted) collocations, and grammar patterns are the prevailing ones that have been discussed in empirical studies (Columbus, 2013), and are discussed in a more detailed manner. It is worth noticing that the differences between phraseological features are not always clear-cut. Usually, researchers focus on one or a few of these phraseological features in their studies to make their research scopes manageable.

4.1.1　Idioms

Idioms, "word strings of varying lengths which have a figurative or metaphorical interpretation" (Columbus, 2013, p. 29), rank among the most commonly investigated phraseological features. Idioms can largely be viewed as expressions including literal and non-literal phrases "which are not the sum of their parts" (Columbus, 2013, p. 29). For each idiom, none or a few of the component words can function as a semantic equivalent of the complete idiom. For example, in *kick the bucket* (to die), s*pill the* *beans* (to let out the secret), and *lose your marbles* (to go crazy), *bucket*, *bean*, and *marbles* are used figuratively rather than literately. The meanings of idioms are often not easily deduced based on the meanings of their constituent words, and thus more difficult for learners than for native speakers who have access to a considerably larger amount of language input with idioms embedded (Oakey, 2010).

Early research tended to view idioms as words with spaces, indicating that the relationship between idioms and their meanings was arbitrary (e.g. Bobrow & Bell, 1973; Swinney & Cutler, 1979), and "idioms are stored and accessed as whole units" (Holsinger, 2013, p. 375). Recent research, nevertheless, has discovered that there exist structural / grammatical relationships between words in an idiom, e.g. structural priming (Konopka & Bock, 2009). In addition, the rapid access of idiomatic expressions also occurs with less idiosyncratic multi-word units (Tabossi et al., 2008). A review of previous research suggests that idiomatic expressions behave as words with spaces and grammatical structures simultaneously (Cacciari & Tabossi, 1988; Cutting & Bock, 1997; Sprenger et al., 2006). Consistent with the view that literal processing plays a causal role in the access of idiomatic meaning, Cacciari and Tabossi (1988) proposed the configuration hypothesis, which speculates that the processing of idioms depends on the predictability of the intended meaning. Later, Cutting and Bock (1997) proposed a distributed representation for idioms by drawing upon errors in speech data. Specifically, idioms were represented as structural or phrasal frames directly associated with conceptual meanings. Similarly, Sprenger et al. (2006) viewed idioms as superlemmas, "(operating) as a grammatical function over the component lemmas of the idioms" (Holsinger, 2013, p. 375). The superlemma hypothesis postulates that idiom production initiates with the conceptual meaning and is then realized through individual composing lemmas. When attempting to express the conceptual meaning, the speaker chooses one expression among semantically competitive expressions, such as *die*, *pass away*, and *kick the bucket*. When a specific expression is decided on, the mechanism travels to individual composing lemma, such as *kick* and *bucket*. This process is reversed during comprehension. Syntactic context not matching the expected structure of an idiom would not lead to the conceptual level (e.g. *The bucket was kicked* would not be associated with the idiomatic meaning *died*.). Holsinger (2013), nevertheless, perceived the superlamma hypothesis somewhat unclear in terms of whether related lemmas (e.g. *pail* as related to *bucket*) promoted the activation process leading to idiomatic conceptual meaning.

4.1.2   Lexical Bundles

From the perspective of Corpus Linguistics, lexical bundles are frequently co-occurring word strings (also known as "*n*-grams") with no semantic or pragmatic bond (Columbus, 2013). Lexical bundles differ from idioms in that bundles are "strictly statistical" and "syntactically predictable and semantically regular" (Columbus, 2013, p. 30). Take the lexical bundle *I would like to* for example. Its meaning is more predictable than *let the cat out of the bag* (an idiom) because of its components.

   Lexical bundles function as basic building blocks of discourse (Biber et al., 2004). An abundance of empirical research has been conducted to investigate the use of lexical bundles in different registers, including conversations, research articles (Cortes, 2004), university textbooks, introductions (Biber et al., 2004), and doctoral dissertations and Master's theses (Hyland, 2008). The significance of Biber et al. (2004) lies in that this research offers a systematic taxonomy of analyzing lexical bundles by annotating structures and functions. To be specific, with reference to structures, Biber et al. (2004) divided lexical bundles into bundles incorporating verb phrase fragments, lexical bundles including dependent clause fragments, and lexical bundles including noun phrase fragments and prepositional phrase fragments. Each category was further categorized in a fine-grained manner. For example, lexical bundles incorporating dependent clause fragments were divided into: 1st / 2nd person pronoun + dependent clause fragment (e.g. *I want you to…*), *wh*-clause fragments (e.g. *what I want to…*), *if*-clause fragments (e.g. *if you want to…*), (verb / adjective+) *to*-clause fragment (e.g. *to be able to…*), and *that*-clause fragments (e.g. *that there is a…*). In terms of function, Biber et al. (2004) divided lexical bundles into stance bundles (including epistemic stance bundles, attitudinal / modality stance bundles), discourse organizing bundles (including topic introduction / focus bundles and topic elaboration / clarification bundles), and referential bundles (identification / focus bundles, imprecision bundles, bundles specifying attributes, time / place / text-deixis bundles). Epistemic stance bundles were further categorized into personal epistemic bundles that "express certainty or uncertainty" (e.g. *I don't know why the voltage is here…*) and impersonal epistemic bundles which "express degrees of certainty rather than uncertainty" (e.g. *are more likely to*) (Biber et al., 2004, p. 389). Attitudinal / modality stance bundles, expressing personal "attitudes towards the actions or events described in the following proposition" (Biber et al., 2004, p. 390), include desire bundles (e.g. *I don't want to…*), obligation / directive bundles (e.g. *You need to know…*), intention / prediction bundles (e.g. *what we're going to take a look…*), and ability bundles (e.g. *I want you to be able to…*). Topic introduction / focus bundles are used to indicate the introduction of a new topic (e.g. *I want to talk about…*), and topic elaboration / clarification bundles signal a further explanation or clarification (e.g. *…you know I mean I expect you to…*). Nested under referential bundles, identification / focus bundles are used to highlight important information (e.g. *For those of you who came late…*) and introduce a discussion (e.g. *One of the things they stress…*). Imprecision bundles function to "indicate that a specified reference is not necessarily exact, or to indicate that there are additional references of the same type that could be provided (e.g. *something like that*)" (Biber et al., 2004, p. 394). The third subcategory of referential bundles specifies attributes of the head noun such as quantities or amounts (e.g. *have a lot of power*). Time / place / text-deixis bundles "refer to particular places, times, or locations (e.g. *in the United States*)" (Biber et al., 2004, p. 395).

Biber et al. (2004) compared lexical bundles in university classroom instruction and textbooks to those occurring in conversations. The former ones were "characterized by high interaction, expression of personal stance, and real-time production circumstances", and the latter ones were "characterized by an informational rather than personal focus, and extensive opportunity for crafting, revising, and editing the written text" (Biber et al., 2004, p. 374). The analysis of lexical bundles in university classroom instruction and textbooks was realized by drawing upon the TOEFL 2000 Spoken and Written Academic Language Corpus (Biber et al., 2002, 2004), which includes spoken and written academic language in six disciplines, including Business, Education, Engineering, Humanities, Natural Science, and Social Science. The identification of lexical bundles normally relies on an arbitrary threshold of frequency. Adopting a conservative threshold, Biber et al. (2004) set a high frequency cut-off of 40 times per million words to be selected as frequent lexical bundles for analysis, and only four-word bundles were selected. Idiosyncratic uses of lexical bundles were fully considered by excluding lexical bundles occurring in less than five different texts. Lexical bundles were categorized according to different dimensions, including structures (lexical bundles including verb phrases, dependent clauses, noun phrases and prepositional phrases), and functions (stance expressions, discourse organizers, referential expressions, and special conversational functions). Biber et al. (2004) provided an in-depth analysis of lexical bundles used in classroom teaching, textbooks, conversation, and academic prose. Biber et al. (2004) found that classroom instruction used significantly more stance lexical bundles and discourse organizing bundles than that used in conversations and more referential bundles than that used in academic prose.

Similar to research on many other linguistic features (e.g. Brett, 1994; Kanoksilapathem, 2003; Yang & Allison, 2003), lexical bundles have also been indentified in different sections of research articles. For example, Cortes (2013) extracted the introduction sections of research articles from the Published Research Article Corpus (Gray & Cortes, 2010). The Lexical Bundle Program (Cortes, 2004) was adopted to extract lexical bundles from all these introductions. Moves and steps of these introductions were analyzed according to the framework proposed by Swales (1990, 2004). In addition, all lexical bundles identified were tagged according to their structures and functions as specified in Biber et al. (2004). Cortes' (2013) research successfully connected lexical bundles in introductions with moves and steps that served communicative functions. Her findings could be used to help academic language learners utilize lexical bundles skillfully.

Empirical studies have also investigated language learners' lexical bundle use. For example, Bychkovska and Lee (2017) identified Chinese undergraduate students' misuse of lexical bundles in argumentative essays by comparing Chinese and native undergraduate students' argumentative essays. A total amount of 101 high-quality essays written by native students and 105 high-quality essays written by Chinese students were analyzed by adopting Biber's structural and functional framework (Biber et al., 1999; Biber et al., 2004). Native speakers' writings were extracted from Michigan Corpus of Upper-Level Student Papers (a corpus of A-graded papers written by L1 and L2 senior students and graduate students from various disciplines in the Humanities and Social Sciences). Chinese students' essays were selected from the Corpus of Ohio Learner and Teacher English, consisting of ESL students' argumentative essays and teachers' written feedback at Ohio University. Bychkovska and Lee (2017) extracted four-word lexical bundles that occurred at least 40 times per million words by using the clusters / n-gram function embedded in a publicly available concordance tool Antconc. In terms of dispersion, the cut-off criterion was set as occurring in at least five different texts to prevent idiosyncratic uses of lexical bundles. The results demonstrated that Chinese students used more bundle types and tokens. Native students used more verb phrase bundles, while Chinese students used more stance bundles. In addition, even though lexical bundles were highly frequent in the target discourse community, grammatical errors were associated with lexical bundle misuses, suggesting the necessity of drawing language learners' attention to structures and functions of lexical bundles.

4.1.3 Collocations

From a theoretical perspective, the term "collocation", referring to the frequent co-occurrence of two or more words, is a semantic, textual, and statistical concept (Partington, 1998). Depending on the writers' priorities, the definition of collocation varies from a combination of two or more words (e.g. an adjective or a verb which tends to be used with a limited number of nouns), to longer, more complex combinations (e.g. phrases, idioms, and proverbs, which can be made up of a fixed or variable number of grammatical and / or lexical words) (Oakey, 2010). Oakey (2010) exemplified two methodological approaches to investigating collocations: native speakers' intuitive judgment and the corpus-based analysis of language data.

Native speakers' judgment, a method frequently used in the field of lexical semantics to investigate and describe lexical relations, determines whether a collocation is acceptable. Native speakers' intuitive judgment suggests the existence of "semi-systematic collocational restrictions" (Oakey, 2010, p.15), which constraints the collocates of the base word. For example, *purse* can be used with *lips* but not *brow* or *forehead*. Knowledge of these restrictions can be applied in lexicography to improve the definition of the base word in a collocation.

The corpus-based method investigates the language system itself, rather than individual users' intuitive knowledge of the language system. There are different ideas on how far to the left and right of a word its collocational relations extend. Sinclair (1991) speculated that the collocates span around four or five words to the left or right of the base word, while other corpus linguists pointed out that words differed in terms of their own unique span (Mason, 1999). Hoey (1991) even regarded the whole text that the base word appeared in as its collocational span. Any word within the span is considered as a collocation of the base word. When a word is located at the end of a sentence, its collocational span may include the first few words of the next sentence, so empirical collocational relations between words extend across sentence boundaries. Given the substantial number of running words in many corpora, close examination of the base word line by line is difficult to achieve. Nevertheless, the calculation of the occurrence of each word in different collocations can be easily obtained, and the identification of words co-occur with a certain word can also be easily achieved (Oakey, 2010).

From a statistical standpoint, collocations are defined as the regular co-occurrence of words within a given span. The statistical strength of co-occurrence is measured through MI scores, *t* scores, and log-likelihood statistic (Webb et al., 2013). According to Webb et al. (2013), even though defining collocation from a statistical standpoint promoted the efficiency of identifying collocates for a base word and reduces subjectivity, this approach did not consider semantic factors, such as concreteness of meaning (Walker & Hulme, 1999), transparency of meaning (Fernando, 1996; Moon, 1998; Nesselhauf, 2003), L1 and L2 congruence (Nesselhauf, 2003), and function (Forsberg, 2010; Wouden, 1997). Thereafter, collocations were sometimes distinguished from idioms according to their different degrees of semantic transparency (Fernando, 1996; Moon, 1998; Nesselhauf, 2003).

The method of Contrastive Interlanguage Analysis has been widely adopted to compare the collocation used by native speakers and nonnative speakers (Bestgen & Granger, 2014; Chen & Baker, 2010; De Cock, 2000). These studies indicate that L2 learners generally use more limited collocations and overuse or underuse certain collocations (Bestgen & Granger, 2014). Nevertheless, this type of point-in-time research is limited in unveiling L2 learners' longitudinal development of collocations (Li & Schmitt, 2009, p. 97). Probably due to the difficulty of collecting large longitudinal corpora of L2 language production, pseudolongitudinal studies have been conducted by collecting data simultaneously across different proficiency levels. Developmental trends are identified by comparing the linguistic devices used by different proficiency groups (e.g. Vidakovic & Barker, 2010). However, one noticeable issue with pseudolongitudinal studies lies in their exclusive focus on the frequency of phraseological features. Little attention is paid to the degree of association within collocations (Bestgen & Granger, 2014). Though frequency change data is an important data that reflects language development, it does not account for the frequency of the individual words in the sequence. "The fact that a sequence of words is above a certain frequency threshold does not necessarily imply psycholinguistic salience or pedagogical relevance" (Simpson-Vlach & Ellis, 2010, p. 490). Erequent words are more likely to occur in highly frequent collocations than low-frequency words. To overcome this weakness, Durrant and Schmitt (2009) adopted two important indexes, MI and *t* score. MI identifies collocations consisting of low-frequency words (e.g. *tectonic plates*), and *t* score identifies collocations consisting of high-frequency words (e.g. *such a long way*) (Bestgen & Granger, 2014).

Given the importance of collocations to L2 learners' language proficiency indicated by point-in-time research and pseudolongitudinal studies, the acquisition of collocations has gradually drawn researchers' attention. The majority of empirical studies have focused on the effectiveness of explicit teaching of collocations (Boers et al., 2004; Chan & Liou, 2005; Laufer & Girsai, 2008; Lindstromberg & Boers, 2008; Sun & Wang, 2003; Webb & Kagimoto, 2009, 2011), with a few on incidental learning (e.g. Webb et al., 2013). The explicit instruction mainly adopts glossed sentences and cloze tasks (Webb & Kagimoto, 2009), concordancers (Chan & Liou, 2005; Sun & Wang, 2003), and contrastive analysis and translation (Laufer & Girsai, 2008). As to incidental learning, Webb et al. (2013) identified a positive association between the effectiveness of collocation learning and the frequency of encounters (1, 5, 10, and 15 encounters).

4.2　Corpus-Based Approach to the Acquisition of Phraseology

A corpus is defined as a large, principled collection of naturally occurring texts (written or spoken) stored electronically (Reppen, 2001). The corpus approach is identified with four major characteristics: (1) empirically analyzing language use in natural texts; (2) analyzing a large and principled collection of natural texts; (3) extensive use of computers for analysis; (4) involving both quantitative and qualitative analytical techniques. These characteristics enable Corpus Linguistics to answer many questions, which cannot be answered by other means. Many of the questions answered by Corpus Linguistics are closely associated with different areas of language teaching, including phraseology, lexicogrammar, registers, nuances of language and syllabus design (Bennett, 2013). Therefore, Corpus Linguistics has a great potential of informing language pedagogy. However, pedagogic applications of Corpus Linguistics have also received criticisms (Swales, 2002; Vannestål & Linquist, 2007; Widdowson, 2003). These criticisms against pedagogic applications of Corpus Linguistics are actually constructive. Recent improvement in applied corpus studies has sufficiently addressed the issues in pedagogies inspired by Corpus Linguistics. The following section first provides a review of current pedagogic applications of Corpus Linguistics, and then responds to most frequently reported criticisms of these pedagogies, and concludes with a summary of the usefulness of Corpus Linguistics in language pedagogy and possible future research.

4.2.1　Pedagogic Applications of Corpus Linguistics

Pedagogic applications of Corpus Linguistics can be categorized into three aspects: corpus-influenced materials, corpus-cited texts, and corpus-designed activities. Corpus-influenced materials refer to textbooks and other materials influenced by corpus findings. Corpus-cited texts are references presenting corpus findings in grammar and vocabulary, and are usually accessed by teachers (Bennett, 2013). The three major corpus-cited texts are the *Longman Grammar of Spoken and Written English* (1999), the *Cambridge Grammar of English: A Comprenensive Guide*, and the *Oxford Collocations Dictionary* (2002).

　　Corpus-designed activities are activities designed for students to inquire questions concerning language use through accessing corpus directly (Bennett, 2013). Data-Driven Learning (DDL) developed by Tim Johns (Johns, 1991) can be regarded as one of the earliest designs of corpus-designed activities (Bennett, 2013). DDL requires students to function as corpus researchers by asking questions and finding answers through direct inquiry in a corpus. Teachers' role is shifted to a director or facilitator of the student-initiated research. The convention of encouraging students to manipulate a corpus directly has also been inherited in recent pedagogic approaches informed by Corpus Linguistics, including comparing corpus data produced by experts and nonexperts (Friginal, 2013), consulting a corpus depending on students' own needs (Bernardini, 2002; Yoon & Hirvela, 2004), and compiling their own corpus for consultation (Charles, 2012, 2014; Lee & Swales, 2006).

4.2.1.1　Comparing Different Corpus Data

To evaluate the effectiveness in helping college-level students develop their research report writing skills through DDL, Friginal (2013) compared a corpus of published forestry articles with a corpus of students' research reports. The 28 students enrolled in a professional forestry program were divided into two equal groups, one group receiving 6 hours of instruction for two weeks accompanied by corpus analysis, and the other group receiving traditional research report writing instruction. Frignal's (2013) compared the distributional data of the target features, produced by both groups before and after the instruction with the distributional data from the corpus of published articles. The value of Corpus Linguistics in pedagogy has been sufficiently supported by Frignal's (2013) conclusion that the distribution of the target features in students' work improved due to corpus instruction.

4.2.1.2　Consulting a Corpus Depending on Students' Own Needs

Viewing students' corpus use as related to their proficiency levels, Yoon and Hirvela (2004) recruited one intermediate level ESL class and one advanced level ESL class at a large American university taught by the same experienced teacher. The intermediate class was involved in hands-on practice with corpus analysis, while the advanced class used corpus on their own. A survey was employed to investigate learners' actual use of corpora and their attitudes towards corpus use in the L2 language classroom. The results indicated that students perceived corpus as useful for facilitating their writing process and learning common usage of words and collocations. However, since the two classes experienced completely different activities, the uncontrolled situation prevented the researchers from uncovering corpus use by learners at different levels.

4.2.1.3　Using Corpora Compiled by Students

Lee and Swales (2006) reported a 13-week academic writing course, where the participants, doctoral students, relied on two self-compiled corpora as the major resource: one corpus of their own writing (term papers, dissertation drafts, unedited journal drafts) and the other of expert writing (electronic versions of published papers in the students' own field or subfield). However, Lee and Swales (2006) failed to provide clear information as to how the activities were organized during the 13 weeks (i.e. What linguistic features were discussed? How were these features selected? What was the role of the teacher?). Rather, two activities focusing on V-ing pattern and near-synonyms were cited as examples. Even though at the end of the course, participants reported how they felt their rhetorical consciousness was raised and demonstrated the willingness of using corpus linguistic techniques in future language learning, it was somewhat disappointing that the evaluation of the course only consisted of the researcher's subjective comments.

Different from Lee and Swales' (2006) evaluation of their pedagogic activities through students' comments, Charles (2012) collected data through 5-point Likert scale questionnaires. During the six weeks between the initial and final questionnaires, EAP students learned about academic writing by exploiting self-constructed discipline-specific corpora. The majority of the participants found working with concordances not very difficult and that analyzing concordance lines not very time-consuming. Charles (2012) also reflected on the advantages and disadvantages of using corpora compiled by students. She found that the small size of the corpora made corpus analysis more easily affected by language issues of individual papers, because many articles were published due to their merits of research rather than the quality of their language. The advantage of using corpus compiled by students was that the students established more connection with their corpus, because these articles were selected from their own fields.

According to students and teachers involved in these studies, Corpus Linguistics has affected language teaching positively. However, the majority of these studies, except Friginal (2013), did not evaluate improvement in students' language production. Insufficient empirical evidence renders the pedagogic value of Corpus Linguistics seemingly vulnerable to several criticisms. The next section presents the major criticisms against the corpus approach and argues for the value of pedagogies inspired by Corpus Linguistics.

4.2.2 Application of Corpus Linguistics to Pedagogy

Recent publications evaluating the new pedagogies informed by Corpus Linguistics have gradually adopted a critical view (Flowerdew, 2009). The most frequently reported criticisms against corpus linguistic techniques are: (1) The corpus approach encourages a bottom-up rather than top-down text processing; (2) The corpus data presents language in a decontextualized manner, which makes it difficult to transfer corpus data directly into teaching materials; (3) The inductive approach typical of corpus-based pedagogy may not always be beneficial for all learners (Flowerdew, 2009). The subsequent sections will examine each of the criticisms and argue that recent improvement in corpus-based pedagogy has great potential to address these issues.

One of the most frequently debated issues is that corpus investigation encourages bottom-up processing of text while ignoring the top-down approaches to academic discourse represented by Swales' genre analysis (Charles, 2007; Flowerdew, 2009). As pointed out by Swales (2002), the top-down approach, widely adopted in EAP material construction, prioritized macro-textual features and then introduced linguistic features that served as linguistic realizations of the macro-textual features. The bottom-up approach, on the other hand, initiated with corpus analysis with a focus on linguistic features and then identified the macro-textual functions they intended to serve. Flowerdew (1998, 2003) also observed that many applied corpus studies exerted little effort to link lexico-grammatical patterns to their functions in the discourse.

Nevertheless, recent years have witnessed great improvement in the field of applied corpus studies that have successfully bridged the gap between lexico-grammatical patterns at the local level and their functions in the discourse as a whole. Charles (2007) successfully reconciled top-down and bottom-down approaches through initial discourse-based tasks followed by controlled and context-sensitive corpus search performed by students. Forty international graduate students from 27 different research fields at Oxford University participated in this study. Charles (2007) used two corpora consisting of eight MPhil theses in politics / international relations and eight doctoral theses in Materials Science. Each class was divided into the discourse session, where students were encouraged to notice how the writer deals with a weakness in his work by anticipating a criticism from the reader and dealing with it, and the exploration session where students were asked to identify further examples of this strategy. A majority of the students participated in this study found corpus use encouraging and would like to continue to use corpora in future English classes.

Another criticism that could diminish the value of the pedagogic application of Corpus Linguistics is that corpus data is decontextualized and may not be used as pedagogic materials directly (Widdowson, 2003). Conversely, Charles (2007) argued that compared to paper-based materials, corpus actually is able to provide students with a greater sense of contextualization. First, published teaching materials in the EAP context tend to include extracts from the target genres, because texts are usually too lengthy to be presented in paper-based materials. When working with corpus, students can access the context of each concordance line at their request and can even access the original file, which may facilitate the development of contextual knowledge. Charles (2007) judged corpus as more appropriate than paper-based materials in offering a sense of contextualization also because printed extracts are isolated from the material that precedes and follows.

Even though consensus has not been reached in terms of whether corpus data is decontextualized, many researchers actually agree with Widdowson that pedagogic processing is indispensable for transferring corpus data into pedagogy. Flowerdew (2008) acknowledged the necessity of pedagogic processing by pointing out that students may learn how to write reports to university authorities by exploring a corpus of reports addressing external clients. However, the direct transfer of the pattern, grammatical metaphor noun + will + verb (e.g. *Implementation of barriers will reduce noise.*), into internal reports to university authorities is not appropriate. However, what are the specific pedagogic procedures that could be implemented to facilitate the transfer from corpus data to pedagogy? Two suggestions have been provided in the literature: negotiation accompanied by corpus consultation (Flowerdew, 2008; Gavioli & Aston, 2001) and incorporation of contextual information in a corpus, including gender, age, academic position, and other types of metadata (Krishnamurthy & Kosem, 2007). However, as with many valuable pedagogic innovations in Corpus Linguistics, many of the proposed approaches have not been reported being implemented in real language classroom, thus not empirically evaluated.

The inductive approach associated with corpus-based pedagogy, as exemplified in data-driven learning, has gradually received more criticisms (Vannestål & Linquist, 2007; Widdowson, 2003). Some students attended the inductive corpus-based grammar course held by Widdowson (2003) commented that reading about grammatical rules in the book was more rewarding than corpus analysis. Emphasizing on learners' different cognitive styles, Meunier (2002) and Flowerdew (2008) pointed out that generating rules from a list of concordance lines might appeal to field-dependent students, whereas field-independent learners tend to prefer explicit instruction rather than inductive learning typical of corpus-based pedagogy.

Apart from students' cognitive styles, the choice between an inductive or deductive approach has been related to the nature of a particular enquiry (Flowerdew, 2009). Students tend to perform inductive learning of grammatical rules more efficiently, since the differences between structures are usually clear-cut (Tribble & Jones, 1990). However, inductive learning of an aspect of phraseology can be very problematic (Vannestål & Lindquist, 2007), since it is difficult for students to extrapolate the tendencies in the language given conflicting example that students may encounter (Hunston & Francis, 2000; Flowerdew, 2009) and the daunting number of concordance lines required for the extrapolation (Coxhead, 2008). In view of the great difficulties of inducing phraseological tendencies by students, Flowerdew (2009) added intervention in the form of clues or hints as an optional stage between interaction and induction to the "3Is" strategies of corpus-based enquiries proposed by Carter and McCarthy (1995) which only consist of illustration (looking at data), interaction (discussion and sharing observations and opinions), and induction (generating rules for a particular feature). Teachers' intervention may lead to a combined approach proposed by Meunier (2002) that could potentially cater to a wider range of learners.

Gavioli (2005) advanced the argument by pointing out that the concern is "which type filter they (teachers) should exercise and in what way" (Gavioli, 2005, p. 30) rather than whether teachers should provide intervention when students access corpus. Following the call for specific types of teacher intervention, Charles (2007) demonstrated and evaluated empirically one possibility of teacher invention (reviewed under the section "Bottom-up Processing of Text"). Different from traditional data-driven learning, where teachers and students attempt to answer questions posed by students, teachers in Charles' (2007) research drew students' attention to one specific strategy of defining one's research against criticism (using *while* at the initial position of a sentence) among many possibilities exhibited in the students' self-compiled corpus, and then directed students to investigate *while* within sentences. Charles (2007) admitted that although the advantages of discovery learning might be compromised, teacher intervention could avoid the pitfalls of free corpus searches that have been frequently utilized in inductive learning with a corpus.

Based on the review of applied corpus studies, we can draw the conclusion that Corpus Linguistics has affected contemporary language pedagogy positively in all aspects. Although several issues have been identified with pedagogic applications of Corpus Linguistics, recent improvement in the field of applied corpus studies has proposed informative solutions that can further polish language pedagogies using corpus. However, it is still worth noticing that many of the innovations in pedagogic use of corpus are restricted to claims. For those that have been realized in classroom teaching, students' learning gains are actually not assessed. Therefore, future research could seek to apply the innovative pedagogies in language classrooms and assess the effectiveness of the pedagogies through providing stronger evidence.

4.3 Grammar Patterns and Pattern Grammar

4.3.1 Defining Grammar Patterns

Although grammar patterns are one type of phraseological features similar to idioms, lexical bundles, and collocations, grammar patterns have generally been under-investigated (Green, 2019). Grammar patterns are "in a sense, examples of lexical phrases" (Hunston & Francis, 2000, p. 14), multi-word units that are starting to be identified before language corpora are commonly used. However, grammar patterns and lexical phrases differ in the coverage of language. The existence of language corpora assisted Sinclair (1991) in articulating a corpus-driven language description—the idiom principle, which states that:

> A language user has available to him or her a larger number of semi-preconstructed phrases that constitute single choices, even though they might appear to the analyzable into segments (Sinclair, 1991, p. 110).

The idiom principle broadens the idea of a multi-word unit to incorporate more than simply the lexical phrases (Hunston & Francis, 2000). With the assistance of computer technology, grammar patterns, "all the words and structures which are regularly associated with the word and which contribute to its meaning" (Hunston & Francis, 2000, p. 38), were successfully identified and extracted from the Bank of English through a corpus-driven approach (Groom, 2005; Hunston & Francis, 2000; Sinclair, 1991, 2004), which is a way of investigating language by generating hypotheses based on the observation of a large collection of naturally occurring texts stored electronically (Hunston & Francis, 2000). To be specific, the patterns of a word were identified by manually analyzing concordance lines with the target word appearing in the center. The concordance lines were right-sorted or left-sorted according to the target word in alphabetical order.

In the process of compiling the second edition of the *Collins Cobuild English Dictionary* (1995), the need of representing grammar patterns in a comprehensive and transparent manner emerged. Hunston and her associates noticed some problems in the coding system that they employed in compiling the first edition of *Collins Cobuild English Language Dictionary* (1987), which involves functional labels, such as "object", "complement", and "adjunct". The first problem was that analysts were not able to reach a consensus in terms of whether four miles is an object or an adjunct in the sentence *She walked four miles*, suggesting the low reliability of this coding system. Another issue with the previous coding system was its low transparency. Seeing the coding [V Obj Abj], a learner might still not be able to use the verb to explain in practice. To address these two issues, the simplest and most superficial word-class labels were adopted to represent grammar patterns.

Take the grammar pattern "V N with N" of the verb *provide* for example, "V" is capitalized to indicate that this is the pattern of the target verb. In a pattern, the preposition, adverb, or other lexical item is italicized to indicate that it is used as a lexical item but not a code (e.g. *with* in the pattern "V N with N"). The basic passive form of a verb pattern is coded as "be V-ed". In addition, some "new" word classes are proposed to contribute to a transparent coding system of grammar patterns, including N-VAR (nouns referring to substance), N-MASS (mass noun), N-UNCOUNT (uncountable noun), N-COUNT (countable noun), N-FAMILY, COLOUR (including both adjective-like and noun-like behavior), ergative verbs, shell nouns (words used with expansion in the surrounding text), and reciprocal adjectives and nouns. Ergative verbs are those verbs with two major patterns, one transitive pattern and the other intransitive pattern. "A reciprocal adjective indicates that a feeling or situation applies to two or more people or things equally and reciprocally" (Hunston & Francis, 2000, p. 191) (e.g. *The two situations are comparable.*). Reciprocal nouns are nouns that act similarly. Some word classes are problematic in that (1) some words do not fit into one specific category, and (2) some words do not seem to belong to any of these word classes. For example, *worth* could be treated as an adjective in *This bicycle is not worth what you paid for it* (Quirk et al., 1985, p. 1064), or a preposition in *Two gold-hilted swords, each worth 10,000, were sold at Sotheby's last Monday* (Quirk et al.,

1985, p. 667).

Hunston and Francis (2000) argued that frequent co-occurrences of words did not necessarily indicate the presence of a pattern. Take the verb *train* for example. Even though *train* can be followed by a variety of prepositions, it generally has the following grammar patterns: "V as N", "V N as N" (or "be V-ed as N"), "V in N", and "V N in N" (or "be V-ed in N"). In sentences such as *They are specially trained in underground rescue*, the preposition *in* is not constrained by the verb *train* but simply indicating location. Therefore, the grammar pattern "V in N" cannot be identified in this sentence. We thus draw the conclusion that the definition of grammar patterns is not only associated with frequency and structure. Most importantly, the identification of grammar patterns depends on whether the structure is constrained by the key word.

From the perspective of Corpus Linguistics, grammar patterns permeate each individual sentence. Although the question of how frequent certain grammar patterns are is yet to be answered, researchers have found that each discourse moves from one pattern to the next (Hunston & Francis, 1998). The phenomenon that patterns flow into one another is termed as "pattern flow", and it occurs when an item that is a component of one pattern is also the starting point of another pattern (Mason & Hunston, 2004). Figure 4.1 shows a traditional hierarchical representation of the pattern flow in the clause *if you decide you want to get pregnant*, with one clause being an element in another clause (Mason & Hunston, 2004, p. 259).

		V		*that*			
				V	*to*-inf		
						V	adj
If	*you*	*decide*	*you*	*want*	*to*	*get*	*pregnant*

Figure 4.1   Illustration of Pattern Flow (Mason & Hunston, 2004, p. 259)

Furthermore, contrary to traditional grammar that ignores lexis, Pattern Grammar has established an association between grammatical structures and lexis. According to Pattern Grammar theory, a word can be a component of several different patterns, and a pattern can also be seen as associated with a variety of different words (Hunston & Francis, 2000). The connection between patterns and meanings was articulated as the hypothesis that "the different senses of words will tend to be distinguished by different patterns, and secondly, that particular patterns will tend to be associated with lexical items that have particular meanings" (Hunston & Francis, 2000, p. 83). Corpus-driven research has confirmed these two hypotheses and stated these significant findings in multiple publications (Hunston et al., 1997; Hunston & Francis, 2000; Hunston, 2003). Hunston et al. (1997) illustrated the first observation that different patterns of a word are associated with different meanings by providing a list of different patterns of the verb *reflect*. Each pattern is associated with a certain meaning of *reflect* (shown in Table 4.2).

Table 4.2　Meanings and patterns of the verb *reflect* (adapted from Hunston et al., 1997)

Meaning	Example	Pattern
1. Show that an attitude or situation exists.	The riots reflected the bitterness between the two communities.	V N
2. Light or heat bounces off a surface.	The sun reflected off the snow-covered mountains.	V Prep
	The glass reflects light naturally.	V N
3. Image can be seen in a mirror or water.	His image seemed to be reflected many times in the mirror.	be V-ed
4. Think deeply about something.	We should all give ourselves time to reflect.	V
	I reflected on the child's future.	V on / upon N
5. A thought occurs to someone.	He reflected that he ought to write a line to Veronica.	V *that*-clause
6. Give a good or bad impression.	The affair hardly reflected well on the British.	V Adv on N
	Your behavior reflects on the second itself.	V on N

The second observation of Pattern Grammar is that particular patterns tend to be associated with lexical items that share particular meanings. All verbs associated with each pattern have been divided into several subgroups based on their basic meanings. Each meaning group is labeled with one (or more) of the verbs in this meaning group. This association between patterns and meaning is demonstrated through the pattern "V of N".

As shown in Table 4.3, 20 verbs associated with the pattern "V of N" were grouped into three meaning groups based on their basic meanings (Since this pattern contains a long list of verbs, these sample verbs were selected for easiness of presentation.). These meaning groups were labeled THE "TALK" GROUP, THE "THINK" GROUP, and THE "REEK" GROUP respectively, using one verb from each sublist. Following the two observations concerning grammar patterns, knowledge of patterns in this project refers to not only knowledge of correct forms of patterns, but also knowledge of meanings with which different patterns are associated.

Table 4.3   Meaning groups, basic meanings, and verbs associated with the pattern "V of N"
(summarized from Francis et al., 1996)

Meaning group	Basic meaning	Verbs identified as having similar meanings
THE "TALK" GROUP	Concerned with talking	Boast, speak, tell, complain, talk, warn
THE "THINK" GROUP	Concerned with thinking or having an opinion	Approve, daydream, dream, conceive, despair, repent, disapprove, think
THE "REEK" GROUP	Indicate something resembles something else or seems to be something	Reek, smell, stink, smack, speak, taste

4.3.2   Empirical Research from Corpus Linguistic Perspective

Empirical evidence on the value of grammar patterns is also scarce in view of the increasing attention being paid to multi-word units in teaching English as a second / foreign language (Howarth, 1998). Rather, research on grammar patterns is descriptive in nature. The dominant number of studies utilizes corpora as research tools for investigating correspondences between pattern distribution and word form (Hunston, 2003), distributions of patterns across disciplines and genres (Charles, 2007; Groom, 2005), and comparisons of patterns used by apprentice and expert writers (Römer, 2009). The majority of these empirical efforts focused on the "introductory *it*" pattern exclusively, with a few exceptions. Various terms have been used to refer to the "introductory *it*" pattern, including subject extraposition (e.g. Quirk et al., 1985; Biber et al., 1999; Herriman, 2000, 2013), the "introductory *it*" pattern (e.g. Francis, 1993; Groom, 2005; Larsson, 2017; Peacock, 2011; Römer, 2009), the "anticipatory *it*" pattern (e.g. Ädel, 2014), *it*-clause (Hewings & Hewings, 2002) and "*it*-extraposition" (Kaltenböck, 2005; Zhang, 2015).

4.3.2.1 Association Between Form and Meaning

Focusing on the subjective extrapolation (i.e. "introductory *it*" pattern), Herriman (2000) intended to uncover the association between the types of matrix predicates and different clause types. Matrix predicates, usually taking the initial position in an extrapolation sentence, manifest the speaker's opinions or attitudes. For example, in the sentence *It is likely that he has left* (Quirk et al., 1985, pp. 1355–1377), the matrix predicate *likely* functions to express the speaker's assessment of the possibility of the *that*-clause *he has left*. Nevertheless, the impersonal pronoun *it* makes the statement appear to be more objective by "disguis[ing] the source of the opinion" (Halliday, 1994, p. 355). Earlier research suggested that matrix predicates with semantic differences tended to be used with different clause types. For example, by studying a corpus of contemporary Australian English, Collins (1994) found that the matrix predicates of extraposed finite and nonfinite clauses were semantically associated with emotion and rationality (e.g. *It is a pity / true / clear*.), deontic conditions (e.g. *It is better / desirable*.) and potentiality (e.g. *It is possible / impossible*.), while the matrix predicates of infinitival and nonfinite clauses tend to be used to express difficulty (e.g. *It is difficult / hard*.) and usuality (e.g. *It is usual / common*.). Herriman's (2000) research stands out because of its wide coverage and systematic examination of matrix predicates and different types of clauses by including four types of extraposed clauses (two finite clause types: *that*-clause and *wh*-clause; two non-finite clause types: infinitive clause with and without *for*-PP [preposition phrase] subjects and *-ing* clause). The matrix predicates were semantically classified into epistemic ("concerned with the likelihood of the content of the extraposed clause being true"), deontic ("represent[ing] obligation"), and dynamic modality ("frequently involv[ing] some property or disposition of a participant in the sentence, typically his or her ability or power to carry out a course of action") (Herriman, 2000, p. 585). Based on an in-depth analysis of subjective extraposition in the Lancaster-Oslo / Bergen corpus, Herriman (2000) discovered the relation between matrix predicates and the four types of clauses, and provided detailed frequency information of the combinations of predicates and clause types.

To relate the distribution of patterns in general corpora to their linguistic contexts, Hunston (2003) compared the frequency of two complementation patterns (*that*-clause and *wh*-clause) in the large general corpus Bank of English by focusing on the verb *decide* and 10 random verbs (*accept, calculate, discern, establish, hear, mention, recommend, say, surmise,* and *find out*) respectively. The results suggested that the patterns tended to co-occur differentially with word forms. For instance, the *wh*-clauses generally occurred most frequently with the base form, while the *that*-clauses occurred most frequently with the *-ed* form. However, not all of the 26 verbs studied followed this observation. As Hunston (2003) pointed out, the findings supported the hypothesis that word forms comprising a lemma tend to appear in different grammatical contexts.

The concept of "semantic sequences" refers to "recurring sequences of words and phrases that may be very diverse in form", and "therefore usefully characterized as sequences of meaning elements rather than as formal sequences". (Hunston, 2008, p. 271) For example, Hunston (2008) proposed two frequently occurring semantic sequences: theory / argument + arises from + the observation + *that*-clause, and the observation + *that*-clause + consistency +theory / argument. In addition, three alternatives identifying and extracting semantic sequences from a corpus were presented from the most specific (searching a particular lexical word or phrase) to the most general (searching a very frequent grammatical item). As to the method of searching for a lexical word or phrase, concordance lines containing the target word / phrase (e.g. *make sure*) were analyzed hierarchically and linearly as shown in Figure 4.2 and Figure 4.3. In addition, collocates of *make sure* to the left were divided into several meaning groups, including volition, obligation, necessity, importance, possibility and achievement, and miscellaneousness.

1	2				
Somebody knew	that the one way to make sure every child learns the word Queen was to create an extra bank holiday.				
	3			4	5
	the one way to make sure every child learns the word Queen			was	to create an extra bank holiday
	6	7		13	14
	the one way	to make sure every child learns the word Queen		create	an extra bank holiday
		8	9		
		Make sure	every child learns the word Queen		
			10	11	12
			every child	learn	the word Queen

Figure 4.2　Hierarchical analysis (Hunston, 2008, p. 274)

Somebody certainly knew	that the one way	to make sure	every child in the country learns	the word Queen	was to create
knew prospects *that*-clause (V *that*)					
	Way prospects *to*-inf…*was*…*to*-inf (N *to*-inf *V*-link *to*-inf)				
		make sure prospects *that*-clause (PHR *that*)			
			learns prospects noun group (V N)		
					create

Figure 4.3　Linear analysis (Hunston, 2008, p. 274)

Another approach to exploring semantic sequences of grammar patterns begins with a specific pattern (e.g. "Noun that"). "The noun in this pattern indicates the epistemic status of the proposition expressed in the *that*-clause, and *that* projected *that*-clauses of this kind are important to disciplinary epistemology" (Hunston, 2008, p. 278). To test the hypothesis that words / phrases tend to be associated with certain semantic sequences idiosyncratically, *speculation that* and *discovery that* were examined closely. On the basis of frequency analysis, Hunston (2008) proposed frequently occurring sequences of *speculation that* and *discovery that* respectively. Hunston (2008) presented the third method of examining semantic sequences of small words in specialized discourse by adopting examples included in Gledhill (2000). Figure 4.4 shows the concordance lines obtained by Gledhill (2000) after applying the "keyword" function of the WordSmith Tool to Biochemistry papers.

```
Treatment with dismutase yielded modest increase in the levels of lactase
     butyrate-treated cells yielded few increases in the level of fetal matter
cells preexposed to butyrate yielded an increase in the level of spleen weight
treatment with cAMP yielded a significant increase in the level of …lesions
     in vitro doses yielded a similar increase in the levels of …resorption
```

Figure 4.4   The Concordance lines obtained by Gledhill (2000, p. 128)

On the basis of the concordance lines in Figure 4.4, Hunston (2008) deduced the semantic sequence as: biochemical process + verb of result + change in measurement + in + biochemical entity.

Hunston (2009) compared Pattern Grammar and FrameNet, a computational linguistic project influential in Linguistics and natural language processing, in terms of how structural forms were registered to associated meanings. FrameNet was constructed in accordance with the theory of Frame Semantics, which identifies semantic frames and analyzes meanings and syntactic behaviors of words (Fillmore et al., 2003). The target unit of FrameNet analysis is "a pairing of a word with a sense" (Fillmore et al., 2003, p. 236) and different senses of a word are categorized into different semantic frames. For example, the *hot* describing temperature and the *hot* describing taste experience correspond to two different semantic frames according to FrameNet analysis. "FrameNet begins with groups of words that share meaning, examines their recurrent co-text, identifies frame elements and notes the mapping of element on to co-text. Pattern grammar begins with recurring co-occurrences (colligation) and identifies shared meaning among the node lexical items" (Hunston, 2009, p. 1). Pattern Grammar views meaning as closely associated with structural patterns. FrameNet, on the other hand, treats meaning as independent of patterns. With some overlaps, FrameNet and Pattern Grammar also yield different results. For example, FrameNet groups *recover from* and *heal from* together. *Recover from* and *suffer from* were grouped together by Pattern Grammar but not by FrameNet. Hunston (2009) emphasized that both FrameNet approach and Pattern Grammar were facing the challenge of forming appropriately general semantic frames adopted.

With a focus on the occurrence of "N_1 of N_2" pattern in the introduction sections of the research articles on Applied Linguistics, Liu and Lu (2020) annotated the corpus of introductions for rhetorical moves and steps, and analyzed the "N_1 of N_2" pattern in terms of frequency, discourse functions, and rhetorical functions. The corpus used by Liu and Lu (2020), the Corpus of Social Science Research Article Introductions, consisted of 100 research articles published in the top five Applied Linguistics journals between 2012 and 2016. The corpus was annotated with rhetorical moves and steps on the basis of an extensively adapted version of Swales' (1990, 2004) Created A Research Space model. A move, "a stretch of discourse that carries out a broad-brush rhetorical function (e.g. establishing a niche)" (Liu & Lu, 2020, p. 4), includes several steps. In addition, the corpus was analyzed using the Stanford Parser and Stanford Tregex sequentially, and each incidence of the "N_1 of N_2" pattern was retrieved automatically and tagged with general functions according to Sinclair's (1991) functional taxonomy. In Liu and Lu's (2020) project, four functions emerged: focus, support, quantification / classification, and event, with each function consisting of several subcategories. For example, the "focus" function included "part + of + whole" (e.g. *the end of the introduction*) and "attribute + of + entity" (e.g. *the purpose of this study*). On the basis of quantitative analysis and in-depth discourse analysis, researchers found that "N_1 of N_2" constructions, although occurring across all rhetorical steps, were distributed more frequently in several rhetorical steps. This finding supports the usefulness of Pattern Grammar approach to language and underlines the importance of constructions in academic English.

4.3.2.2 Grammar Pattern Use: Across Disciplines

Some researchers choose to explain the frequency of patterns in a discipline-oriented manner with a focus on academic prose. However, these studies usually center around a limited number of patterns. Groom (2005) compared the distribution of "it V-link Adj *that*-clause" (e.g. *It is clear that the problem of evidence continues to vex new historicist criticism.*) and "it V-link Adj *to*-inf " (e.g. *It is important to compare unemployment rates on a consistent basis.*) in four corpora consisting of research articles in History and Literacy Criticism, and book reriews in History and Literary Criticism. These two patterns were selected since the use of *it* as a grammatical subject distinguished the highly personal and subjective presentation of knowledge, which were valued in academic discourse (Hewings & Hewings, 2002). A classification system for pattern—meaning associations adapted from Francis et al. (1998) was utilized to semantically categorize adjectives that occurred with the two target patterns, "it V-link Adj *that*-clause" and "it V-link Adj *to*-inf". To be specific, six meaning groups were identified, namely ADEQUACY, DESIRABILITY, DIFFICULTY, EXCEPTION, IMPORTANCE and VALIDITY. Based on frequency analysis of the four corpora, the pattern "it V-link Adj *that*-clause" used as VALIDITY was identified as the dominant pattern / meaning association in History and Literature research articles; the pattern "it V-link Adj *to*-inf" used as DIFFICULTY, was identified as the dominant pattern / meaning association in History and Literature review papers, suggesting that genre is a "controlling variable for all 'introductory *it*' pattern with *is* as a finite verb" (Groom, 2005, p. 265). Qualitative in-depth analysis of concordance lines revealed that the semantic association between structural patterns and meaning groups was largely determined by rhetorical purposes. Researches concluded that the choice of patterns was associated with different communicative priorities and epistemological percepts of the written genres and disciplinary discourses (Groom, 2005).

Adopting a similar research design, Charles' (2007) findings were consistent with Groom's (2005) conclusion. Charles (2007) chose to investigate disciplinary variation of the pattern "nouns followed by a complement clause" (e.g. *the argument that the Justices exhibit strategic behavior*...), since this pattern had been frequently used in academic discourse as a stance marker. Two corpora of Politics / International Relations (190,000 words) and Materials Science (300,000 words) were selected for the analysis. Stance can be constructed through the choice of nouns in the pattern "Noun that" (Noun is capitalized to indicate the key word of the pattern) to express attitudinal stance (the writer's personal feeling or opinions, e.g. *disadvantage* that indicates negative attitudes) and epistemic stance (the status of information, e.g. *assumption* that suggests that the proposition has not been proven). In addition, the "Noun that" pattern can be used to indicate the stance in relation to readers. The "Noun that" pattern is realized as a nominalization followed by *that* complement functioning to forward an argument known to the readers, suggesting that the writer has been taking the readers' concerns into consideration. The "Noun that" pattern can also be utilized to construct a "seemingly objective" stance by avoiding a person marker. For example, although the sentence *There is a possibility that quenching will cause stresses in crystal stance* carries the writer's stance, it leaves little leeway for readers to argue. Besides different types of stance markers, the "Noun that" pattern was also analyzed according to the semantic categories of the nouns. Similar to Groom (2005), semantic criteria specified in Francis et al. (1998) were adopted to tag the "Noun that" pattern semantically, including IDEA (e.g. *idea, assumption*), ARGUMENT (e.g. *argument, claim*), EVIDENCE (e.g. *evidence, indication*), POSSIBILITY (e.g. *probability, chance*), and OTHER (nouns not covered by other meaning groups). The result indicated that the "Noun that" pattern was over three times as frequent in the Politics / International Relations corpus as in the Materials Science corpus. Charles (2007) attributed this difference in distribution to the fact that many nouns in the Politics corpus referred to propositions put forward by political entities, which tended to be rare in Materials Science. Adopting the notion in Pattern Grammar that nouns in a pattern could be divided into semantic groups, researchers found that writings in the Politics corpus primarily used ARGUMENT nouns (e.g. *argument, assertion*) to demonstrate their stance toward others' research. By contrast, EVIDENCE nouns (e.g. *evidence, observation*) appeared more frequently in Materials Science for evaluating the writers' own research.

4.3.2.3 *Grammar Pattern Use: Novice and Expert Compared*

Another line of research on grammar patterns is designed to uncover the differences between novice and expert (or nonnative and native) writers' use of grammar patterns in academic discourse. To uncover the differences between native speakers and nonnative speakers in establishing interpersonal relationships between writers and the audiences in journal articles and dissertations, M. Hewings and A. Hewings (2002) compared published journal articles in Business Studies and MBA students' dissertations in terms of the use of clauses consisting of an anticipatory *it* and extraposed subject (e.g. *It is interesting to note that no solution is offered.*), since "it-clause" was associated with four interpersonal roles, including hedging ("withholding the writer's full commitment to the content of the extraposed subject."), marking the writer's attitude ("expressing the writer's attitude towards the content of the extraposed subject"), emphatics ("emphasizing the force or the writer's certainty in the content of the extraposed subject"), and attribution ("leading the reader to accept the writer's judgements as being soundly based") (Hewings & Hewings, 2002, p. 373). M. Hewings and A. Hewings (2002) concluded that student writers tended to express persuasion more overtly than published writers.

Römer (2009) also explored the use of the "introductory *it*" pattern, a very common pattern in academic discourse and causes problems for EFL learners (Groom, 2005; Hewings & Hewings, 2002). Römer's study (2009) analyzed four corpora, including three apprentice corpora and one expert corpus. The apprentice corpora included 450 argumentative essays written by German undergraduate students included in the International Corpus of learner English, 45 essays produced by students majoring in Linguistics / Literacy extracted from the Cologne-Hanover

Advanced Learner Corpus, and 162 high quality writing samples by the fourth-year undergraduates and graduate students in Linguistics, Philosophy, Psychology, and Sociology. The expert corpus consisted of 90 published research articles in Linguistics, Philosophy, and Social Sciences. The three apprentice corpora represented the texts produced by upper-intermediate language learners, advanced language learners, and English native speakers (college students) respectively. Therefore, the comparison between these corpora revealed the proficiency development from a low level to a high level. Michael Barlow's Collocate and William Fletcher's kfNgram were used to extract *n*-grams with different length and collocates of the searched words. Phrase-frames emerged from the analysis and were adopted to indicate pattern variability. Concordance lines not containing the "it be (Adv) Adj" pattern were excluded. On the basis of absolute normalized frequencies of "introductory *it*" patterns, Römer (2009) identified "it is (Adv) Adj *to*-infinitive" and "it is (Adv) Adj *that*-clause" as the most frequent patterns across corpora. The variability of pattern use was realized through lexical choices in the adverbial and adjective slots in the identified subpatterns. These lexical choices were further classified according to the semantic groups proposed by Francis, Hunston, and Manning (1998) and functional labels proposed by Groom (2005), namely ADEQUACY, DESIRABILITY, DIFFICULTY, EXPECTATION, IMPORTANCE, and VALIDITY. Deviations have been found between the expert and novice writers' pattern use in terms of frequencies, types, and functions of the subpatterns, highlighting the necessity of apprenticing academic students to lexical-grammatical patterns typical in academic discourse.

Ädel (2014) established the association between the selected subpatterns of "anticipatory *it*" and rhetorical moves, and investigated the differences between native and nonnative speakers in terms of "anticipatory *it*" use in different rhetorical moves. The pattern of "anticipatory *it*" includes finite extraposed clause (i.e. *that*-clause) and non-finite extraposed clause (i.e. "*to*-infinitive"). Rhetorical moves are defined as "rhetorical instruments that realize a subset of specific communicative purposes associated with a genre, and as such they are interpreted in the context of the communicative purposes of the genre in question" (Bhatia, 2006, p. 84). The concept of "moves" was originally introduced by Swales (1990) to analyze research articles, and has been expanded to the analysis of a wider range of genres, including letters of application (Upton & Connor, 2001) and grant proposals (Connor, 2000). Rhetorical moves that are used in a variety of genres are termed as "super moves". For example, "commenting on key concepts or definitions" "emphasizing limitations of the study" and "indicating areas for further research" are frequently adopted rhetorical moves in a range of research genres.

The corpus of Ädel's (2014) research included 62 learners' essays produced by Swedish students of Linguistics and 82 native speakers' essays (British) extracted from the Stockholm University Student English Corpus. The dispersion index of the tokens was checked to prevent that the subpatterns were produced by a particular student. Ädel (2014) specified 10 rhetorical moves, including "commenting on specific findings, commenting on method, attributed commenting on key concepts or definitions, indicating future research, stating aims / justification for study, introducing complexity, emphasizing limitations of study, expressing implied directives, and unclear (for uncategorical moves)" (Ädel, 2014, p. 73).

To identify the differences between native and nonnative speakers in terms of the use of "anticipatory *it*" in different rhetorical moves, Ädel (2014) adopted the well-established methodology, Contrastive Interlanguage Analysis (CIA), which involved not only the comparison between nonnative and native language speakers, but also the comparison between learner populations with different L2 backgrounds. The aim of CIA is to "highlight a range of features of non-nativeness in learner writing […], i.e. not only errors but also instances of under-and overrepresentation of words, phrases and structures" (Granger, 2002, p. 12). By comparing subpatterns (patterns of specific words, e.g. "it be evident that", "it be possible to") produced by these two groups, Ädel (2014) found that L2 learners and native speakers used the subpatterns for the same rhetorical moves. Howener, learners overused *important* and *clear* subpatterns, suggesting that the specificity of these overused subpatterns was not grasped sufficiently. Ädel (2014) called for future research that could investigate the mechanism behind language learners' underuse and overuse of certain linguistic features.

Larsson (2016) investigated the syntactic and lexical variability of the "introductory *it*" pattern in expert and novice writers' writing, represented by the Louvain Corpus of Research Articles and the Advanced Learner English Corpus respectively. Variability was interpreted as a continuum, where the fixed expressions were located at one end, while highly variable items were located at the other end of the continuum. Larsson (2016) classified the "introductory *it*" pattern according to the two volumes *Collins Cobuild Grammar Patterns 1: Verbs* and *Collins Cobuild Grammar Patterns 2: Nouns and Adjectives*. The "introductory *it*" pattern was first extracted by searching all the occurrence of *it*. Manual analysis was applied afterwards to exclude patterns incorrectly identified. The differences between the two target groups, language learners and expert writers, in the use of "introductory *it*" pattern was statistically tested through the Pearson Chi-squared test and the Kruskal-Wallis rank sum test. A log-rate generalized linear model, appropriate for subcorpora with noticeably different sizes (Powers & Xie, 2000), was adopted to identify possible interaction effects between predictors. In the expert data, 43 subpatterns of the "introductory *it*" pattern (e.g. "it be V-ed Adj *that*-clause", "it be V-ed Adj *to*-inf", "it be V-ed Prep *that*-clause") were identified. The variability of the "introductory *it*" pattern was measured in terms of type-token ratios, relative frequency of the predicate lemmas, and the additional features (including tokens with prepositional phrases, adverbs inserted, tokens with negations, modal verbs attached to the verb group, and tokens in the past tense). Larsson (2016) found that "it V *that*-clause", "it V Adj *to*-inf", "it V Adj *that*-clause", and "it be V-ed" were the most frequent subpatterns in the expert corpus and each subpattern demonstrated preferences for different phraseological contexts. Similarly, the four subpatterns were significantly more preferred by language learners. Specific to the variability of pattern use, the experts' and learners' language production did not differ greatly in terms of type-token ratios and the additional features. Nevertheless, significant differences were identified between the two groups regarding the relative frequencies of the predicate lemmas, especially the "it V Adj *to*-inf" subpattern. This subpattern and the most frequent predicate lemma (POSSIBLE) were overused by learners. Larsson (2016) underlined the importance of expanding the methodology to investigate other grammar patterns, and to explore the variability of the use of "introductory *it*" pattern in other fields outside academic writing.

To explore the mechanism behind language learners' and native speakers' use of grammar patterns, Larsson (2017) developed a functional classification for the "introductory *it*" pattern, "a functionally diverse pattern of great importance to academic discourse" (Larsson, 2017, p. 57). The "introductory *it*" pattern, consisting of an introductory *it* and a clausal subject, has two major functions: "observational (affectively neutral statements) and stance marking functions (express the writer's affective attitude)" (Larsson, 2017, p. 57). Compared to previous classification frameworks, Larsson's (2017) version is claimed to be more replicable for not depending on semantics, but on a wide variety of functions of the "introductory *it*" pattern, including attitude marker, observation, hedge, hedge attitude marker, emphatic attitude marker, and hedged emphatic attitude marker. The practical use of the "introductory *it*" pattern was investigated through three dimensions: academic discipline (Linguistics and Literature), nativeness, and levels of achievement (lower graded vs. higher-graded nonnative students). Three corpora were incorporated to represent the language production by three groups of students respectively. The Advanced Learner English Corpus included nonnative students' writing labeled with different achievement levels. The combination of subsets of the Michigan Corpus of Upper-level Student Papers and the British Academic Written English corpus was used as a native-student reference corpus. The "introductory *it*" pattern was identified by a semi-automated process, where the corpora were processed using WordSmith Tools and manual analysis. Given that the variables are nominal, a Pearson's Chi-squared test and a log-rate generalized linear model were performed using R (a free software environment for statistical computing and graphics) to uncover the differences between native and nonnative speakers in use of "introductory *it*" pattern. Similar to M. Hewings and A. Hewings (2002), the results suggested that nonnative students underused the pattern for hedge noticeably in both Linguistics and Literature. The emphatic attitude makers, on the other hand, were overused by nonnative students. With relevance to levels of achievement, low-achieving students significantly overused attitude markers, while the high-achieving nonnative students used this function slightly less frequent than native students.

4.4 Pedagogical Considerations

4.4.1 The Necessity of Frequency Lists from Corpus Linguistic Perspective

Although approaching grammar patterns from different perspectives, these aforementioned studies yielded pedagogical implications and contributed to the teaching of grammar patterns. First, teaching the grammatical contexts with which complementation patterns were associated could help students produce patterns in a more accurate and native-like manner (Hunston, 2003). Pedagogical implications also included that drawing students' attention to differences between novice and expert academic writers' use of patterns could help students become more accepted writers in their communities of practice (Charles, 2007; Groom, 2005; Römer, 2009).

Despite the claimed pedagogical implications, empirical findings that contribute to real language learning are still difficult to find. It seems that all current studies focus on a very narrow scope of patterns by investigating a small number of typical patterns, such as introductory *it* clause, *that*-clause, and *wh*-clause. In addition, none of these mentioned studies set the effectiveness of teaching grammar patterns as their primary research goal. Therefore, questions, such as how to teach grammar patterns effectively or what are the factors influencing the effectiveness of teaching grammar patterns, still remain empirically unanswered.

The promising achievements of corpus-driven research, the eloquently argued importance of Pattern Grammar, and the thorough discussion on pedagogical considerations in teaching grammar patterns have sufficiently prepared researchers and teachers to teach grammar patterns and evaluate teaching effectiveness. However, empirical efforts assumed a widespread and uncritical acceptance of pattern grammars.

Teaching grammar patterns by adopting the theory of Pattern Grammar is claimed to be beneficial to students, because this method of learning may promote four crucial aspects of language learning: understanding, accuracy, fluency, and flexibility (Hunston et al., 1997). Hunston et al. (1997) explained the benefits of learning patterns as follows. Firstly, knowledge of patterns could promote understanding, since the broad meaning of a certain word could be deduced based on other words that were nested under the same meaning group with the target word. The meaning group also provided students with clues to guess the meaning of an unknown word in a text. Secondly, knowledge of patterns could promote the accuracy of learners' language production given that producing correct sentences relied on knowledge of grammar patterns. Thirdly, fluency was demonstrated through the production of stretches of language without excessive hesitations or false starts (Hunston et al., 1997). Since language could be seen as a flow of patterns, accurate and automatic production of patterns could help language flow more fluently. Finally, introducing vocabulary and patterns together could encourage learners to develop the flexibility in their language production, since one meaning could be expressed through more than one pattern (Hunston, et al., 1997). Overall, the pattern approach to grammar could provide language learners multiple benefits and had great potential in aiding language teaching and learning.

The call for teaching learners knowledge of patterns never aimed to challenge or eradicate prevailing trends of communicative language teaching. Instead, the pattern approach to grammar centers on a complementary teaching component (Hunston & Francis, 1998). The role of patterns is set as a reference for grammatical consciousness raising, given that language courses completely built around individual patterns are not realistic or pedagogically sound (Hunston & Francis, 1998).

Compared with other types of syllabi, it is suggested that incorporation of Pattern Grammar into a lexical approach is more convenient, since both lexical approach and Pattern Grammar prioritize lexis and emphasize the association between lexis and grammar (Howarth, 1998; Hunston & Francis, 1998). The lexical approach intends to develop learners' knowledge of words and multi-word units with emphasis on the importance of comprehending and producing multi-word units (Olga, 2001). A lexical syllabus centers on vocabulary identified from a corpus by predicting a group of words learners are most likely to encounter. Given that patterns are presented based on the core lexical items, it is convenient to generate a list of patterns for vocabulary covered in a lexical syllabus (Francis et al., 1996). Although most logically associated with a lexical syllabus, the pattern approach to grammar can form a part of any syllabus, including a grammatical syllabus, a functional syllabus or a notional syllabus (Howarth, 1998; Hunston et al., 1997). A grammatical syllabus usually includes a list of structures, tenses, and other grammatical points. Introducing knowledge of patterns can complement the grammar-oriented syllabus with knowledge of meaning and vocabulary and help students establish connections between grammar and vocabulary (Francis et al., 1996). On the other hand, functional syllabi provide a list of communicative functions, such as requests and denials, and notional syllabi are organized based on notional categories (concepts such as time, quantity, and space). Since little explicit attention has been given to vocabulary in both functional and notional syllabi, the incorporation of knowledge of patterns could provide students a balanced learning experience with a focus on learning objectives and the development of vocabulary knowledge. Incorporating patterns into an already fully designed syllabus seems to impose "an unreasonable additional load upon learners already struggling to remember large amounts of vocabulary and understand detailed grammatical systems" (Hunston et al., 1997, p. 210). However, the associations between patterns and words make the load upon learners not as great as it appears (Hunston et al., 1997).

As previously discussed in Chapter 4, Data-Driven Learning (DDL), developed by

Tim Johns (1991), is closely associated with the teaching of multi-word units (Bennett, 2013). DDL requires students to examine corpus data by asking questions and finding the answers through direct inquiry in corpora. The teacher's role is shifted to a director or a facilitator of the student-initiated research. The inductive approach associated with data-driven learning, however, has been criticized (Vannestål & Lindquist, 2007; Widdowson, 2003). Some students who attended an inductive corpus-based grammar course held by Widdowson (2003) commented that reading about grammatical rules was more rewarding than corpus analysis. Emphasizing on learners' different cognitive styles, Meunier (2002) and Flowerdew (2008) pointed out that generating rules from a list of concordance lines might appeal to field-dependent students, who tended to perceive the field as a unified system (Brown, 2000), whereas field-independent learners, who demonstrated stronger analytical and problem solving abilities than field-dependent learners, tended to prefer explicit instruction. Besides students' cognitive styles, the choice between an inductive approach and a deductive approach has been related to the nature of a particular inquiry (Flowerdew, 2009). Inductive learning of an aspect of multi-word units can be very problematic (Vannestål & Lindquist, 2007), since it is difficult for students to extrapolate the tendencies in language given conflicting examples that students may encounter (Hunston & Francis, 2000; Flowerdew, 2009), and the daunting number of concordance lines required for the extrapolation (Coxhead, 2008). Therefore, a deductive approach, as exemplified in the pattern approach to grammar, can potentially complement the inductive approach to teaching grammar patterns.

Another important consideration related to the teaching of multi-word units, including grammar patterns, is that it is desirable to focus on a specific register (Howarth, 1998). Following this recommendation, this book is intended for target EAP learners. These students are expected to be competent in basic language skills of listening, speaking, reading, and writing in academic contexts. Learners' knowledge of academic vocabulary is the foundation to acquire these skills (Akbarian, 2010; Barrow et al., 1999). However, current academic vocabulary pedagogy has not incorporated patterns, and thus lends little support to teaching patterns of academic vocabulary. For instance, the most current Academic Vocabulary List (Gardner & Davis, 2014) and the Academic Word List (Coxhead, 2000) provide academic words in isolation without listing patterns of these academic words. As a consequence, EAP learners and teachers tend to focus merely on individual academic words without considering the grammar patterns of these academic words (Coxhead, 2008).

4.4.2 The Necessity of Frequency Lists from the Perspective of Construction Grammar

Researchers focusing on constructions and grammar patterns have been using corpora as evidence to support their propositions, which contributes to an updated interpretation of the grammar patterns (Hunston & Francis, 2000) in terms of construction (Goldberg, 1995; 2006). Construction Grammar is the approach to the description of language that grew up within the tradition of Cognitive Linguistics rather than the tradition of Corpus Linguistics. Until recently, there has been little dialogue between the two fields. Corpora are increasingly used as evidence for constructions as they are for patterns. Patterns are perceived as purely observational phenomena, while constructions attempt to model the mental representation of language. Dąbrowska (2015), for example, perceived Construction Grammar as a valid alternative to universal grammar. Ellis et al. (2016) used corpus evidence to demonstrate the acquisition of verb complementation constructions by learners of English. The associative-cognitive CREED theory rooted in Cognitive Linguistics predicts that high-frequency constructions are more likely to be learned than low-frequency ones (Ellis, 2007). The associative-cognitive CREED theory claims that:

> The learner's initial noticing of a new word can result in an explicit memory that binds its features into a realization of its whole form... As a result of this, a detector unit for that word, whose job is to signal the words' presence, ... whenever its features are present in the input, is added to the learners' perception system (Ellis, 2007, p. 79).

This claim can also be applied to constructions. The Associative-Cognitive CREED theory contributes to second language acquisition in that it explains the interaction between explicit and implicit learning processes. According to Ellis (2007), explicit learning establishes the initial form-meaning mappings, which are gradually integrated into learners' interlanguage through subsequent input, where frequency plays a role. The associate-cognitive CREED framework (Ellis, 2007) views language learning as governed by general laws of human learning, consisting of an associative type of learning, (see Pavlov's experiments with dogs as an example), and cognitive learning, (Chapelle, 2009; Ellis, 2007). Therefore, a frequency list of grammar patterns is necessany to facilitate the learning and teaching of grammar patterns.

4.5 Summary

Chapter 4 reviews literature on Pattern Grammar and grammar patterns from the perspective of Corpus Linguistics. In this chapter, grammar patterns are perceived as one typical phraseological feature similar to idioms, lexical bundles and collocations. Theoretically, Pattern Grammar describes the relationship between form and meaning on the basis of corpus-driven research. To be specific, Pattern Grammar speculates that words with the same pattern tend to share similar meanings, while words with similar meanings tend to be associated with the same grammar patterns. Previous empirical research on grammar patterns can be largely grouped into three types: the detailed association between form and meaning, the pattern use across academic disciplines, and the pattern use of novice and expert writers. Finally, pedagogical implications on teaching grammar patterns from both the perspective of Corpus Linguistics and the perspective of Cognitive Linguistics are summarized to further emphasize the importance of creating a frequency list of grammar patterns so as to inform the practical teaching of grammar patterns.

References

Ackerley, K. (2017). Effects of corpus-based instruction on phraseology English. *Language Learning & Technology*, 3, 195-216.

Ädel, A. (2014). Selecting quantitative data for qualitative analysis: A case study connecting a lexicogrammatical pattern to rhetorical moves. *Journal of English for Academic Purposes*, 16, 68-80.

Akbarian, I. (2010). The relationship between vocabulary size and depth for ESP / EAP learners. *System*, 38(3), 391-401.

Barrow, J., Nakanishi, Y. & Ishino, H. (1999). Assessing Japanese college students' vocabulary knowledge with a self-checking familiarity survey. *System*, 27, 223-247.

Bennett, R. G. (2013). *Using corpora in the language learning classroom: Corpus Linguistics for teachers*. Ann Arbor, MI: University of Michigan Press.

Bernardini, S. (2002). Exploring new directions for discovery learning. In B. Kettemann & G. Marko (eds.), *Teaching and learning by doing corpus analysis: Proceedings of the Fourth International Conference on Teaching and Language Corpora*. Amsterdam: Rodopi, 165-182.

Bestgen, Y. & Granger, S. (2014). Quantifying the development of phraseological competence in L2 English writing: An automated approach. *Journal of Second Language Writing*, 26, 28-41.

Bhatia, V. K. (2006). Analyzing genre: Some conceptual issues. In M. Hewings (ed.), *Academic writing in context: Implications and application*. Birmingham: University of Birmingham Press, 79-92.

Biber, D. & Barbieri F. (2006). Lexical bundles in university spoken and written registers. *English for Specific Purposes*, 26, 263-286.

Biber, D., Conrad, S. & V. Cortes. (2004). If you look at ...: Lexical bundles in university teaching and textbooks. *Applied Linguistics*, 25, 371-405.

Biber, D., Stig, J., Leech, G., Conrad, S. & Finegan, E. (1999). *Longman grammar of spoken and written English*. Harlow: Longman.

Bobrow, S. & Bell, S. (1973). On catching on to idiomatic expressions. *Memory and Cognition*, 1, 33-346.

Boers, F., Demecheleer, M. & Eyckmans, J. (2004). Etymological elaboration as a strategy for learning figurative idioms. In P. Bogaards & B. Laufer (eds.), *Vocabulary in a second language: Selection, acquisition and testing*. Amsterdam: John Benjamins, 53-78.

Brett, P. (1994). A genre analysis of the result sections of sociology articles. *English for Specific Purposes*, 13, 47-59.

Bychkovska, T. & Lee, J. J. (2017). At the same time: Lexical bundles in L1 and L2 university student argumentative writing. *Journal of English for Academic Purposes*, 30, 38-52.

Cacciari, C. & Tabossi, P. (1988). The comprehension of idioms. *Journal of Memory and Language*, 27, 668-683.

Carter, R. & McCarthy, M.(1995). Grammar and the spoken language. *Applied Linguistics*, 16(2), 141-158.

Chan, T. P. & Liou, H. C. (2005). Effects of web-based concordancing instruction on EFL students' learning of verb-noun collocations. *Computer Assisted Language Learning*, 18, 231-251.

Chapelle, C. A. (2009). The relationship between second language acquisition theory and computer-assisted language learning. *The Modern Language Journal*, 93(1), 741-753.

Charles, M. (2007). Reconciling top-down and bottom-up approaches to graduate writing: Using a corpus to teach rhetorical functions. *Journal of English for Academic Purposes*, 6(4), 289-302.

Charles, M. (2012). Proper vocabulary and juicy collocations: EAP students evaluate do-it-yourself corpus-building. *English for Specific Purposes*, 31(2), 93-102.

Charles, M. (2014). Getting the corpus habit: EAP students' long-term use of personal corpora. *English for Specific Purposes*, 35, 30-40.

Chen, Y. H. & Baker, P. (2010). Lexical bundles in L1 and L2 academic writing.

Language Learning & Technology, 14, 30-49.

Church, K. & Hanks, P. (1990). Word association norms, mutual information and lexicography. *Computational Linguistics*, 16, 22-29.

Collins Cobuild English dictionary (1987). London: Collins CoBUILD.

Collins Cobuild English dictionary (1995). 2 nd ed. London: Collins CoBUILD.

Collins, P. (1994). Extraposition in English. *Functions of Language*, I(1), 7-24.

Columbus, G. (2010). Processing MWUs: Are different types of MWUs psycholinguistically valid? An eye-tracking study. In D. Wood (ed.), *Perspectives on formulaic language in communication and acquisition*. New York: Continuum, 194-210.

Columbus, G. (2012). *An analysis of the processing of multiword units in sentence reading and unit presentation using eye movement data: Implications for theories of MWUs*. (Doctoral dissertation, University of Alberta). Retrieved from https://doi.org/10.7939/R3M717.

Columbus, G. (2013). In support of multiword unit classifications: Corpus and human rating data validate phraseological classifications of three different multiword unit types, *De Gruyter Mouton*, 4, 23-43.

Connor, U. (2000). Variation in rhetorical moves in grant proposals of US humanists and scientists. *Text*, 20(1), 1-28.

Cortes, V. (2004). Lexical bundles in published and student writing in history and biology. *English for Specific Purposes*, 23, 397-423.

Cortes, V. (2013). The purpose of this study is to: Connecting lexical bundles and moves in research article introductions. *Journal of English for Academic Purposes*, 12, 33-43.

Cowie, A. P. (1994). Phraseology. In R. E. Asher (ed.), *The encyclopedia of language and Linguistics*. Oxford: Oxford University Press, 3168-3171.

Cowie, A. P. (1998). *Phraseology: Theory, analysis, and applications*. Oxford: Clarendon Press.

Coxhead, A. (2000). A new Academic Word List. *TESOL Quarterly*, 34(2), 213-238.

Coxhead, A. (2008). Phraseology and English for Academic Purposes: Challenges and opportunities. In F. Meunier & S. Granger (ed.), *Phraseology in foreign language learning and teaching.* Amsterdam: John Benjamins Publishing Company, 149-162.

Coxhead, A., Dang, T. N. Y. & Mukai, S. (2017). Single and multi-word unit vocabulary in university tutorials and laboratories: Evidence from corpora and textbooks. *Journal of English for Academic Purposes*, 30, 66-78.

Cutting, J. & Bock, K. (1997). That's the way the cookie bounces: Syntactic and semantic components of experimentally elicited idiom blends. *Memory & Cognition*, 25, 57-71.

Dabrowska, E. (2015). What exactly is Universal Grammar, and has anyone seen it? *Frontiers in Psychology, 6*, 1-17.

De Cock, S. (2000). Repetitive phrasal chunkiness and advanced EFL speech and writing. In C. Mair & M. Hundt (eds.), *Corpus Linguistics and linguistic theory: Papers from the Twentieth International Conference on English language research on computerized corpora.* Amsterdam: Rodopi, 51-68.

Durrant, P. & Schmitt, N. (2009). To what extent do native and non-native writers make use of collocations?. *International review of Applied Linguistics in language teaching*, 47, 157-177.

Ellis, N. (2007). The associative-cognitive CREED. In B. Van Patten & J. Williams (eds.), *Theories in second language acquisition.* Mahwah, NJ: Erlbaum, 77-96.

Ellis, N. C., Römer, U. & O'Donnell, M. B. (2016). *Usage-Based approaches to language acquisition and process: Cognitive and corpus investigations of Construction Grammar.* Malden, MA: Wiley.

Ellis, P. B., Hunston, S. & Manning, E. (1996). *Collins Cobuild grammar patterns 1: Verbs.* London: Collins CoBUILD.

Fernando, C. (1996). *Idioms and idiomaticity.* Oxford: Oxford University Press.

Fillmore, J. C., Johnson, R. C. & Petruck, R. L. M. (2003). Background to FrameNet. *International Journal of lexicography*, 16(3), 235-250.

Flowerdew, L. (1998). Corpus linguistic techniques applied to Text Linguistics.

System, 26(4), 541-552.

Flowerdew, L. (2003). A combined corpus and systemic-functional analysis of the problem-solution pattern in a student and professional corpus technical writing. *TESOL Quarterly*, 37(3), 489-511.

Flowerdew, L. (2008). Corpus Linguistics for academic literacies mediated through discussion activities. In D. Belcher & A. Hirvela (eds.), *The oral-literate connection: Perspectives on L2 speaking, writing and other mediate interactions*. Ann Arbor, MI: University of Michigan Press, 268-287.

Flowerdew, L. (2009). Applying Corpus Linguistics to pedagogy: A critical evaluation. *International Journal of Corpus Linguistics*, 14(3), 393-417.

Forsberg, F. (2010). Using conventional sequences in L2 French. *International Review of Applied Linguistics*, 48, 25-51.

Francis, G., Hunston, S. & Manning, E. (1998). *Collins Cobuild grammar patterns 2: Nouns and adjectives*. London: Collins CoBUILD.

Friginal, E. (2013). Developing research report writing skills using corpora. *English for Specific Purposes*, 32(4), 208-220.

Gavioli, L. (2005). *Exploring corpora for ESP learning*. Amsterdam / Philadelphia: John Benjamins.

Gavioli, L. & Aston, G. (2001). Enriching reality: Language corpora in language pedagogy. *ELT Journal*, 55(3), 238-246.

Gledhill, C. (2000). *Collocations in science writing*. Tübingen: Gunter Narr.

Goldberg, A. (1995). *Constructions: A Construction Grammar approach to argument structure*. Chicago: Chicago University Press.

Goldberg, A. (1996). Optimizing constraints and the Persian complex predicate. *Berkeley Linguistic Society*, 22, 132-146.

Goldberg, A. (2006). *Constructions at work: The nature of generalization in language*. Oxford: Oxford University Press.

Granger, S. (2002). A bird's-eye view of learner corpus research. In S. Granger, J. Hung. & S. Petch-Tyson (ed.), *Computer learner corpora, second language acquisition and foreign language teaching*. Amsterdam: John Benjamins, 3-33.

Granger, S. & Meunier, F. (2008). *Phraseology: An interdisciplinary perspective*. Amsterdam / Philadelphia: John Benjamins Publishing Company.

Granger, S. & Paquot, M. (2008). Disentangling the phraseological web. In Granger, S. & Meunier, F. (eds.), *Phraseology: An interdisciplinary perspective*. Amsterdam: John Benjamins, 27-49.

Gray, B. & Cortes, V. (2010). Perception vs. evidence: An analysis of *this* and *these* in academic prose. *English for Specific Purposes*, 30, 31-43.

Green, C. (2019). Enriching the Academic Word List and Secondary Vocabulary Lists with lexicogrammar: Toward a Pattern Grammar of academic vocabulary. *System*, 87(1), 1-10.

Groom, N. (2005). Pattern and meaning across genres and disciplines: An exploratory study. *Journal of English for Academic Purposes*, 4(3), 257-277.

Halliday, M. A. K. (1994). *An introduction to Functional Grammar*. 2nd ed. London: Edward Arnold.

Herriman, J. (2000). Extraposition in English: A study of the interaction between the matrix predicate and the type of extraposed clause. *English Studies*, 81(6), 582-599.

Herriman, J. (2013). The extraposition of clausal subjects in English and Swedish. In K. Aijmer, & B. Altenberg (eds.), *Advances in Corpus-Based Contrastive Linguistics: Studies in honour of Stig Johansson*. Amsterdam: John Benjamins Publishing Company, 233-259.

Hewings, M. & Hewings, A. (2002). "It is interesting to note that…": A comparative study of anticipatory "it" in student and published writing. *English for Specific Purposes*, 21(4), 367-383.

Hoey, M. (1991). *Patterns of lexis in text*. Oxford: Oxford University Press.

Holsinger, E. (2013). Representing idioms: Syntactic and contextual effects on idiom processing. *Language and Speech*, 56(3), 373-394.

Howarth, P. (1998). Phraseology and second language proficiency. *Applied Linguistics*, 19(1), 24-44.

Hunston, S. (2003). Lexis, wordform and complementation pattern: A corpus study. *Functions of Language*, 10(1), 31-60.

Hunston, S. (2008). Starting with small words: Patterns, lexis and semantic sequences. *International Journal of Corpus Linguistics*, 13(3), 271-295.

Hunston, S. (2009). FrameNet and Pattern Grammar. From https://www.researchgate. net/profile/Susan-Hunston/publication/255655794_FrameNet_and_Pattern_ Grammar/links/02e7e53cb9839f38a6000000/FrameNet-and-Pattern-Grammar.pdf.

Hunston, S. & Francis, G. (1998). Verbs observed: A corpus-driven pedagogic grammar. *Applied Linguistics*, 19(1), 45-72.

Hunston, S. & Francis, G. (2000). *Pattern grammar: A corpus-driven approach to the lexical grammar of English*. Amsterdam / Philadelphia: John Benjamins.

Hunston, S., Francis, G. & Manning, E. (1997). Grammar and vocabulary: Showing the connections. *ELT Journal*, 51(3), 208-216.

Hyland, K. (1998). *Hedging in scientific research articles*. Amsterdam: John Benjamins.

Hyland, K. (2008). As can be seen: Lexical bundles and disciplinary variation. *English for Specific Purposes*, 27, 4-21.

Johns, T. (1991). Should you be persuaded: Two samples of data-driven learning materials. *English Language Research Journal*, 4, 1-16.

Kaltenböck, G. (2005). *It*-extraposition in English: A functional view. *International Journal of Corpus Linguistics*, 10(2), 119-159.

Kanoksilapatham, B. (2003). *A corpus-based investigation of scientific research articles: Linking move analysis with multidimensional analysis*. Unpublished doctoral dissertation. Georgetown University.

Krishnamurthy, R. & Kosem, I. (2007). Issues in creating a corpus for EAP pedagogy and research. *Journal of English for Academic Purposes*, 6(4), 356-373.

Konopka, A. & Bock, K. (2009). Lexical or syntactic control of sentence formulation? Structural generalizations from idiom production. *Cognitive & Psychology*, 58, 68-101.

Larsson, T. (2016). *The introductory it pattern in academic writing by non-native-speaker students, native-speaker students and published writers: A corpus-based study*. (Doctoral dissertation, Uppsala University). Retrieved from https://www.dissertations.se/dissertation/c4b236a04e/.

Larsson, T. (2017). A functional classification of the introductory *it* pattern: Investigating academic writing by non-native-speaker and native-speaker students. *English for Specific Purposes*, 48, 57-70.

Laufer, B. & Girsai, N. (2008). Form-focused instruction in second language vocabulary learning: A case for contrastive analysis and translation. *Applied Linguistics*, 29, 694-716.

Lee, D. & Swales, J. (2006). A corpus-based EAP course for NNS doctoral students: Moving from available specialized corpora to self-compiled corpora. *English for Specific Purposes*, 25(1), 56-75.

Li, J. & Schmitt, N. (2009). The acquisition of lexical phrases in academic writing: A longitudinal case study. *Journal of Second Language Writing*, 18, 85-102.

Lindstromberg, S. & Boers, F. (2008). The mnemonic effect of noticing alliteration in lexical chunks. *Applied Linguistics*, 29, 200-222.

Liu, Y. & Lu, X. (2020). N1 of N2 constructions in academic written discourse: A Pattern Grammar analysis. *Journal of English for Academic Purposes*, 47, 1-11.

Longman Grammar of Spoken and Written English (1999). London: Pearson Education.

Mason, O. (1999). Parameters of collocation: The word in the center of gravity. In J. M. Kirk (ed.), *Corpora Galore: Analyses and techniques in describing English*. Amsterdam: Rodopi, 267-280.

Mason, O. & Hunston, S. (2004). The automatic recognition of verb patterns: A feasibility study. *International Journal of Corpus Linguistics*, 9(2), 253-270.

Martinez, R. & Schmitt, N. (2012). A phrasal expression list. *Applied Linguistics*, 33(3), 299-320.

McCarthy, M. & Carter, R. (2006). *Cambridge grammar of English: A comprehensive guide*. Cambridge: Cambridge University Press.

Mel'cuk, I. A. (1998). Collocations and lexical functions. In. A. P. Cowie (ed.), *Phraseology: Theory, analysis, and applications*. Oxford: Clarendon Press, 23-53.

Meunier, F. (2002). The role of learner and native corpora in grammar teaching. In S. Granger, J. Hung & S. Petch-Tyson (eds.), *Computer learner corpora, second language acquisition, and foreign language teaching*. Amsterdam, Netherlands: John Benjamins, 119-142.

Moon, R. (1998). *Fixed expressions and idioms in English*. Oxford: Oxford University Press.

Nesselhauf, N. (2003). The use of collocations by advanced learners of English and some implications for teaching. *Applied Linguistics*, 24, 223-242.

Oakey, D. (2010). Introduction to chapter 2: English vocabulary and collocation. In S. Hunston & D. Oakey (eds.), *Introducing Applied Linguistics: Concepts and skills*. London / New York: Routledge Taylor & Francis Group, 12-23.

Olga, M. (2001). *Lexical approach to second language teaching*. (ERIC No. ED455698). Retrieved from Institute of Education Sciences: https://eric. ed.gov/?id=ED455698.

Oxford collocations dictionary (2002). 2nd ed. Oxford: Oxford University Press.

Partington, A. (1998). *Patterns and meanings: Using corpora for English language research and teaching*. Amsterdam: John Benjamins.

Pawley, A. & Syder, F. H. (1983). Two puzzles for linguistic theory: Nativelike selection and nativelike fluency. In J. C. Richards & R. W. Schmitt (eds.), *Language and communication*. London & New York: Longman, 191-226.

Peacock, M. (2011). A comparative study of *introductory it* in research articles across eight disciplines. *International Journal of Corpus Linguistics*, 16, 72-100.

Powers, D. A. & Xie, Y. (2000). *Statistical methods for categorical data analysis*. San Diego: Academic Press.

Quirk, R., Greenbaum, S., Leech, G. & Svartvik, J. (1985). *A comprehensive grammar of the English language*. London: Longman.

Reppen, R. (2001). Writing development among elementary students: Corpus based perspectives. In R. Simpson & J. Swales (eds.), *Corpus Linguistics in North America*. Ann Arbor, MI: University of Michigan Press, 211-225.

Römer, U. (2009). The inseparability of lexis and grammar: Corpus linguistic perspectives. *Annual Review of Cognitive Linguistics*, 7, 140-162.

Schmitt, N. (2000). Key concepts in ELT: Lexical chunks. *ELT Journal*, 54(4), 400-401.

Schmitt, N. & Carter, R. (2004). Formulaic sequences in action: An introduction. In N. Schmitt (ed.), *Formulaic sequences: Acquisition, processing, and use*. Amsterdam: John Benjamins Publishing Company, 1-22.

Simpson-Vlach, R. & Ellis, N. C. (2010). An academic formulas list: New methods in phraseology research. *Applied Linguistics*, 31(4), 485-512.

Sinclair, J. (1991). *Corpus, concordance, collocation*. Oxford: Oxford University Press.

Sinclair, J. (2004). *Trust the text: Lexis, corpus, discourse*. London: Routledge.

Sprenger, S., Levelt, W. & Kempen, G. (2006). Lexical access during the production of idiomatic phrases. *Journal of Memory and Language*, 54, 161-184.

Sun, Y. C. & Wang, L. Y. (2003). Concordancers in the EFL classroom: Cognitive approaches and collocation difficulty. *Computer Assisted Language Learning*, 16, 83-94.

Swales, J. (1990). *Genre analysis: English in academic and research settings*. Cambridge: Cambridge University Press.

Swales, J. M. (2002). Integrated and fragmented worlds: EAP materials and Corpus Linguistics. In J. Flowerdew (ed.), *Academic Discourse*. Harlow, UK: Longman, 150-164.

Swales, J. (2004). *Research genres: Exploration and applications*. Cambridge: Cambridge University Press.

Swinney, D. & Cutler, A. (1979). The access and processing of idiomatic expressions. *Journal of Verbal Learning and Verbal Behavior*, 18, 523-534.

Tabossi, P., Fanari, R. & Wolf, F. (2008). Processing idiomatic expressions: Effects of semantic compositionality. *Journal of Experimental Psychology: Learning, Memory, and Cognition*, 34, 313-327.

Tribble, C. & Jones, G. (1990). *Concordances in the classroom*. Harlow, UK: Longman.

Upton, T. & Connor, U. (2001). Using computerized corpus analysis to investigate the text linguistic discourse moves of a genre. *English for Specific Purposes*, 20(4), 313-329.

Van Lancker-Sidtis, D. (2004). When novel sentences spoken or heard for the first time in the history of the universe are not enough: Toward a dual-process model of language. *International Journal of Communication Disorders*, 39(1), 1-44.

Vannestål, M. E. & Lindquist, H. (2007). Learning English grammar with a corpus: Experimenting with concordancing in a university grammar course. *ReCALL*, 19(3), 329-350.

Vidakovic, I. & Barker, F. (2010). Use of words and multi-word units in skills for life writing examinations. *Cambridge ESOL: Research Notes*, 41, 7-14.

Walker, I. & Hulme, C. (1999). Concrete words are easier to recall than abstract words: Evidence for a semantic contribution to short-term serial recall. *Journal of Experimental Psychology: Learning Memory, and Cognition*, 25, 1256-1271.

Webb, S. & Kagimoto, E. (2009). The effects of vocabulary learning on collocation and meaning. *TESOL Quarterly*, 43, 55-77.

Webb, S. & Kagimoto, E. (2011). Learning collocation: Do the number of collocates, position of the node word, and synonymy affect learning. *Applied Linguistics*, 32, 259-276.

Webb, S., Newton, J. & Chang, A. (2013). Incidental learning of collocation. *A Journal of Research in Language Studies*, 63(1), 91-120.

Widdowson, H. G. (2003). *Defining issues in English language teaching*. Oxford: Oxford University Press.

Wouden, T. V. D. (1997). *Negative contexts: Collocation, polarity and multiple negation*. London: Routledge.

Wray, A. (2002). *Formulaic language and the lexicon*. Cambridge: Cambridge University Press.

Wulff, S. (2008). *Rethinking idiomaticity: A usage-based approach*. London / New York: Continuum.

Wulff, S. (2009). Converging evidence from corpus and experimental data to capture idiomaticity. *Corpus Linguistics and Linguistic Theory*, 5(1), 131-159.

Yang, R. & Allison, D. (2003). Research articles in Applied Linguistics: Moving from results to conclusion. *English for Specific Purposes*, 22, 365-385.

Yoon, H. & Hirvela, A. (2004). ESL student attitudes towards corpus use in L2 writing. *Journal of Second Language Writing*, 13(4), 257-283.

Zhang, G. (2015). *It is suggested that...* or *it is better to...*? Forms and meanings of subject *it*-extraposition in academic and popular writing. *Journal of English for Academic Purposes*, 20, 1-13.

CHAPTER 5

Developing a Grammar Pattern List for the 115 Most Frequent Academic Verbs

5.1 Research Background

The frequency of academic words is essential to the vocabulary pedagogy in EAP, because it informs instructional decisions concerning which words are to be prioritized given the limited in-class time and independent study time (Coxhead, 2000). Driven by the pedagogical needs of accessing words frequently used in academic writing, many corpus linguists have developed academic word lists by adopting different methods and procedures. The most widely cited lists include the AWL (Coxhead, 2000) and the AVL (Gardner & Davies, 2014). In constructing the AWL, words were selected based on word families, which were defined as stems (headwords) plus all closely related affixed forms (Coxhead 2000, p. 216), because learners are likely to comprehend the affixed forms if they have knowledge of the stem (Bauer & Nation, 1993). Gardner and Davies (2014), nevertheless, found this word selection criterion problematic for not taking grammatical parts of speech into consideration. According to Gardner and Davies (2014), one word form is likely to be used as different grammatical parts of speech, and grammatical parts of speech are associated with meaning differences. For example, the word form *report* means "an official document" when used as a noun or "telling people something happened" when used as a verb. Gardner and Davies (2014) thereafter created the AVL by incorporating grammatical parts of speech and treating the same word forms with different grammatical parts of speech as seperate entities.

Since researchers in second language acquisition (SLA) and Corpus Linguistics recognize formulaic expressions as an indispensable dimension of vocabulary knowledge (Milton, 2009; Read, 2000), lists focusing on different aspects of formulaic expressions in academic texts have been compiled to complement the aforementioned classic vocabulary lists (AWL and AVL). The Academic Formulas List (Simpson-Vlach & Ellis, 2010) and the Academic Collocation List (Ackermann & Chen, 2013) are two typical examples of lists of formulaic expressions that appear frequently in academic writing.

Following this trend of developing frequency lists of formulaic expressions, this book proposes a method for developing a frequency list of grammar patterns, a type of formulaic expression that has not received sufficient attention from the field of language research and pedagogy in SLA (Römer et al., 2014). In this book, we narrow our scope to extract grammar patterns of the first 115 verbs that rank among the 500 most frequent academic words in the AVL. Despite the narrowed focus, the extraction meothodology adopted in the project can be replicated and used to extract grammar patterns for content words (including nouns, verbs, adjectives and adverbs) in any given corpus.

The ground-breaking work presented in the *Collins Cobuild English Dictionary* (1995), which encompasses the grammar patterns extracted from the Bank of English by Hunston, Francis, Manning, and Mason, serves as an important resource for the development of the current study's verb pattern list. *Collins Cobuild English Dictionary*, focusing primarily on the generic patterns (e.g. "be V-ed about", "V N V-ing", "V N V-ed"), provides no information concerning the frequency ranking of the patterns of specific words (e.g. *be concerned about*, *increase from*, and *develop out of*). This book takes the existing resource a step further and generates frequency information for the grammar patterns of specific words. We believe that the complementary frequency information will facilitate more efficient teaching of grammar patterns in language pedagogy. This book also proposes a method for extracting grammar patterns in the *Collins Cobuild English Dictionary* through a rule-based computational approach. Our methodology is replicable for similar future endeavors and is likely to add to the body of literature on methods for word list development.

5.2 Research Purposes

This book has two main purposes: (1) testify a rule-based approach to extracting grammar patterns for the most frequent academic verbs in the Academic Vocabulary List (Gardner & Davies, 2014); (2) derive a tentative grammar pattern list for the 115 most frequent academic verbs. Extracting grammar patterns through a rule-based programming approach tends to be time-consuming compared with statistical methods (e.g. extraction on the basis of mutual information index), since researchers need to code all possible patterns of the most frequent academic verbs and use the script to extract grammar patterns from a given corpus. Nevertheless, the list of grammar patterns developed by rule-based approach ties more closely to the Pattern Grammar theory, thus enjoying higher pedagogical practicality.

5.3 Research Significance

By utilizing computational approach to grammar pattern extraction, this book is significant in multiple aspects.

Firstly, the power of the rule-based approach to extracting grammar patterns is testified. Currently, the majority of linguistic features are extracted through statistical methods (e.g. extraction of collocations on the basis of index), while the possibility of using the rule-based approach is less investigated. The statistical methods have demonstrated high accuracy and convenience (Many statistical methods that have been adopted in the extraction of linguistic features are embedded into ready-made softwares that do not require high coding skills.). Nevertheless, the pedagogical use of the lists extracted through statistical methods is somewhat restricted, since grammar patterns in such lists do not seem to match those included in the Pattern Grammar theory, which specifies the dual connections between individual words and grammar patterns. To be specific, words used with the same grammar patterns tend to have the same meanings, and words with the same meanings are likely to occur with the same grammar patterns. Nevertheless, the grammar pattern list developed in this book, starting with the previously recognized patterns extracted by Hunston's research team, is closely connected to the Pattern Grammar theory, which is also developed by Hunston's team. Given that the classical works on teaching grammar patterns following Hunston's tradition (*Collins Cobuild English Dictionary*, *Pattern Grammar 1: Verbs*, and *Pattern Grammar 2: Nouns and Adjectives*) have been successfully published, teaching grammar patterns extracted in this book seems to be more pedagogically supported and warranted.

Secondly, the list of grammar patterns for the 115 most frequent academic verbs can largely complement the widely used AVL developed by Gardner and Davies in 2013, with specific patterns and uses of these EAP words (e.g. "provide N with N," "select N from N", "base N on N"), which can potentially enrich the practical teaching of these academic words. Apart from specifying the 115 most frequent verb patterns in academic English discourse, this book also clarifies the frequency of occurrence of these patterns. This frequency information empirically reflects the skewed input proposed from the perspective of Construction Grammar, and also makes it more possible to realize the skewness in the practical teaching of grammar patterns. Namely, in the process of vocabulary instruction, teachers could allocate students' attention to more frequent patterns of a specific word, so as to facilitate their comprehension of the skewed input and receptive learning to the greatest extent. In addition, given that students tend to have difficulties or make mistakes with less frequent grammar patterns of a specific word, the frequency information of grammar patterns could also help teachers predict students' errors in language output and plan their teaching accordingly.

Lastly, the pattern extraction methods proposed in the current research project, a rule-based approach, can be utilized in future endeavors to extract grammar patterns from a wider list of verbs and other content words (e.g. nouns, adjectives). The lists to be developed in future endeavors will also facilitate the teaching of grammar patterns from the perspective of the Pattern Grammar theory, thus further systematizing the instruction in grammar patterns. Currently, the teaching of phraseological features, such as collocations, grammar patterns, and lexical bundles, mainly relies on the corpus-based approach (discussed in Chapter 4), an approach characterized by students exploring corpora to discover the practical use of a particular linguistic feature. However, the pedagogic use of corpus is largely restricted to claims. For those few that have been realized in classroom teaching, students' learning gains are not clearly assessed. Besides, students with field-independent cognitive styles find the corpus-based learning implicit and not very helpful. In addition, students find that learning phraseological features inductively is more challenging than tearning grammatical rules, since the rules of using phraseological features are less clear-cut (Hunston & Francis, 2000; Flowerdew, 2009; Tribble & Jones, 1990). Therefore, the explicit teaching of grammar patterns facilitated by frequency information is indispensible.

5.4 Methodology

This section elaborates on the materials and procedures involved in the extraction of the grammar patterns of the 115 most frequent verbs in the AVL (Gardner & Davies, 2014).

5.4.1 Materials

The key materials used include (1) a corpus from which the frequent academic verb patterns were extracted; (2) a previously published pattern list, on which the extraction of verb patterns was based; (3) a corpus compiled by the researchers to evaluate the accuracy of the pattern extraction system; (4) Prolog, a programming language used to program grammatical relations of the target grammar patterns, and SWI-Prolog, the environment where Prolog language can be programmed; (5) Perl, a programming language used in this book to activate a series of functions, such as reading corpus files, applying Stanford CoreNLP, and extracting grammar patterns; (6) Stanford CoreNLP, a natural language processing package that provides POS tagging and dependency analysis of the imported texts; (7) Cywrite Analyzer, a tool used to apply both POS tags and Stanford Typed Dependencies to importing sentences and outputting the images of sentences attached with POS tags and Stanford Typed Dependencies; (8) Antconc, a corpus analysis tool, adopted by human analysts to extract all sentences with target verbs so as to accelerate the process of manually identifying grammar patterns of the target verbs.

5.4.1.1   Corpus Used for Pattern Extraction

The 2.4-million-word corpus used for extracting patterns contains textbooks and published academic journal articles selected from five major academic disciplines (Health Science, Life Science, Physical Science, Social Science, and Engineering). The rationale of including these registers is that textbooks serve as the major source of academic language for university students (Biber et al., 2004; Lei & Liu, 2016; Ward, 2007), while published journal articles represent the discourse community that university students are apprenticed to (Durrant, 2016; Gardner & Davies, 2014; Liu, 2012). Table 5.1 presents the composition of the current corpus.

Table 5.1   Composition of the corpus used for pattern extraction

Academic discipline	Textbooks' number of words	Published journal articles' number of words	Total number of words
Health Science	357,478	109,683	467,161
Life Science	260,287	165,534	425,821
Physical Science	286,071	267,935	554,006
Social Science	263,698	255,896	519,594
Engineering	276,245	221,414	497,659

The size of this corpus, even though slightly smaller than those adopted by previous research in Corpus Linguistics (e.g. Durrant, 2016; Hyland, 2008; Lei & Liu, 2016; Simpson-Vlach & Ellis, 2010), passes the threshold of a million tokens that Sinclair (1991) postulated as sufficient to yield useful in-depth linguistic information.

5.4.1.2 The Academic Vocabulary List

The AVL was extracted from a 120-million-word academic subcorpus of the Corpus of Contemporary American English (COCA) by Gardner and Davies (2014). Accepting the AVL indicates the recognition of the existence of an "academic core" (specifically discussed in Chapter 2). It is certainly understandable that researchers and scholars who do not accept the existence of such an "academic core" would question the validity and usability of the AVL (Gardner & Davies, 2014). Nevertheless, it cannot be denied that the AVL showcases an improved methodology in word list development.

To be specific, lemmas rather than word families were determined to be the basic items for analysis, since word forms nested under the same word family may have various meanings, while one lemma tends to be associated with one homogenous meaning. Take the word *report* for example. The AWL (Coxhead, 2000), adopting word families as the units of analysis, does not distinguish between *report* as a verb and *report* as a noun. While in the AVL, these two entities are recognized as separate lemmas, clearly disentangling the two meanings associated with the two lemmas.

In addition, four indexes—ratio, range, dispersion, and discipline measure—were adopted to distinguish an academic core. In terms of ratio, Gardner and Davies (2014) specified that the frequency of the word should be at least 50% in the academic section than in the nonacademic section of COCA. The threshold range was required that the word must occur at least 20% of the expected frequency in at least 7 out of the 9 disciplines. The Julliand D figure, ranging from 0.01 (only occurring in an extremely small portion of a corpus) to 1.00 (perfectly spreading in the complete corpus), was employed as the dispersion measure, indicating the evenness of a word's distribution across the corpus. The AVL was created by using 0.80 as the minimum dispersion value, which empirically excluded many technical and discipline-specific words, such as *taxonomy*, *sect*, *microcosm*. The discipline measure, specifying that no word should occur more than three times the expected frequency in any of the nine disciplines of COCA, was used to further eliminate technical and discipline-specific words. Through all these procedures aforementioned, the AVL resulted, with lemmas listed together with their part of speech, follows a descending order of frequency of occurrence. The first 500 words in the Academic Vocabulary List is attached to Gardner and Davies's (2014) article, while the complete list is available online (www.academicwords.info) in both lemma-based and word-family-based versions. In this book, we focus on the 115 most frequent academic verbs included in the first 500 words of the AVL.

5.4.1.3 Previously Presented Grammar Patterns

The grammar patterns of English verbs were generally derived from two publications: *Collins Cobuild Grammar Patterns 1: Verbs* (Francis et al., 1996), and *Collins Cobuild English Dictionary*.

The first publication, *Collins Cobuild Grammar Patterns 1: Verbs* (Francis et al., 1996), adopts a pattern-oriented manner, listing each pattern with the verbs that can be used in this specific pattern (Another book of the same series, *Collins Cobuild Grammar Patterns 2: Nouns and Adjectives*, presents the gammar patterns of frequent English nouns and adjectives in a pattern-oriented manner.). In addition, grammatical components of structures involved are also specifically marked, and passive voice structures of the specific patterns are listed, if there is any. Take the pattern "V N at N" for example. The passive pattern is provided as "be V-ed at N". Three different structures are associated with the pattern: "(1) verb with object and prepositional object (e.g. *He shot a glance at her.*), (2) verb with object and prepositional object complement (e.g. *I put the price at £1000.*), and (3) verb with object and adjunct (e.g. *She shouted insults at him.*)" (Francis et al., 1996, p. 356). For the first structure, no passive voice is possible, and this pattern is associated with six different verbs, including *dart, flash, sneak, direct, shoot,* and *throw.* For the second structure, the pattern "V N at N" is specified as "V N at amount" (e.g. *The magazine reckoned his personal wealth at £2.1 billion.*), with "be V-ed at amount" as its passive form (e.g. *The share price was set at £1.75.*) (Francis et al., p. 358). Six verbs, including *estimate* (usually passive), *peg* (usually passive), *reckon*, *maintain*, *put* and *set* (usually passive), are associated with the second structure of the pattern "V N at N". For the third structure, both active and passive voice are possible. Furthermore, verbs associated with the third structure are grouped into five meaning groups: the point group, the throw group, the shout group, the buy group, and verbs with other meanings (referring to verbs that do not share a meaning). Generally, verbs grouped into the same meaning group share a similar meaning. For example, the "point group" includes verbs (e.g. *aim*, *jab*, and *point*) that are concerned with "pointing something or aiming something, which may be (1) a part of your body such as your fist or finger, (2) a weapon, or (3) a torch or other instrument" (Francis et al.,1996, p. 359). Also, the main verbs in grammar patterns could also be phrasal verbs, such as *clamp down*, *crack down*, and *gang up*. Although the book is organized in a pattern-oriented manner, it is still possible for the readers or users to identify patterns of a specific verb in an efficient manner by referring to the "Pattern Finder" and "Verb Index" located approaching the end of the book. Since the book *Collins Cobuild Grammar Patterns 1: Verbs* was designed to help language learners at an intermediate level or higher to learn grammar patterns in a data-driven approach, not all English verbs are included. Rather, only verbs immediately relevant to the target language learners are included, tagged, and grouped into meaning groups. The frequency information of verb patterns is also somewhat insufficient. In the "Verb Index" and "Frequency Information", black diamond shapes are used to indicate the frequency of each verb, with five diamonds being the most frequent and no diamond being the least frequent. If there is an entry for the main verb, phrasal verbs of the main verb are not provided with frequency information. Therefore, the frequency of verb-pattern combinations (verbs used with specific patterns, such as "divide N into N") is not presented. In addition, using diamonds to signify frequency is useful to some extent for students or teachers to set a learning goal or for material developers to arrange content, but using diamonds is less precise compared with specifying the specific frequency of occurrence.

The second publication is the *Collins Cobuild English Dictionary*, where the patterns are presented in a word-oriented manner, with each verb linked to all the patterns the verb can be used in. Similar to a normal dictionary, all words are organized in an alphabetical order. While different from a normal dictionary which features information of each word based on the frequency of different meanings, the *Collins Cobuild English Dictionary* displays information of words based on the frequency of different patterns. Take the verb *announce* for example—five entries corresponding to five different meanings are listed. Each entry is further related to all the patterns that share this specific meaning, and examples are provided to facilitate language learners to obtain contextual information and usage of the specific pattern. The first meaning entry is "if you announce something, you tell people about it publicly or officially". Under this meaning entry, three patterns are listed: "V *that*-clause" (eg. *He will announce tonight that he is resigning from office.*), "V N" (eg. *She was planning to announce her engagement to Pepter.*), and "it be V-ed *that*-clause" (eg. *It was announced that the groups have agreed to a cease-fire.*) (1995, p. 60). All the examples provided in the *Collins Cobuild English Dictionary* were selected from the Bank of English to demonstrate the practical use of various grammar patterns.

The grammar patterns in these two publications were extracted from the Bank of English through a corpus-driven approach, a way of investigating language by generating hypotheses based on observations of a large, principled collection of naturally occurring texts (written or spoken) stored electronically (Hunston & Francis, 2000). The Bank of English is considered as a sufficient representation of the entire English language, as this corpus contains over 250 million words collected from various sources, such as newspapers, magazines, websites, books, and daily conversations in English speaking countries, mainly including Britain, the United States, Canada, Australia, New Zealand, and South Africa. Harper Collins Publishers and the University of Birmingham hold copies of the Bank of English, which can be used for academic purposes.

However, the frequency information of these grammar patterns is not fully reflected in these two works, leaving English teachers and material designers not sufficiently supported in terms of which patterns to prioritize in practical teaching and material development. This book, therefore, is intended to address such deficiencies by deriving a frequency list for grammar patterns of verbs frequently appearing in the academic register.

5.4.1.4 Corpus for Evaluation

To evaluate the performance of the pattern extraction system, we compiled a corpus of manageable size to test the accuracy of the system. The test corpus consists of 10 research articles in Applied Linguistics totaling 77, 085 words. Linguistic articles were selected because their academic genre resembled the target database used for extracting grammar patterns and the genre was familiar to the human raters, extensively trained Applied Linguists, whose manual anlaysis was compared with the output of the pattern extraction program. Choosing a genre familiar to the raters provided further potential to ensure the accuracy and efficiency of their manual analysis.

5.4.1.5 Prolog and SWI-Prolog

Prolog, developed in Marseille France in 1972 by Alain Clomerauer's team, is a logic programming language that can be utilized in different fields, such as Artificial Intelligence and Computational Linguistics (https://en.wikipedia.org/wiki/Prolog). As one of the first logic programming languages, Prolog is well suitable for tasks that involve rule-based logical queries (e.g. searching databases, voice control systems, and filling templates). Prolog, therefore, is widely adopted for queries of syntactical and semantic relations, which are typically logical relations. Logical relations can be described by Prolog through clauses. Generally, for each input / query, Prolog outputs "yes" or "no", indicating true or false by judging whether the input / query fits the logical relations previously programmed. For example, Table 5.2 displays the logical relations / rules programmed with Prolog. The codes in this table are quoted from online wikipedion (https://en.wikipedia.org/wiki/Prolog), and the textual explanations of these codes, following the # sign, are provided by the author of this book to promote the readability of these codes. Relations are described by Prolog through two different types of clauses: facts and rules. In Table 5.2, Lines 1–4 are describing the facts clarified by the sentences signaled using a "#" sign. For example, the fact described in Line 1 is that "Trude is the mother of Sally". Lines 5–7 are rules that specify the logical relations between the previously described facts. For example, the logical relation indicated by Line 6 is that "if X being Y's father is true, X being Y's parent is also true".

Table 5.2   Relations Specified in Prolog Code

Code	Explanation
mother_child (trude, sally).	Trude is the mother of Sally.
father_child (tom, sally).	Tom is the father of sally.
father_child (tom, erica).	Tom is the father of Erica.
father_child (mike, tom).	Mike is the father of Tom.
Sibling (X, Y):-parent_child (Z, X), parent_child (Z, Y).	Sibling is defined as two chidren, X and Y sharing the same parent Z.
parent_child (X, Y) :-father_child (X, Y).	If X being Y's father being true, X being Y's parent being also true.
parent_child (X, Y) :-mother_child (X, Y).	If X being Y's mother is true, X being Y's parent is also true.

After facts and rules are clearly described, queries can be posed to testify whether these queries are true or false. When the following query (?-sibling [sally, erica]) is provided, Prolog testifies that this relation specified in the query is true, indicating that the query that whether Sally and Erica are siblings is judged as true by Prolog given the logical relations specified in Table 5.2.

Specific to this book, grammatical structures / relations of various patterns are specified through Prolog clauses, including facts (specifying the components of all structures in a pattern) and rules (describing the logical relations between different components). When a query (whether a POS-tagged sentence includes a grammar pattern specified by the rules) is sent, Prolog is able to judge whether the query is true (indicating that a pattern is successfully identified), or false (suggesting that no such pattern is identified).

SWI-Prolog employed in this project is a free Prolog environment, the official website of which (https://www.swi-prolog.org) provides several different versions to download for tree, including stable release (infrequently updated, and appropriate for running basic Prolog codes), development release (updated every two to four weeks, and appropriate for developers and users of certain applications), daily builds for Windows, and browse GIT repository (recommended for developers with convenient access to patches). The stable release is adopted in this book for basic coding discerning the logical relations between linguistic units in English sentences. Besides the installation packages, the official website of SWI-Prolog also offers tutorials for users at various levels and with needs various.

5.4.1.6 Perl

Perl, originally released in 1988 by Larry Wall, is a "highly capable, feature-rich programming language with over 30 years of development" (https://www.perl.org/about.html). The Perl language uses other programming languages (such as C and shell script) as references, and has gained popularity since the late 1990s. Perl is powerful in text processing and regular expressions, therefore it is suitable for the current task involving syntactic structure match. In this book, Perl is also utilized to handle a large number of files, transform the corpus into strings of words, and sequentially activate POS tagger—Standford parser and Prolog.

5.4.1.7 Stanford CoreNLP

Standford CoreNLP, developed by the Stanford NLP Group, is a one-stop-shop for natural language processing. Its natural language processing techniques allow users to derive a series of linguistic annotations for an input text, mainly including token, sentence boundaries, parts of speech, named entities, numeric and time values, dependency and constituency parses, coreference, sentiment, quote attributions, and relations for eight different languages—Arabic, Chinese, English, French, German, Hungarian, Italian, and Spanish (https://stanfordnlp.github.io/CoreNLP/). These linguistic annotations can be performed selectively in accordance with practical needs.

The identification of sentence boundaries or sentence splitting, usually the first step of text analysis, refers to the process of isolating sentences in a text so that each sentence is processed separately. Tokenization is the process of transforming all running words into tokens. For example, the sentence *She is powerful* can be split into separate tokens "She", "is", "powerful", and ".". To practice lemmatization, Stanford CoreNLP returns the base form of input words (i.e. lemmas) on the basis of morphological rules. For example, the lemma for "studied" is "study". POS tagging identifies the part of speech for each individual token. For example, in the sentence *She is powerful*, "She" is tagged as a pronoun. The entity recognition process (https:// stanfordnlp.github.io/CoreNLP/ner.html) is able to label entities (e.g. person and company names) by employing one or more machine learning sequence models. The labelling of time and date still relies on rule-based components. For English specifically, the Stanford CoreNLP annotator is able to recognize 12 classes of entities, including named entities (person, location, organization), numerical entities (money, number, ordinal, percent), and temporal entities (date, time, duration, set).

Dependency parser of Stanford CoreNLP provides three dependency-based outputs: basic uncollapsed dependencies, enhanced dependencies, and enhanced + + dependencies (https://stanfordnlp.github.io/CoreNLP/depparse.html). Dependency parsing has to be performed on the basis of prior POS tagging. "A dependency parser analyzes the grammatical structure of a sentence, establishing relationships between head words and words which modify those heads" (https://nlp.stanford.edu/ software/nndep.html). Besides dependency parsing, Stanford CoreNLP also provides constituency parsing, which analyzes sentences by identifying constituency structures (phrase-structure tree). If constituency parses can be converted to dependency representation (only achievable for English and Chinese at this stage), a dependency representation is also provided (https://stanfordnlp.github.io/CoreNLP/parse.html). A clear description of these two complementary techniques of parsing can only be achieved through a review of dependency structure and phrase structure. The concept of dependency grammar was first introduced by Lucien Tesnière. Constituency grammar, on the other hand, was initiated by Noam Chomsky in *Syntactic Structures* (1957). Dependency grammar speculates that words are attached to one another to form greater units, while phrase structure indicates that words combine with each other to form greater units (Osborne, 2018). Dependency generates minimal tree structures through one-to-one mapping, while phrase structure, characterized by one-to-one / more mapping, displays more fine-grained structures (Osborne, 2018).

Stanford CoreNLP also offers coreference resolution that identifies expressions referring to the same entity. For example, the word *it* may refer to the book *Collins Cobuild Grammar Patterns 1: Verbs* in a text. This function is realized through coreference systems: machine-learning based coreference, only requiring dependency parses that are faster than constituency parses, and neural identification systems (most accurate but slow, and relying on neural-network solutions) (https://stanfordnlp. github.io/CoreNLP/coref.html). In this book, a series of Stanford CoreNLP functions, including sentence splitting, tokenization, lemmatization, POS tagging, dependency parsing and constituency parsing, are employed.

5.4.1.8   CyWrite Analyzer

Cywrite Analyzer was originally designed as a component of the web-based automated writing evaluation tool, CyWrite (Chukharev-Hudilainen & Saricaoglu, 2014). Cywrite was developed by Evgeny Chukharev-Hudilainen at the Applied Linguistics and Technology Program of Iowa State University. Apart form a holistic score, Cywrite also provides formative feedback on learners' writing samples. Keystroke logging and eye tracking technology are also combined and incorporated into Cywrite to probe into students' writing process. The interface of Cywrite, resembling a custom text editor, requires no specialized software, thus preserving students' conventional writing habits as with Microsoft Wordpad, and facilitating the data collection process. Meanwhile, Cywrite provides basic text producing and editing functions, such as typing, copy, paste, character formatting (bold, italic, underline), and paragraph alignment (left, center, and right). Besides these basic functions, the eye-tracking function can be performed with Cywrite by plugging any commercial eye-tracking devices that are packed with an application interface that captures real-time gaze data (Chukharev-Hudilainen et al., 2019).

The Cywrite Analyzer module utilized in this book, originally designed to facilitate the formative feedback function in Cywrite, incorporates both POS tags and Stanford Typed Dependencies. POS tags and Stanford Typed Dependencies can be coordinated and activated sequentially by the Cywrite Analyzer module to mark input texts with POS tags and provide dependency analysis for the tagged texts.

5.4.1.9   Antconc

Antconc (http://www.laurenceanthony.net/software/antconc/), designed by Laurence Anthony, is a free corpus analysis tool that provides several powerful functions, mainly including basic concordance, concordance plot, clusters, collocates, word list, and keyword list. The concordance function allows the user to search a word or phrase, and list all concordance lines with the searched word / phrase aligned in the middle and highlighted. A click on the searched word embedded in the concordancing lines leads the user to the original text, to which the specific word belongs. This function provides users with convenient access to the contextual information of a target word / expression. Besides, users can highlight up to three words to the left and right of the searched word / expression. The word list function is able to list all words in the inputted files / corpus according to their frequency of occurrence.

The *n*-gram search allows users to retrieve *n*-grams by specifying the number of co-occurring words and the threshold frequency of occurrence. Offering a very similar function, the cluster tool of Antconc allows users to search a target word and specify the number of words that cluster with the target word. A minimum frequency of occurrence can also be set to narrow down the results.

The collocate tool of Antconc is able to retrieve words that are associated with the searched collocates (i.e. the base words) and provide the strength of each associative pair. The span of each search (i.e. the number of words to the left and / or right of the collocate) is also required for this case.

The keyword list function lists all keywords with their frequencies and ranks the keywords according to the descending order of the Keyness value. The current versions of Antconc are compatible with most frequently used operating systems (e.g. Windows, Macintosh OS X, and Linux). Besides English, Antconc can also be used to analyze texts written in other languages, such as French, German, Spanish, Chinese, Japanese, and Korean. For non-English texts, default encoding UTF-8 should be used. A guide to Antconc can be downloaded from http://www.laurenceanthony.net/software/antconc/. In this book, the basic function, concordancing, is used to help the researchers retrieve all sentences that include the target verbs. The analysis of the verb pattern in each concordance line was completed manually.

5.4.2　Procedures

5.4.2.1　Identification of Patterns of Frequent Verbs

To identify the most frequent academic verb patterns, a pattern extraction system was developed by drawing upon the new AVL and *Collins Cobuild English Dictionary*, and integrating tenets of natural language processing. The development process involved three key steps. First, the 115 most frequent academic verbs were obtained from the top 500 words / lemmas, "words with a common stem, related by inflection only, and coming from the same part of speech" (Gardner & Davies, 2013, p. 308), in the AVL. Then, all possible patterns of each selected verb were collected by manually searching each entry for the verb in the *Collins Cobuild English Dictionary*. Finally, the NLP approach was adopted to extract all the identified patterns for the 115 most frequent academic verbs from our corpus. Because in this study we were interested in the patterns of specific verbs (e.g. *be concerned about, increase from*, and *develop out of*) rather than the generic patterns (e.g. "be V-ed about", "V N V-ing", and "V N V-ed"), we solely focused on the extraction of those grammar patterns containing the target verbs. We hereafter termed the patterns of specific verbs as "verb-pattern combinations".

The NLP-based pattern extraction system consisted of two sequential modules: (1) activation of Stanford CoreNLP with the Cywrite Analyzer; (2) the rule-based pattern extraction with Prolog, which is a logical programming language commonly adopted for textual data analysis (Bramer, 2013). Stanford CoreNLP, a language parser, automatically (1) split input text into sentences and tokens, (2) labeled each token with POS tags (shown in Figure 5.1), (3) parsed each sentence and output syntax trees (shown in Figure 5.1), (4) identified Stanford Typed Dependencies (shown in Figure 5.1), (5) produced a hierarchical and textual description of the syntactic structure of each sentence (shown in Figure 5.2), and (6) saved all the textual descriptions in an Extensible Markup Language (XML) file readily analyzable for the rule-based extraction module (Chukharev-Hudilainen & Saricaoglu, 2014). Figure 5.1 illustrates the syntax tree of the example sentence *Native students are provided with mentors*. (The target verb-pattern combination is "provide N with N".). This tree also includes POS tags above the tokens and Stanford Typed Dependencies below the tokens.

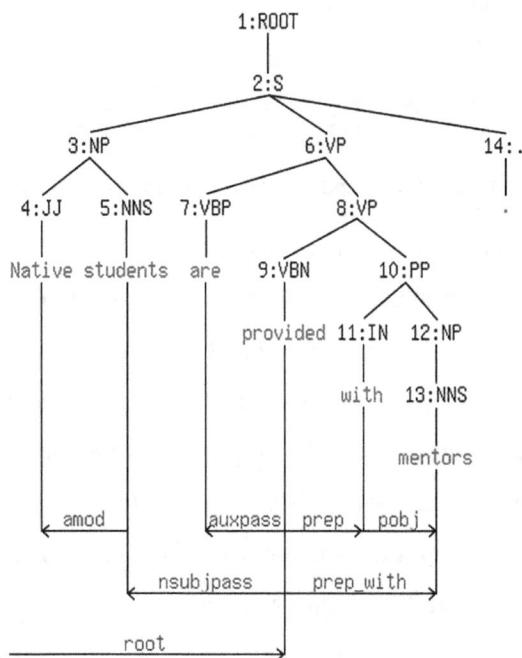

Figure 5.1　The Syntactic tree of the example sentence

The syntactic structure of the example sentence was also produced in the form of a textual description (shown in Figure 5.2) and saved in an XML document, which was analyzed afterwards in the rule-based extraction module.

```
<parse>(ROOT
  (S
  (NP (JJ Native) (NNS students))
  (VP (VBP are)
  (VP (VBN provided)
  (PP (IN with)
  (NP (NNS mentors)))))
  (. .)))
```

Figure 5.2　The textual description of the syntactic tree

The rule-based extraction module was programmed with Prolog. To extract the patterns, the Prolog code was written to specify the structure of each pattern by describing the syntax trees produced in the Cywrite Analyzer module incorporating both POS tags and Stanford Typed Dependencies. One of the strings of the Prolog code used to extract the passive form of the verb-pattern combination "V N with N" (as an example) is presented in Figure 5.3.

```
'bevedwith(X) :-
type(verb,X),dep(auxpass,X,_),token(with,W),precedes(X,W),
(dep(prep_with,X,_);dep(prepc_with,X,_);immed_precedes(X,W)).',
```

Figure 5.3　The Prolog code for the passive form of "V N with N"

When the patterns described matched the syntactic structures of sentences parsed in the Cywrite Analyzer module, these sentences were extracted with the specific patterns labeled. As shown in the example output (see Figure 5.4), the pattern "provide N with N" was extracted from the example sentence *Native students are provided with mentors* with *provide* as the target verb. All patterns were numbered for convenient tracking. For example, the pattern "V N with N" was numbered as "166_1" in our list. "Feature Counts" indicates the total number of the target patterns extracted from a sentence. Here for pattern "V N with N", "Feature Counts" equals 1, indicating that one target verb-pattern combination "provide N with N" was extracted from the example sentence.

```
Native students are provided with mentors
[pattern166_1]
          X = provided (node9)
[Feature Counts]
          pattern166_1: 1
```

Figure 5.4　The extraction of the target verb pattern combination

5.4.2.2　*Evaluation of the Pattern Extraction System*

This section elaborates on our evaluation procedure in which output made by the extraction system and analysis made by human raters were compared to calculate the accuracy performance of the pattern extraction system.

1. Obtaining output from the extraction system

The evaluation procedure included obtaining output from the extraction system and obtaining output from human raters. The current pattern extraction system was applied to the test corpus to extract all coded verb-pattern combinations in text. The sentences containing the extracted verb-pattern combinations were subsequently retrieved of the test corpus and compared with the results from human analysis.

2. Obtaining output from human raters

Several methodological steps were taken to obtain the analysis by human raters. Firstly, the self-compiled corpus was imported into Antconc, a concordance software program.Secondly, after a search of the target verb lemmas in Antconc, all the sentences containing the target lemmas were then automatically extracted and listed as concordance lines in Antconc. As shown in Figure 5.5, a search of the target lemma *provide* yielded all the sentences that contained this lemma. Using Antconc to compile sentences with the target verb lemma increased work efficiency by drawing the raters' attention exclusively to the sentences containing the target lemma, so the raters did not have to read every single sentence in the corpus to identify the target grammar patterns.

Thirdly, the two human raters manually analyzed each concordance line and independently tagged the patterns of the target verb. The interrater reliability was 96.3%. Differences between the two raters' analysis were then identified and negotiated to achieve an agreed version. Finally, the patterns identified by human raters were compared against the output from the extraction system. The next section explains how the data were analyzed to evaluate the performance of the pattern extraction system.

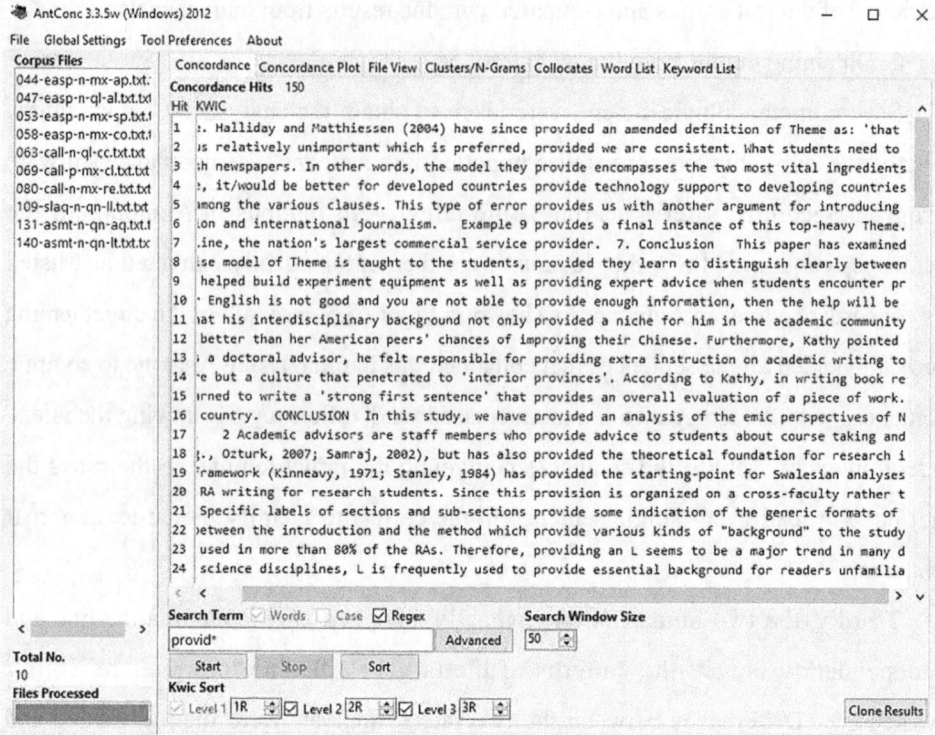

Figure 5.5   The concordance lines with the target verb *provide*

5.4.3   Data Analysis

Precision and recall, measures widely used to evaluate NLP systems (Melamed et al., 2003), were used to assess the performance of the current pattern extraction system. When comparing a set of "candidate" items Y to a set of "reference" items X, precision equals the intersection of the two sets divided by the candidate set ($\frac{|X \cap Y|}{|X|}$), while recall equals the intersection of the two sets divided by the reference set ($\frac{|X \cap Y|}{|X|}$) (Melamed et al., 2003). Specific to this book, candidate items are items that were retrieved by the pattern extraction system, and the reference items are items identified by human raters. The intersection set include grammar patterns simultaneously identified by both the pattern extraction system and human raters. Precision reflects the percentage of extracted patterns that are accurate, while recall indicates the percentage of manually identified patterns that are successfully extracted by using the rule-based approach.

5.4.4 Results and Discussion

The results of this project can be broadly grouped into two parts: (1) precision and recall of the pattern extraction system; (2) a pattern frequency list extracted for the 115 most frequent academic verbs.

5.4.4.1 Precision and Recall

The precision of the pattern extraction system was 95.2%, and the recall was 82.0%. These results suggest that 95.2% of the retrieved verb-pattern combinations were accurate, and the majority (82.0%) of the verb-pattern combinations existing in the evaluation corpus were successfully recognized and retrieved by the pattern extraction system.

5.4.4.2 The Pattern List

All the verb-pattern combinations for the 115 most frequent verbs in the AVL list were extracted. A Perl script was written to sort the verb-pattern combinations based on frequency. This section presents part of the pattern list of the 115 most frequent academic verbs in a verb-oriented order and a pattern-oriented order respectively, since the two different versions of the list are too long to present in the main body of this chapter.

As exemplified in Table 5.3, grammar patterns for each academic verb are ranked based on their frequency of occurrence in a descending order. To associate our list with the AVL, we rank the verbs based on their frequency order in the AVL.

Table 5.3 Part of the grammar pattern list for the 115 most frequent academic verbs in a verb-oriented order

Verbs	Patterns	Frequencies
require	V N	996 (including 385 passive forms)
	V N *to*-inf	379 (including 225 passive forms)
	V *that*-clause	88
	be V-ed of	5
report	V N	341 (including 253 passive forms)
	V N to N	175 (including 159 passive forms)
	be V-ed *to*-inf	141
	V *that*-clause	50
	be V-ed as	36 (including 7 active forms)
	V to N	32
	be V-ed for	24
	It be V-ed *that*-clause	19
	V on N	10

This list of verb patterns is pedagogically useful in several ways. Firstly, provided with the list, English language teachers and material designers would be able to make more informed decisions as to which patterns of a specific academic verb should be introduced earlier than others. To date, implicit learning realized through data-driven learning has been the most widely adopted method for teaching formulaic expressions (Charles, 2007; Yoon & Hirvela, 2004). However, inductive learning of one aspect of formulaic expressions can be problematic (Vannestål & Lindquist, 2007), since it is difficult for students to extrapolate the tendencies of language use given the conflicting examples students may encounter (Flowerdew, 2009; Hunston & Francis, 2000) and the daunting number of concordance lines required to perform the extrapolation (Coxhead, 2008). Secondly, guided by the current list, explicit teaching of academic verb patterns can be more conveniently and systematically enacted. As shown in Table 5.3, the verb *report* can be used with nine patterns in an academic register. EAP students are not likely to identify and learn all nine patterns independently, even though they are expected to use academic verbs with flexibility. Hence, drawing upon this list, teachers or material designers can manipulate students' exposure to patterns of *report* by introducing its more frequent patterns first and then its less frequent patterns. Thirdly, with a clear goal of determining which specific patterns of an academic verb to search and explore, students can also work more efficiently to retrieve authentic sentences with the target patterns of a specific verb and learn practical uses of the lexis.

Table 5.4 presents part of the pattern list for the 115 most frequent academic verbs in a pattern-oriented order. Verbs frequently used with each grammar pattern are listed based on frequency of the specific verb-pattern combinations in a descending order.

Table 5.4 Part of the grammar pattern list for the 115 most frequent academic verbs in a pattern-oriented order

Patterns	Verbs	Frequency
V	occur (1,526), increase (1,259), exist (808), form (233), arise (195), differ (183), develop (170), emerge (158), indicate (134), reduce (101), perform (96), reflect (84), vary (81), improve (65), interpret (60), permit (43), lack (40), yield (23), publish (17), organize (16), locate (11), engage (10), result (4)	5,317
V *that-* clause	suggest (619), indicate (314), note (279), assume (278), demonstrate (226), ensure (160), argue (151), state (139), imply (118), conclude (112), reveal (92), require (88), observe (75), recognize (69), propose (57), predict (52), report (50), provide (36), determine (24), maintain (21), establish (21), illustrate (17), estimate (15), emphasize (13), emerge (12), reflect (4)	3,042
V on N	depend (719), focus (374), rely (203), reflect (35), exist (14), report (10), improve (2)	1,357
V to N	refer (397), contribute (234), relate (233), apply (219), extend (67), increase (34), occur (32), report (32), tend (18), yield (5), demonstrate (5)	1,276

Note: The numbers in parentheses refer to the frequency of the verb-pattern combinations.

The frequency list in a pattern-oriented order carries pedagogical value and enables English language teachers to prioritize verb-pattern combinations of higher frequency in their teaching process, since each generic pattern can be associated with numerous English verbs. Access to this current list of grammar patterns could also facilitate language learners' independent study of grammar patterns in an order that takes frequency and use into consideration. Take the pattern "V to N" for example. In the most frequent 115 academic verbs, 11 verbs can be used with the pattern "V to N" (Table 5.4). It is, therefore, more efficient for students to learn more frequently used verb-pattern combinations, such as "contribute to N" "relate to N" and "refer to N", and then extend their efforts to less frequently used combinations.

Consistent with previous research that adopted usage-based approach to the study of grammar patterns, this current project also identified Zipfian distribution of grammar patterns, with only a few verb-pattern combinations accounting for the lion's share of each pattern (Goldberg et al., 2004; Römer et al., 2014). Usage-based studies have emphasized the importance of frequency in learning grammar patterns, and showed that Zipfian distributional properties make grammar patterns learnable (Römer et al., 2014), since the highly frequent verb-pattern combinations serve as prototypes with which other semantically related verb-pattern combinations can be associated (Goldberg et al., 2004).

The idea of linking semantically associated verb-pattern combinations is also reflected in a pattern approach developed through a corpus-driven approach (Hunston & Francis, 1998). At the core of the pattern approach is the observation that words used with the same pattern tend to share similar meaning. Researchers in favor of the pattern approach have speculated that this approach could promote the efficiency of students' learning patterns by establishing the connection between individual word behaviors based on meaning. While they have long realized that "one of the questions that arises from considering the role of pattern in text is how frequent certain patterns are" (Hunston & Francis, 1998, p. 67). Lacking information on frequency of specific verb-pattern combinations, the published verb pattern teaching material, *Collins Cobuild Grammar Patterns 1: Verbs* ranked the base verbs alphabetically. For example, verbs with the pattern "V *that*-clause" and the meaning of "say" are listed alphabetically as follows: *accept, acknowledge, admit, advise, advocate, affirm, agree, allege, allow, announce, argue, ask...* (Francis et al., 1996, p. 98). Teaching patterns following alphabetical order seems not to be pedagogically sound. The current frequency list of verb patterns will contribute to a more efficient pattern approach to grammar by narrowing teaching scope to the most frequent verb patterns and grouping the patterns based on meanings.

5.5 Summary

This book successfully extracted a pattern list for the 115 most frequent verbs in academic English discourse using a self-built pattern extraction system with the help of Stanford CoreNLP and Cywrite Analyzer. The development of this list contributes to the ongoing call for efforts to create frequency lists for formulaic expressions in academic discourse. The accuracy of the pattern extraction system measured through precision and recall is high. However, it is worth bearing in mind that the result, obtained from the test corpus of only 77,085 words, does not confirm the accuracy of the pattern extraction system when applied to the 2.4-million-word target corpus. It also should be noted that the list only covers grammar patterns of the 115 most frequent academic verbs. To benefit language learners in a wider context, the current list needs to be expanded to cover patterns of more words. The extraction method proposed in this book can be replicated to generate such lists.

The development of the current pattern extraction system can potentially advance studies on grammar patterns to a greater degree. Current studies on grammar patterns compare native / novice writers' and nonnative / expert writers' use of patterns, explore the differences in pattern use across different disciplines, and investigate the grammatical contexts of pattern use. However, these studies have focused on a limited number of grammar patterns, such as *that*-clause and *wh*-clause (Hunston, 2003), "it V-link Adj *that*-clause" and "it V-link ADJ *to*-inf" (Groom, 2005), nouns followed by a complement clause (Charles, 2007), and small sets of verb patterns, mostly "V preposition N" types (Römer & Berger, 2019; Römer et al., 2014; Römer et al., 2017). By replicating the current pattern extraction approach and applying it to corpora of varied registers and genres, studies on grammar patterns are likely to uncover practical uses of a significantly wider range of grammar patterns.

Additionally, this book may inspire other methods of extracting grammar patterns, which could contribute to a more accurate list. Relying on *Collins Cobuild English Dictionary* (1995) to identify possible grammar patterns, this rule-based programming approach may fail to extract patterns that were not identified previously. This issue could be successfully addressed by adopting machine-learning-based techniques, which may well yield a fully automatic pattern extraction program.

A few methods of extracting grammar patterns have been proposed mostly from the computational linguistic perspective (e.g. Watson, 2003). Despite the fact that Watson (2003) showcased a Boyer-Moore algorithm for grammar pattern matching, information such as specific patterns identified and accuracy of the algorithm was not provided, rendering Watson's (2003) work somewhat irrelevant to the efforts of creating a list of grammar patterns. Manson and Hunston (2004) proposed a method of automatic recognition of grammar patterns, shallow parsing, referring to the level of completeness of the structural description at the level of constituent elements, rather than full syntactic structure. Therefore, this shallow parsing process is more simplified and robust than other parsers that process and analyze input text thoroughly. Qtag, the probabilisitic POS tagger, and a noun group recognizer were applied sequentially to identify verbs, the patterns, and the marked noun groups involved. Impossible constituents were further filtered out. "If a preposition is not required by a pattern, it will be attached to a preceding noun group, otherwise it will become part of the pattern" (Manson and Hunston, 2004, p. 257). After the text is divided into potential groups and clauses, pattern recognition is realized by an exhaustive search that "filters out those patterns whose individual components cannot be found in the text. The remaining patterns are then ranked according to a weighting" (Mason & Hunston, 2004, p. 258). As to accuracy, the pattern recognition method proposed by Manson and Hunston (2004) was able to assign 85 correct patterns for 100 lines. In addition, one pattern (*decide between*) not listed in *Collins Cobuild English dictionary* was successfully identified. However, intervening words (words and phrases that are

188

located between one element of the pattern and the next) caused difficulties in pattern recognition. For example, the pattern recognizer identified the pattern "V *wh*-clause" of *decide* in the sentence *Mehari said yesterday he would decide next week whether the jury ...* as the pattern "V". This error was attributed to the fact that the adverbial *next week* prevented the pattern recognizer from identifying the *wh*-clause. Mason and Hunston postulated that NLP techniques may provide deeper analysis and minimize the influence of intervening words; meanwhile, they argued that "automatic pattern recognition is unlikely to be successful because verb + preposition combinations are inherently ambiguous" (2004, p. 262). Sinclair, nevertheless, defended automatic recognition of grammar patterns by stating that "ambiguity is much rarer in practice than it is in theory" (1991, p. 262). Mason and Hunston (2004) randomly selected 100 sentences with *decide on* from the Bank of English, and found out that 87% of the instances were the target pattern "V on", while only 13% of cases were prepositional phrases beginning with *on*. Verbs with multiple patterns also caused difficulties in pattern recognition, especially when patterns and senses do not correspond to each other on a one-to-one mapping. Mason and Hunston (2004) found that the verb *decide* has 17 patterns used with five different senses. The automatic recognition procedure can only distinguish pattern structures but not senses. Mason and Hunston (2004) observed that the distribution of grammar patterns does not follow Zipfian distribution (Zipf, 1949), since words with two or more patterns do not significantly outnumber words with one pattern. When encountering alternative patterns, the pattern recognition method adopted by Mason and Hunston (2004) prioritizes a longer matching pattern. If two pattern alternatives have the same number of elements, the one with more tokens is selected. To be specific, the sentence *Modern women may decide their place is at home with the children* can be recognized as the pattern "V *that*-clause" or the pattern "V N" of *decide*. In this case, the pattern "V *that*-clause" is selected over "V N" since the former pattern includes more tokens. Another problem difficult to solve was non-canonical patterns that do not follow the prototypical order. For example, in the sentence *The question a director has to decide is how...*, the direct object of *decide* is moved before the base verb *decide*. The empirical data revealed that only 6% of the patterns of *decide* were non-canonical patterns, suggesting that non-canonical patterns are not very influential. In addition, adding "transformed" rules specifying passive voice of the patterns could reduce the errors in identifying canonical patterns. Therefore, the current proiect listed passive voice of grammar patterns seperately to reduce the errors associated with canonical patterns. Finally, tagging errors also contributed to the erroneous identification of grammar patterns. Verbs tagged as nouns occurred more frequently than nouns tagged as verbs, since nouns usually occur in a more restrictive context. Mason and Hunston (2004) pointed out that this type of errors reduced the possibility of superfluous verbs, since verbs tagged as nouns would not be recognized as associated with verb patterns. To increase recall, nevertheless, the tagger adopted by Mason and Hunston (2004) allowed for two most likely tags. In this situation, verbs with the pattern "V" and contractions would cause ambiguity that cannot be resolved by the pattern matcher.

Green (2019) also developed a frequency list for the grammar patterns of frequent academic verbs identified in Gardner and Davies' study (2014). The identification methods used in Green (2019), termed as collostructional analysis (Stefanowitsch & Gries, 2003), consist of three statistical methods established on the basis of the associations between vocabulary and grammar: collexeme analysis, the distinctive collexeme analysis, and the covarying collexeme analysis (Green, 2019). In the process of creating the Lexicogrammar of Academic Vocabulary List (LAV list), Green (2019) adopted the collexeme analysis, operating on the basis of statistical relation between a given word and grammatical context. The threshold of collexeme value was computed using the package Collostructions in R and set as 1.3, which indicates statistically significant ($p < 0.05$) colligations. In addition, Green (2019) adopted the following criteria in identifying patterns (i.e. colligations): "a collexeme value above 1.3, a minimum of three or more grammatical constituents, and a minimum of 10 colligations per million words between word and grammatical pattern for nouns and 5 per million for verbs" (Green, 2019, p. 5).

Part of the final product of Green's (2019) research, the LAV list, is presented in Table 5.5 and Table 5.6 in a pattern-oriented manner and word-oriented manner respectively. A comparison between Green's (2019) LAV list and the current list of grammar patterns suggests some overlaps between the two lists. For example, *consist* with the pattern "nsubj-v-prep-of" and "nsubj-v-ccomp" are also identified as very frequent in this book. Not relying on the previously published grammar patterns in the *Collins Cobuild English Dictionary*, the pattern extraction method used in Green (2019) definitely has greater potential of identifying patterns previously not recognized. Nevertheless, the precision and recall values of the LAV list (Green, 2019) were not reported, leaving the accuracy of the list somewhat unclear. In addition, Green (2019) admitted that the LAV list was not able to establish connection with Pattern Grammar or Construction Gramma. The little connection between the LAV list and previous published grammar patterns could render it comparatively more difficult to apply the Pattern Grammar theory to the practical learning of grammar patterns. To be specific, to adopt meaning groups in practical teaching of grammar patterns may well require teachers to translate the patterns with symbols listed in Table 5.5 and Table 5.6 into patterns specified by the Pattern Grammar theory. While in some cases, a corresponding relation between the two systems of patterns cannot be established. For example, it might be not very convenient to build direct connection between *enable* with the pattern "nsubj-v-dobj-xcomp" according to the LAV list and *enable* with the pattern "V N to-inf" following the Pattern Grammar tradition. It is unquestionable that the LAV list also bears great pedagogical implications despite the difficulty of connecting the LAV list to the well-established Pattern Grammar theory.

Table 5.5　Part of the LAV list in a word-oriented order (Green, 2019, p. 6)

AWL: General Academic		SVL: Biology		SVL: Economics	
Verb	Pattern	Verb	Pattern	Verb	Pattern
consist	nsubj-v-prep-of	code	nsubj-v-prep_for	pay	v-prep-for
occur	nsubj-v-advcl	carry	v-prt-dobj	tend	nsubj-v-xcomp
enable	nsubj-v-dobj-xcomp	bind	nsubj-v-prep_to	fall	mark-nsubj-v

Table 5.6　Part of the LAV in a pattern-oriented order (Green, 2019, p. 7)

	AWL	Freq p / m	SVL Biology	Freq p / m	SVL Physics	Freq p / m
Verbs	nsubj-v-ccomp	2,003	mark-nsubj-v-dobj	1,934	v-prep-in	1,221
	mark-nusbj-v-dobj	1,495	nsubjpass-v-prep_in	275	mark-nsubj-v-dobj	1,168
	nsubj-v-xcomp	1,399	nsubjpass-v-agent	535	nsubjpass-v-xcomp	924
Nouns	det-pobj-prep	6,838	det-amod-pobj-prep	1,986	det-pobj-prep	7,932
	det-amod-pobj	5,755	podb-conj-and	1,554	det-amod-pobj	7,700
	det-dobj-prep	4,215	det-amod-dobj-prep	1,418	det-dobj-prep	4,395

Finally, the current list of verb patterns does not address the concern that a core list of formulaic expressions fails to consider disciplinary variability. Some scholars have challenged the practice of developing general academic word lists (or general lists of formulaic expressions) (Ackerman & Chen, 2013; Hyland & Tse, 2007), because (1) words may associate with different meanings across disciplines, and (2) highly frequent academic words may also be frequent in general contexts (Gardner & Davies, 2014). Concerning the two criticisms, this book sides with Gardner and Davies (2014) in arguing that generalized word lists cannot be discarded before a computer program is developed to accurately tag the distinct meanings of word forms, and that being included in a frequency general word list does not diminish the importance of a word (or a formulaic expression) that also frequently occurs in academic fields. Nevertheless, we cannot ignore the value of discipline-specific lists. Future lists of grammar patterns could be developed from corpora representing different disciplines to capture cross-disciplinary pattern use. These future discipline-specific grammar pattern lists may have the potential to uncover the frequency distribution of meanings across disciplines, since different patterns of the same word are generally associated with different meanings (Hunston & Francis, 1998). For example, when used with the pattern "V N with N", the verb *provide* may refer to provide something that someone needs or wants, while the verb-pattern combination *provided that* means "supposing that" (e.g. *The other banks are going to be very eager to help, provided that they see that he has a specific plan.*). It can be expected that the frequency of occurrences for the two patterns of *provide* are different across disciplines. Given the close connection between pattern and meaning, we anticipate that discipline-specific lists of grammar patterns could contribute to the ongoing debate concerning the viability of a core list of academic words or formulaic expressions.

As one previous example of creating disciplinary-specific lists of grammar patterns, Green and Lambert (2018) complied the Secondary School Vocabulary Lists (SVL), covering eight core subjects: Biology, Chemistry, Economics, English, Geology, History, Mathematics, and Physics. Following the practice of Gardner and Davies (2014) and Lei and Liu (2016), lemmas rather than word families were regarded as the basic units for analysis in the development of the SVL. CLAW tagger with an error rate of approximately 3% was used to tag the corpus. Six criteria were adopted to select lemmas: (1) with a minimum occurrence of 28.57 per million words in the specific discipline (Coxhead, 2000; Lei & Liu, 2016); (2) occurring over 50% of texts in a discipline to ensure that the lemmas do not only occur in a small portion of texts in a discipline (Gardner & Davies, 2014); (3) with a dispersion value greater than 0.50; (4) with a minimum frequency of 20% in more than 50% of texts to avoid that a lemma occurs in more than 50% of texts but only frequent in a small portion of texts; (5) three times more frequent in the discipline than in other disciplines included in the corpus; (6) with a part of speech as noun, verb, adjective, or adverb, since other word classes have low teachability.

To complement discipline-specific word lists with more lexical information, Green and Lambert (2019) developed a discipline-specific phrase list (the Secondary Phrase List) of noun-noun, adjective-noun, noun-verb, verb-noun, and verb-adverb phrases for eight secondary subjects: Biology (2,011,083 words), Chemistry (1,908,228 words), Economics (2,297,055 words), English (2,110,857 words), Geography (2,221,239 words), History (2,389,034 words), Mathematics (1,404,280 words), and Physics (1,911,574 words). The corpus was tagged with POS using CLAWS

7 with an error rate of approximately 6.4%. The MI value, greater than 3.00, was used to identify bigrams that co-occur frequently. Five different types of erroneously recognized two-word phrases were removed from the final list, even though the objective standard of MI was met: (1) phrases with hyphens; (2) phrases nesting under longer multi-word phrases (e.g. *other hand* in *on the other hand*); (3) bigrams that crossed clause boundaries or commas (e.g. *adenine, cytosine);* (4) textbook organizers (e.g. *focus questions*); (5) biagrams that consist of a name and an abbreviation (e.g. organization *NATO*) (Green & Lambert, 2019).

Another improvement that could be achieved on the basis of the current study is that instead of discussing the pedagogical implications of this Secondary Phrase List relating to previous literature and imaginative scenarios, three experienced teachers were recruited to rate each phrase for pedagogical usefulness on a 5-point scale, with 1 representing "less useful" and 5 "very useful". Five questions were provided as evaluation guidelines, targeting five aspects: (1) correct spelling and readiness for explicit teaching; (2) words with specialized sense in the discipline (Ha & Hyland, 2017); (3) semantic opaqueness (Martinez & Schmitt, 2012); (4) whether the phrase is associated with concepts in the discipline; (5) phrases marking a student's proficiency level (Hyland, 2017). Green and Lambert (2019) also pointed out that future research could incorporate content teachers' rating.

References

Ackermann, K. & Chen, Y. (2013). Developing the academic collocation list (ACL)—A corpus driven and expert-judged approach. *Journal of English for Academic Purposes*, 12, 235-247.

Bauer, L. & Nation, I. (1993). Word families. *International Journal of Lexicography*, 6, 253-279.

Biber, D., Conrad, S. & Cortes, V. (2004). If you look at ...: Lexical bundles in university teaching and textbooks. *Applied Linguistics*, 25(3), 371-405.

Bramer, M. (2013). *Logic programming with Prolog*. New York: Springer.

Charles, M. (2007). Argument or evidence? Disciplinary variation in the use of the "Noun that" pattern in stance construction. *English for Specific Purposes*, 26(2), 203-218.

Chomsky, N. (1957). *Syntactic structures*. Hague: Mouton Publishers.

Chukharev-Hudilainen, E. & Saricaoglu, A. (2014). Causal discourse analyzer: Improving automated feedback on academic ESL writing. *Computer Assisted Language Learning*, 1-23.

Chukharev-Hudilainen, E., Saricaoglu, A., Torrance, M. & Feng, H. (2019). Combined deployable keystroke logging and eyetracking for investigating L2 writing fluency. *Studies in Second Language Acquisition*, 41(3), 583-604.

Collins Cobuild English dictionary (1995). 2nd ed. London: Collins CoBUILD.

Coxhead, A. (2000). A new Academic Word List. *TESOL Quarterly*, 34(2), 213-238.

Coxhead, A. (2008). Phraseology and English for Academic Purposes: Challenges and opportunities. In F. Meunier & S. Granger (eds.), *Phraseology in foreign language learning and teaching*. Amsterdam: John Benjamins, 149-162.

Durrant, P. (2016). To what extent is the academic vocabulary list relevant to university student writing?. *English for Specific Purposes*, 43, 49-61.

Flowerdew, L. (2009). Applying Corpus Linguistics to pedagogy: A critical evaluation. *International Journal of Corpus Linguistics*, 14(3), 393-417.

Francis, G., Hunston, S. & Manning, E. (eds.) (1996). *Collins Cobuild grammar patterns 1: Verbs*. London: Collins CoBUILD.

Francis, G., Hunston, S. & Manning, E. (1998). *Collins Cobuild grammar patterns 2: Nouns and adjectives*. London: Collins CoBUILD.

Gardner, D. & Davies, M. (2014). A new Academic Vocabulary List. *Applied Linguistics*, 35(3), 305-327.

Goldberg, A. E., Casenhiser, D. M. & Sethuraman, N. (2004). Learning argument structure generalizations. *Cognitive Linguistics*, 15, 289-316.

Green, C. (2019). Enriching the academic wordlist and secondary vocabulary lists with lexicogrammar: Toward a Pattern Grammar of academic vocabulary. *System*, 87, 102-158.

Green, C. & Lambert, J. (2018). Advancing disciplinary literacy through English for Academic Purposes: Discipline-specific wordlists, collocation and word families for eight secondary subjects. *Journal of English for Academic Purposes*, 35, 105-115.

Green, C. & Lambert, J. (2019). Position vectors, homologous chromosomes and grammar rays: Producing disciplinary literacy through Secondary Phrase Lists. *English for Specific Purposes*, 53, 1-12.

Groom, N. (2005). Pattern and meaning across genres and disciplines: An exploratory study. *Journal of English for Academic Purposes*, 4, 257-277.

Ha, A. Y. H. & Hyland, K. (2017). What is technicality? A technicality analysis model for EAP vocabulary. *Journal of English for Academic Purposes*, 28, 35-49.

Hunston, S. (2003). Lexis, word form and complementation pattern: A corpus study. *Functions of Language*, 10(1), 31-60.

Hunston, S. & Francis, G. (1998). Verbs observed: A corpus-driven pedagogic grammar. *Applied Linguistics*, 19(1), 45-72.

Hunston, S. & Francis, G. (1999). *Pattern grammar: A corpus-driven approach to the lexical grammar of English*. Amsterdam: John Benjamins.

Hunston, S. & Francis, G. (2000). Pattern grammar: A course-driven approach to the lexical grammar of English. *Computational Linguistics*, 27(2), 318-320.

Hyland, K. (2008). As can be seen: Lexical bundles and disciplinary variation. *English for Specific Purposes*, 27, 4-21.

Hyland, K. (2017). English in the disciplines: Arguments for specificity. *ESP Today-Journal of English for Specific Purposes at Tertiary Level*, 5(1), 5-23.

Hyland, K. & Tse, P. (2007). Is there an "academic vocabulary"?. *TESOL Quarterly*, 41, 235-253.

Jaen, M. M. (2007). A corpus-driven design of a test for assessing the ESL collocational competence of university students. *International Journal of English Studies*, 7(2) 127-147.

Lei, L. & Liu, D. (2016). A new Medical Academic Word List: A corpus-based study with enhanced methodology. *Journal of English for Academic Purposes*, 22, 42-53.

Liu, D. (2012). The most frequently-used multi-word constructions in academic written English: A multi-corpus study. *English for Specific Purposes*, 31, 25-35.

Mason, O. & Hunston, S. (2004). The automatic recognition of verb patterns: A feasibility study. *International Journal of Corpus Linguistics*, 9(2), 153-270.

Martinez, R. & Schmitt, N. (2012). A Phrasal Expression List. *Applied Linguistics*, 33(3), 299-320.

Melamed, I, D., Green, R. & Turian, J. P. (2003). Precision and recall of machine translation. *Proceedings of the 2003 Conference of the North American Chapter of the Association for Computational Linguistics on Human Language Technology*, 61-63, doi: https://doi.org/10.3115/1073483.1073504.

Milton, J. (2009). *Second language acquisition: Measuring second language vocabulary acquisition*. Bristol: Multilingual Matters.

Osborne, T. (2018). *A dependency grammar of English: An introduction and beyond*. Amsterdam: John Benjamins Publishing Company.

Qian, D. & Schedl, M. (2004). Evaluation of an in-depth vocabulary knowledge measure for assessing reading performance. *Language Testing*, 21(1), 28-52.

Read, J. (2000). *Assessing vocabulary*. New York: Cambridge University Press.

Römer, U. & Berger, C. M. (2019). Observing the emergence of constructional knowledge: Verb patterns in German and Spanish learners of English at different proficiency levels. *Studies in Second Language Acquisition*, 41, 1089-1110.

Römer, U., O'Donnell, M. B. & Ellis, N. C. (2014). Second language learner knowledge of verb-argument constructions: Effects of language transfer and typology. *The Modern Language Journal*, 98, 952-975.

Römer, U., Skalicky, S. & Ellis, N. C. (2017). Verb-Argument constructions in advanced L2 English learner production: Insights from corpora and verbal fluency tasks. *Corpus Linguistics and Linguistic Theory*, 1-27.

Simpson-Vlach, R. & Ellis, N. (2010). An Academic Formulas List: New methods in phraseology research. *Applied Linguistics, 31*(4), 487-512.

Sinclair, J. M. (1991). *Corpus, concordance, collocation*. Oxford: Oxford University Press.

Stefanowitsch, A. & Gries, S. T. (2003). Collostructions: Investigating the interaction of words and constructions. *International Journal of Corpus Linguistics*, 8(2), 209-243.

Tribble, C. & Jones, G. (1990). *Concordances in the classroom*. Harlow, UK: Longman.

Vannestål, M. E. & Lindquist, H. (2007). Learning English grammar with a corpus: Experimenting with concordancing in a university grammar course. *ReCALL*, 19(3), 329-350.

Ward, J. (2007). Collocation and technicality in EAP engineering. *Journal of English for Academic Purposes*, 6, 18-35.

Watson, B. W. (2003). A new regular grammar pattern matching algorithm. *Theoretical Computer Science*, 299, 509-521.

Yoon, H. & Hirvela, A. (2004). ESL student attitudes towards corpus use in L2 writing. *Journal of Second Language Writing*, 13(4), 257-283.

Zipf, G. K. (1949). *Human behaviour and the principle of least-effort*. Cambridge, MA: Addison-Wesley.

APPENDIX 1

The Grammar Pattern List for the 115 Most Frequent Academic Verbs in a Verb-Oriented Order

Verb	Pattern	Frequency
provide	V N	1,462 (including 135 passive forms)
	V N with N	139 (including 15 passive forms)
	V *that*-clause	36
include	V N	480 (including 43 passive forms)
	be V-ed in	106
develop	V N	968 (including 225 passive forms)
	V	170
	V out of N	19
	V from N	10
suggest	V *that*-clause	619
	V N	138
	be V-ed	106
require	V N	996 (including 385 passive forms)
	V N *to*-inf	379 (including 225 passive forms)
	V *that*-clause	88
	be V-ed of	5

Continued

Verb	Pattern	Frequency
report	V N	341 (including 253 passive forms)
	V N to N	175 (including 159 passive forms)
	be V-ed *to*-inf	141
	V *that*-clause	50
	be V-ed as	36 (including 7 active forms)
	V to N	32
	be V-ed for	24
	It be V-ed *that*-clause	19
	V on N	10
base	V N on N	41
	be V-ed on	331
describe	V N	684 (including 211 passive forms)
	V N as	150 (including 98 passive forms)
	V *wh*-clause	48
indicate	V *that*-clause	314
	V N	491 (including 80 passive forms)
	V	134
	V *wh*-clause	33
produce	V N	1,028 (including 184 passive forms)
identify	V N	406 (including 58 passive forms)
	V N as	39 (including 11 passive forms)
	V N with N	16 (including 7 passive forms)
	V with N	4
support	V N	452 (including 66 passive forms)
increase	V	1,259
	V N	1,145 (including 192 passive forms)
	V from N	42
	V to N	34
	V by N	19
note	V *that*-clause	279
	V N	335 (including 228 passive forms)
	V *wh*-clause	7
represent	V N	799
	be V-ed	177
	V N as	59 (including 22 passive forms)

Continued

Verb	Pattern	Frequency
determine	V N	1,104 (including 371 passive forms)
	V *wh*-clause	157
	V *that*-clause	24
	V *to*-inf	10
	V *wh-to*-inf	7
occur	V	1,526
	V to N	32
present	V N	189 (including 50 passive forms)
	V N in N	133 (including 85 passive forms)
	V N with N	34 (including 14 passive forms)
	V N to N	26 (including 8 passive forms)
	V N as	24 (including 9 passive forms)
reduce	V N	987 (including 224 passive forms)
	V	101
	V N to N	143 (including 75 passive forms)
involve	V N	561 (including 77 passive forms)
	V N in N	191 (including 164 passive forms)
	V V-ing	93
focus	V on N	347
	V N	78 (including 41passive forms)
relate	V to N	233
	V N to N	164 (including 109 passive forms)
	V N	44 (including 16 passive forms)
establish	V N	384 (including 148 passive forms)
	V N with N	15 (including 4 passive forms)
	V *that*-clause	21
	V N as	11 (including 4 passive forms)
	It be V-ed *that*-clause	11
seek	V N	177 (including 23 passive forms)
	V *to*-inf	90
	V N from N	14 (including 2 passive forms)
	V N for N	8

Continued

Verb	Pattern	Frequency
compare	V N	314 (including 39 passive forms)
	V with N	289
	V N with N	74 (including 18 passive forms)
	V N to N	55 (including 9 passive forms)
argue	V *that*-clause	151
	V for N	12
	It be V-ed *that*-clause	23
	V against N	9
	V over N	7
	V about N	2
state	V *that*-clause	139
	V N	91 (including 41 passive forms)
examine	V N	386 (including 55 passive forms)
reflect	V N	159 (including 37 passive forms)
	V	84
	V on N	35
	V *that*-clause	4
recognize	V N	221 (including 49 passive forms)
	V *that*-clause	69
	V N as	53 (including 34 passive forms)
	be V-ed by	23
maintain	V N	431 (including 87 passive forms)
	V *that*-clause	21
	V N at N	14 (including 5 passive forms)
associate	V with N	519
	be V-ed with N	368 (including 31 active forms)
design	V N	122 (including 33 passive forms)
	be V-ed *to*-inf	65
	be V-ed for	19
address	V N	264 (including 55 passive forms)
	V N to N	11 (including 5 passive forms)
define	V N	414 (including 164 passive forms)
	V N as	177 (including 109 passive forms)
	V *wh*-clause	7

Continued

Verb	Pattern	Frequency
apply	V N	351 (including 150 passive forms)
	V N to N	296 (including 198 passive forms)
	V to N	219
	V for N	36
	V *to*-inf	23
contain	V N	1391 (including 52 passive forms)
form	V N	982 (including 191 passive forms)
	V	233
	V N into N	6 (including 4 passive forms)
	V into N	3
reveal	V N	213 (including 28 passive forms)
	V *that*-clause	92
	be V-ed as	7 (including 6 active forms)
	V *wh*-clause	3
affect	V N	573 (including 149 passive forms)
achieve	V N	661 (including 263 passive forms)
conduct	V N	266 (including 125 passive forms)
	V	18
perform	V N	588 (including 337 passive forms)
	V	96
discuss	V N	429 (including 183 passive forms)
	V *wh*-clause	19
exist	V	808
	V on N	14
improve	V N	477 (including 65 passive forms)
	V	65
	V on N	2
observe	V N	632 (including 444 passive forms)
	V *that*-clause	75
	V N V-ing	14
demonstrate	V N	497 (including 121 passive forms)
	V *that*-clause	226
	V *wh*-clause	14
	V to N	5
	V for N	7

Continued

Verb	Pattern	Frequency
result	V in N	691
	V from N	220
	V	4
experience	V N	195 (including 26 passive forms)
control	V N	370 (including 114 passive forms)
measure	V N	580 (including 244 passive forms)
test	V N	206 (including 71 passive forms)
	be V-ed for	34
tend	V *to*-inf	297
	V to N	18
	V N	7
refer	V to N	397
	V N to N	198 (including 161 passive forms)
obtain	V N	858 (including 370 passive forms)
contribute	V to N	234
	V N to N	29
	V N	28
assume	V N	320 (including 91 passive forms)
	V *that*-clause	278
	be V-ed *to*-inf	75
express	V N	451(including 215 passive forms)
	be V-ed as	66 (including 16 active forms)
promote	V N	203 (including 16 passive forms)
	V N from N	3
participate	V in N	110
engage	V in N	95
	V N in N	29 (including 23 passive forms)
	V N	22 (including 8 passive forms)
	V with N	18
	V	10
publish	V N	138 (including 68 passive forms)
	V	17
encourage	V N to-inf	69 (including 24 passive forms)
	V N	23 (including 10 passive forms)

Continued

Verb	Pattern	Frequency
assess	V N	268 (including 68 passive forms)
	V *wh*-clause	16
view	V N as	91 (including 52 passive forms)
	V N	62 (including 16 passive forms)
	V N in N	9
limit	V N	390 (including 199 passive forms)
	V N to N	119 (including 82 passive forms)
influence	V N	95 (including 29 passive forms)
emerge	V	158
	V from N	50
	V as	38
	V that	12
explore	V N	236 (including 51 passive forms)
	V N for N	18 (including 4 passive forms)
	V for N	2
generate	V N	415 (including 111 passive forms)
perceive	V N	81 (including 34 passive forms)
	V N as	44 (including 18 passive forms
ensure	V *that*-clause	160
	V N	131 (including 4 passive forms)
select	V N	117 (including 52 passive forms)
	V N for N	37 (including 24 passive forms)
	V N from N	6 (including 4 passive forms)
emphasize	V N	53 (including 8 passive)
	V *that*-clause	13
extend	V N	166 (including 31 passive forms)
	V N to N	70 (including 34 passive forms)
	V to N	67
	V from N to N	12
	V beyond	11
	V from N	12
evaluate	V N	314 (including 97 passive forms)

Continued

Verb	Pattern	Frequency
conclude	V *that*-clause	112
	V N	39 (including 18 passive forms)
	V N from N	4 (including 1 passive forms)
consist	V of N	413
	V in N	29
adopt	V N	186 (including 48 passive forms)
	V N as	11 (including 2 passive forms)
depend	V on N	719
	V upon N	81
attempt	V *to*-inf	124
	V N	40 (including 15 passive forms)
predict	V N	365 (including 56 passive forms)
	V *that*-clause	52
	V *wh*-clause	28
employ	V N	143 (including 63 passive forms)
	V N *to*-inf	38 (including 25 passive forms)
	be V-ed in	34 (including 6 active forms)
account	V for	186
	be V-ed for	23
link	V N to N	146 (including 97 passive forms)
	V N	107(including 41 passive forms)
	V N with N	30 (including 15 passive forms)
analyze	V N	325 (including 129 passive forms)
range	V from N to N	55
	V between Pln	10
enable	V N *to*-inf	139
	V N	117 (including 6 passive forms)
organize	V N	104 (including 52 passive forms)
	V	16
locate	V N	69 (including 24 passive forms)
	V	11
enhance	V N	323 (including 58 passive forms)

Continued

Verb	Pattern	Frequency
estimate	V N	309 (including 107 passive forms)
	V *that*-clause	15
	V N at N	12 (including 8 passive forms)
	V *wh*-clause	3
propose	V N	230 (including 119 passive forms)
	V *that*-clause	57
	V *to*-inf	52
vary	V	81
	V from N	63
	V N	95 (including 34 passive forms)
construct	V N	141 (including 34 passive forms)
	V N from N	11 (including 9 passive forms)
rely	V on / upon N	203
cite	V N	25 (including 12 passive forms)
	V N as	11 (including 8 passive forms)
lack	V N	116
	V	40
constitute	V N	176 (including 6 passive forms)
incorporate	V N	154 (including 68 passive forms)
	V N into N	60 (including 47 passive forms)
illustrate	V N	218 (including 61 passive forms)
	V *wh*-clause	26
	V *that*-clause	17
	V N with N	12
arise	V	195
	V from N	134
	V out of N	17
acquire	V N	143 (including 36 passive forms)
	V N from N	5 (including 2 passive forms)
characterize	V N	92 (including 11 passive forms)
	V N as	78 (including 12 passive forms)
	be V-ed by	66
differ	V	183
	V from N	150
	V with N	5

Continued

Verb	Pattern	Frequency
review	V N	156 (including 50 passive forms)
	V for N	2
interpret	V N	106 (including 50 passive forms)
	be V-ed as	87 (including 49 passive forms)
	V	60
display	V N	123 (including 23 passive forms)
	V N to N	9
derive	V N	153 (including 53 passive forms)
	V from N	135
	V N from N	131 (including 104 passive forms)
permit	V N *to*-inf	60 (including 12 passive forms)
	V N	55 (including 16 passive forms)
	V	43
	V N N	2
regard	V N as	175 (including 107 passive forms)
	V N with N	3
transform	V N	112 (including 21 passive forms)
	V N into N	49 (including 16 passive forms)
	V N from N	4 (including 2 passive forms)
imply	V N	135 (including 8 passive forms)
	V *that*-clause	118
facilitate	V N	213 (including 16 passive forms)
yield	V N	214 (including 6 passive forms)
	V	23
	V to N	5
inform	V N	77 (including 30 passive forms)
	V N *that*-clause	14 (including 7 passive forms)

APPENDIX 2

The Grammar Pattern List for the 115 Most Frequent Academic Verbs in a Pattern-Oriented Order

Pattern	Frequency	Total frequency
V N	contain (1,339), provide (1,327), increase (953), produce (844), represent (799), form (791), reduce (763), develop(743), determine (733), require(611), obtain (488), involve (484), describe (473), include(437), affect (424), improve (412), indicate (411), achieve (398), support (386), demonstrate (376), identify (348), maintain (344), measure (336), examine (331), predict (309), generate (304), compare (275), enhance (265), control (256), perform (251), define (250), discuss (246), establish (236), express (236), assume (229), evaluate (217), address (209), yield (208), estimate (202), apply (201), assess (200), facilitate (197), analyze (196), limit (191), observe (188), promote (187), reveal (185), explore (185), recognize (172), constitute (170), experience (169), illustrate (157), seek (154), present (149), conduct (141), suggest (138), adopt (138), test (135), extend (135), ensure (127), imply (127), reflect (122), enable (111), propose (111), Note (107), acquire (107), construct (107), review (106), display (100), derive (100), transform (91), design (89), report (88), incorporate (86), characterize (81), employ (80), publish (70), regard (68), influence (66), link (66), select (65), vary (61), interpret (56), organize (52), state (50), perceive (47), inform (47), view (46), locate (45), permit (39), focus (37), relate (28), attempt (25), conclude (21), engage (14), encourage (13), cite (13)	24,301

Continued

Pattern	Frequency	Total frequency
be V-ed	observe (444), determine (371), obtain (370), perform (337), develop (225), provide (135), require (385), achieve (263), report (253), measure (244), note (228), reduce (224), express (215), describe (211), increase (192), form (191), produce (184), discuss (183), represent (177), define (164), apply (150), affect (149), establish (148), analyze (129), conduct (125), demonstrate (121), limit (119), propose (119), control (114), generate (111), estimate (107), evaluate (97), link (97), assume (91), maintain (87), indicate (80), involve (77), test (71), publish (68), assess (68), incorporate (68), support (66), improve (65), employ (63), illustrate (61), identify (58), enhance (58), predict (56), examine (55), address (55), derive (53), contain (52), select (52), organize (52), explore (51), present (50), review (50), interpret (50), recognize (49), adopt (48), include (43), focus (41), state (41), compare (39), reflect (37), acquire (36), perceive (34), vary (34), construct (34), design (33), extend (31), inform (30), influence (29), reveal (28), experience (26), locate (24), seek (23), display (23), transform (21), conclude (18), relate (16), promote (16), view (16), facilitate (16), attempt (15), cite (12), permit (12), characterize (11), encourage (10), emphasize (8), imply (8), enable (6), constitute (6), yield (6), ensure (4)	9,023
V	occur (1,526), increase (1,259), exist (808), form (233), arise (195), differ (183), develop (170), emerge (158), indicate (134), reduce (101), perform (96), reflect (84), vary (81), improve (65), interpret (60), permit (43), lack (40), yield (23), publish (17), organize (16), locate (11), engage (10), result (4)	5,317
V that-clause	suggest (619), indicate (314), note (279), assume (278), demonstrate (226), ensure (160), argue (151), state (139), imply (118), conclude (112), reveal (92), require (88), observe (75), recognize (69), propose (57), predict (52), report (50), provide (36), determine (24), maintain (21), establish (21), illustrate (17), estimate (15), emphasize (13), emerge (12), reflect (4)	3,042
V on N	depend (719), focus (374), rely (203), reflect (35), exist (14), report (10), improve (2)	1,357
V to N	refer (397), contribute (234), relate (233), apply (219), extend (67), increase (34), occur (32), report (32), tend (18), yield (5), demonstrate (5)	1,276
V in N	result (691), participate (110), engage (95), consist (29)	925

Continued

Pattern	Frequency	Total frequency
be V-ed to	apply (198), refer (161), report (159), relate (109), link (97), limit (82), extend (34), contribute (29), compare (9), display (9), present (8), address (5)	900
V from N	result (220), differ (150), derive (135), arise (134), vary (63), emerge (50), increase (42), extend (12), develop (10)	816
V *to*-inf	tend (297), attempt (124), seek (90), propose (52), apply (23), determine (10)	596
V with N	associate (519), engage (18), differ (5), identify (4)	546
V N to N	apply (98), reduce (68), relate (55), link (49), compare (46), refer (37), limit (37), extend (36), contribute (29), present (18), report (16), display (9), address (6)	504
V of N	consist (413)	413
be V-ed with	associate (337), compare (18), provide (15), link (15), present (14), identify (7), establish (4)	410
V N *to*-inf	require (154), enable (139), permit (48), encourage (45), employ (13)	399
be V-ed as	define (109), regard (107), view (52), express (50), report (29), perceive (18), characterize (12), cite (8), adopt (2), reveal (1)	388
be V-ed in	involve (164), include (106), present (85), engage (23)	378
V N as	regard (68), characterize (66), view (39), represent (37), identify (28), perceive (26), recognize (19), express (16), present (15), adopt (9) , report (7), establish (7), reveal (6), cite (3)	346
be V-ed on N	base (331)	331
V N with N	provide (124), compare (56), associate (31), present (20), link (15), illustrate (12), establish (11), identify (9), regard (3)	281
be V-ed *to*-inf	report (141), assume (75), encourage (24), permit (12)	252
V *wh*-clause	describe (48), indicate (33), predict (28), illustrate (26), discuss (19), assess (16), demonstrate (14), define (7), note (7), estimate (3), reveal (3)	204
be V-ed from	derive (104), construct (9)	113
be V-ed for	test (34), select (24), report (24), design (19), explore (4)	105

Continued

Pattern	Frequency	Total frequency
be V-ed by	characterize (66), recognize (23), inform (7)	96
V V-ing	involve (93)	93
V N in N	present (48), involve (27), view (9), engage (6)	90
V upon	depend (81)	81
be V-ed into	incorporate (47), transform (16), form (4)	67
V from N to N	range (55), extend (12)	67
V for N	apply (36), argue (12), demonstrate (7), review (2), explore (2)	59
It be V-ed *that-* clause	argue (23), report (19), establish (11)	53
V N from N	derive (27), seek (12), acquire (3), conclude (3), select (2), transform (2)	49
V N into N	transform (33), incorporate (13), form (2)	48
V N on N	base (41)	41
V as	emerge (38)	38
V out of N	develop (19), arise (17)	36
V N for N	select (13), explore (12)	25
V by N	increase (19)	19
V N V-ing	observe (14)	14
V N at N	maintain (9), estimate (4)	13
V beyond	extend (11)	11
V between Pln	range (10)	10
V against N	argue (9)	9
V N *that-* clause	inform (7)	7

Continued

Pattern	Frequency	Total frequency
be V-ed *that-* clause	inform (7)	7
V *wh-to-* inf	determine (7)	7
V over N	argue (7)	7
be V-ed of	require (5)	5
V into N	form (3)	3
V N N	permit (2)	2
V about N	argue (2)	2